M000158510

A LOTUS OF ANOTHER COLOR

A LOTUS

OF ANOTHER

COL🪷R

An Unfolding of the South Asian Gay and Lesbian Experience

Edited by Rakesh Ratti

Boston ♦ Alyson Publications, Inc.

Copyright © 1993 by Rakesh Ratti. All rights reserved.

Typeset and printed in the United States of America.

This is a paperback original from Alyson Publications, Inc.,
40 Plympton St., Boston, Mass. 02118.
Distributed in England by GMP Publishers,
P.O. Box 247, London N17 9QR, England.

This book is printed on acid-free, recycled paper.

First edition, first printing: January 1993

5 4 3 2 1

ISBN 1-55583-171-0

Back cover photograph copyright © 1992 by David Hill Photography,
Atlanta, Ga. Photograph on page 4 reprinted with permission from *Trikone*.
All other photographs copyright © 1992 by Giti Thadani.

Library of Congress Cataloging-in-Publication Data

A lotus of another color : an unfolding of the South Asian gay and
   lesbian experience / edited by Rakesh Ratti. – 1st ed.
      p.   cm.
   ISBN 1-55583-171-0 : $9.95
   1. Gays–South Asia.   2. Gay liberation movement.   3. Coming out
(Sexual orientation)   I. Ratti, Rakesh.
HQ76.3.S6L67   1993
305'.90664'0954–dc20
                                                           92-3691
                                                              CIP

To my sister, Kamlesh,
who has personified unconditional love in my life;
her support has made each step of my coming-out process
immeasurably easier.

To the memory of Siddharth,
a kindred spirit who taught me to value every moment;
all of us who knew him celebrate what he gave to us,
both personally and politically.

Acknowledgments

I would like to express my gratitude to Arvind Kumar, Ashok Jethanandani, Ravi Verma, Kamini Chaudhary, ShivOm, Kaushalya Bannerji, Sharmeen Islam, Ramesh M., Franklin Abbot, Byron Patterson, and Julia Perilla-Parker for the support and input they have given during the various stages of this project.

Contents

Ardhanarishwara: Indian mythology not only recognizes the existence of male and female principles within the human body, but honors and deifies it in this representation of Lord Shiva as half man, half woman. (Stone sculpture, Bengal, A.D. 1200)

Introduction

An Indian professor at an Ivy League university, a Pakistani practicing law in Vancouver. A Bangladeshi artist raising awareness in San Francisco. An ebony-eyed Sri Lankan doctor in Boston, a Nepali graduate student in New York City, a married Pakistani civil servant in London. A young shopkeeper with sparkling green eyes in Udaipur, India. A married woman who must see her female lover secretly in New Delhi, an apprehensive high school student in Singapore. An old man who has lived out a lonely life in a rural village, a pair of lovers who defy their world in New Delhi.

What do these men and women have in common? They – we – are all gay, lesbian, or bisexual South Asians. We proudly share the cultural heritage of the Indian subcontinent, a heritage that stretches in an unbroken line 4,000 years old and that is as rich and diverse as that of any continent. This heritage distinguishes us culturally within the Western gay and lesbian communities that many of us join. Similarly, the fact that we are attracted to and love others of our own gender gives us minority status within the South Asian mainstream. These two facets are integral components of our self-definition, yet they are too often compartmentalized within many of us and thus estranged from one another.

(The term *South Asian* refers to an individual who is an inhabitant of, or is descended from the inhabitants of, the following countries: Bhutan, Bangladesh, India, the Maldives, Nepal, Pakistan, and Sri Lanka. The term *Asian* is too often incorrectly applied; in the United

11

States it is used interchangeably with the term *East Asian* – Chinese, Japanese, etc. – and in the United Kingdom it refers exclusively to South Asians. Even when used broadly, this term is misleading. Though they share common struggles and goals, East Asians and South Asians are distinct from one another linguistically, racially, and culturally, and yet Westerners have a tendency to refer to them monolithically. This is merely another form of ethnocentrism, an extension of the "white" and "other" dichotomy that once ignored the individuality of all minority groups.)

In the process of editing this book, I have encountered one common thread that connects all of the personal experiences contained within these pages. Each one of us can recall the sense of isolation that we felt when we first realized that we were gay or lesbian. We were certain that no one else harbored such feelings. We also knew that the South Asians around us – our family, friends, and acquaintances – would not react well to the truth of our sexual orientation. So most of us chose to hide our true nature, at least for a time. Once some of us entered the lesbian and gay subculture of the West, our feeling of isolation did not fade as we had assumed it would; it only changed face. It took us a bit longer to identify a new dimension to the sense of alienation. In our burgeoning gay and lesbian world, we were still anomalies. None of our newly found gay or lesbian friends and acquaintances spoke our languages, shared our history, or really understood our culture.

The fact that this feeling of isolation seems universal among lesbian and gay South Asians should not be difficult to understand. We human beings are social creatures, and we have a need to surround ourselves with others who are like us. In this manner we find social validation and achieve a sense of belonging. Gay and lesbian South Asians should naturally seek out one another and form ties that affirm our existence, that give us a sense of community. Just as our culture and our gayness or lesbianism set us apart from others, so they serve to bring us together with one another.

In 1986 there were two gay and lesbian South Asian organizations: Trikone and Anamika. The two groups had sprouted independently; Anamika formed in 1985 and Trikone was created a few months later. The formation of these groups was a testament to our need to acknowledge the South Asian and gay or lesbian aspects of ourselves and the need to integrate these facets into our individual self-definitions. These two groups also acknowledged what we had to give one another in the form of sharing and support. Today we have a variety of organizations in Canada, England, India, and numerous cities in the United States. These organizations vary in size, in the demographics of their membership, and in the focus of their activities, yet they have one thing in common: they have all helped to dispel feelings of isolation through the creation of nurturing support networks that continue to grow.

The benefits of coming together have been tremendous, yet we gay and lesbian South Asians still continue to be an invisible group. We are relatively unknown in the gay and lesbian communities, and we are similarly overlooked in the mainstream South Asian communities. Whether because of benign neglect or a conscious desire to deny our existence, evidenced by myriad rationales, we too often go unacknowledged in both groups.

The South Asian communities are often uncomfortable with our presence and try to pass off homosexuality as a trait foreign to our native lands. This is not only ludicrous, given the scientific evidence that same-gender attraction is present in all cultures, it is also an obvious lie; images of gays and lesbians are readily available in the history of the subcontinent. There are images of same-gender individuals in intimate positions on temples in Khajuraho and Konarek in India. Most of these temples were built more than a thousand years ago. There are also references to homosexuality as an alternative expression of sexuality in the *Kama Sutra,* the ancient Indian text on the diversities of sex. Babar, the founder of the Mughal dynasty in India, is said to have been gay, as was Abu Nawas, a famous Islamic poet. Homosexuality is as native to the Indian subcontinent as heterosexuality and cannot be dismissed as a Western import.

In the South Asian cultures, sex is an issue that is rarely discussed, and this tends to make the discussion of homosexuality quite taboo. Consequently, gays and lesbians go largely unacknowledged. This avoidance, coupled with the traditional pressures to marry and raise a family, can cause tremendous strain for the individual trying to live his or her life in a healthy, honest way. Millions of gays and lesbians in South Asia find themselves pressured into entering heterosexual marriages; ultimately, these marital bonds become chains that

13

enslave both partners and deny them the full existence they deserve. So many dreams of love are thus rendered unreachable, so much yearning is left unfulfilled because our South Asian world is unwilling to open its eyes to our existence.

Ideally, one would think that we would fare better with the gay and lesbian communities that we South Asians become a part of in the West. One would think that they would warmly embrace our uniqueness, our contribution to their diversity. One would be sadly mistaken. Some individuals do welcome us, some organizations acknowledge our existence, but by and large we have been invisible within the gay and lesbian world. This lack of visibility can be partially explained by our scarcity; within the United States and Canada we don't constitute a very large group. It is highly unlikely that this is the only reason. The neglectful way that the mainstream gay and lesbian communities have treated people of color within their parameters must also be considered. This subculture does not acknowledge that South Asians and other ethnically distinct groups have a different life experience, different societal and familial influences, and different needs; too often we are expected to fit into a generic gay or lesbian mold that is a square hole for our round pegs.

The familial connections we South Asians have are often more sturdy, intricate, and intense than those held by our Western counterparts. Because of the extended family networks that are still a very real part of many of our lives, our sense of, and need for, community is also more deeply embedded. In addition, most of us are raised with a quite monogamous ideal that, for better or worse, can leave us feeling bewildered and betrayed in a gay world that has so often trashed monogamy as a vestige of heterosexual values.

In these ways and many others, we stand with one foot in the South Asian society, the other in the gay and lesbian world. It is natural then that we should support one another in sorting out these conflicts. Beyond simply serving as support networks, our groups, and we as individuals, have the potential to change the way our surrounding world views us.

As diverse and as numerous as gay and lesbian South Asians may be (eighty million in India alone, if one goes by the 10 percent estimate), there is little mention of us in the literature of the East or the West. In 1988, my friend Ravi Verma and I came up with the idea of a book to fill this void. We attempted to put together such an anthology, sent out notices, courtesy of Trikone, but we received little response from gay and lesbian South Asians and eventually shelved the idea. The need stayed with us, however. In 1989, Sasha Alyson approached Trikone with the possibility of doing the current book, unaware of our previous attempt; the universe was providing, as it always does.

As with the first attempt, the response to my second invitation for stories and articles was slow. A great many potential contributors cited their need for discretion as a reason for not sharing their stories, which only served to underscore the need for this anthology. Others did not write because of personal apprehensions about their writing abilities, but they agreed to interviews. These interviews were then restructured into stories, many of which appear in this book. All of the accounts in this anthology are factual, unless otherwise noted. Many of the writers felt a need to shield their identities for a variety of personal reasons; an asterisk next to a name indicates that it is a pen name.

The experiences and perspectives of both men and women fill the pages of this book. We tried to find a South Asian lesbian to serve as a co-editor for this project, but those contacted declined for a variety of reasons. This left us with no small dilemma: should we compile an anthology of male experiences only, or would it be acceptable for a man to serve as the sole editor of writings by both men and women? In the end, after discussing the issue with many South Asian lesbians, and in light of the scarcity of opportunities we are given to express ourselves in print, we chose to go with the latter decision.

The purpose of this book is twofold. Firstly, we hope that the publication of this book will increase our visibility in both the South Asian and the gay and lesbian communities. With the reality of our life experiences laid out before their eyes, these two communities cannot deny our existence so easily. Only if they become aware of our existence can they come to acknowledge, understand, and, ideally, accept us. Ultimately, we seek acceptance, not mere tolerance. Tolerance contains an element of condescension, of hierarchy, while acceptance implies an acknowledgment of equal validity for differing ideas and lifestyles. In striving for this acceptance, however, we must take the lead; we must make an active effort to reach others and thus bring about our own empowerment. We must demand that they re-examine their notions about our existence and re-evaluate the stereotypical ways in which they view us.

The issue of empowerment is integral to the second component of this anthology's purpose. Until now, the mainstream world has defined us, as it does with any subgroup, within its parameters. The pages of this book offer us an opportunity to define ourselves. The power of self-definition is awesome because words are tremendously effective tools for reconstruction. When people who were labeled as faggots and dykes chose to refer to themselves as gays and lesbians, when those who were called niggers chose to call themselves black or African-American, they began to claim for themselves the power of self-definition and thus cut through the world's stereotypes of who they were. While it is true that some of these stereotypes continue to exist, they are but mere shadows of what they were once.

We gay and lesbian South Asians now have the same opportunity to empower ourselves, to show the world our diversity, our reality that differs from its stereotypes of us. Exercising this power can force a new image of us upon the world, an image it must acknowledge and examine. Along with changing how others view us, we can also change how we view ourselves. Defining ourselves can transform our self-concept, imbue it with appreciation and replace old, negative ideas with new, positive ones; it can chip away at our own internalized homophobia and replace it with pride. Self-definition can also help in the sometimes painful process of integrating our South Asian and gay or lesbian selves. In addition, it can help us reach out to those South Asians, of any age and gender, who are awakening to and struggling with their own homosexuality or bisexuality; it can make them aware that they are not alone.

In the process of rendering our self-definition, we are discovering our own diversity and we often find ourselves confronted with many issues. The issues that gay and lesbian South Asians must struggle with, as individuals and as a community, include: sexism and misogyny manifested by many gay men; friction between lesbian and gay male communities; racist attitudes that are rooted in both color and caste consciousness; the reality of bisexuality and its stigmatization in both the heterosexual and homosexual worlds; and the tightrope we must walk in learning from, networking with, and teaching our Western sisters and brothers as we steer our own course and thus try to avoid the colonial hangover of following the lead of the West blindly. These issues and others are presented in this book not as exercises in self-flagellation, but as a sample of the challenges we must overcome as we define ourselves and try to build a cohesive, respectful community.

This book can be but a step in the process of self-definition and the push for visibility. The organizations that we form, such as Trikone, Shamakami, Anamika, Khush, Bombay Dost, and Shakti, and the people who pioneer them, people like Arvind Kumar, Ashok Jethanandani, Sharmeen Islam, Anu, Utsa, Shivananda, Nelson Carvalho, and Kartikeya are integral components of this process. These activists, and this book, are important, yet equally important are the countless individuals who engender understanding and respect from the world around them by living openly as gay and lesbian South Asians.

The courageous people who have shared their stories in this book have helped us all take a step forward. The pages that follow are full of our pain and exhilaration, our challenges and victories, our losses and our loves. We have opened ourselves, allowed the world a glimpse of our private realities. Sharing such intimate parts of ourselves will no doubt leave many of us feeling quite vulnerable. The understanding that may be gained, however, is well worth the price. For us, this book is a chance to explore, affirm, and share who we are, in all of our diversity. For our families and friends, for any and everyone who is a part of our world, this is an invitation to gain some understanding of us as gay, lesbian, and bisexual South Asians.

Uncovering our past/
Inventing our present

*Two women sharing an intimate touch. (Temple
carving from the city of Khajuraho, India)*

Homosexuality in India: Culture and heritage

AIDS Bhedbav Virodhi Andolan (ABVA)

ABVA is a nonprofit organization that is successfully focusing
attention on AIDS awareness in India and is also attempting to
increase the consciousness of Indians regarding gay and lesbian
issues. This chapter is excerpted from the book *Less Than Gay:
A Citizens's Report on the Status of Homosexuality in India*,
published by ABVA in 1991.

The religious backgrounds of a culture and its ancient religious
codes are often important sources by which individuals live their
sexual lives. The Kinsey report (a watershed report on sexuality
published in the United States in 1948) concluded that "nothing in
American society has more influence upon present-day patterns of
sexual behavior than the religious backgrounds of that culture ...
ancient religious codes are still the prime source of the attitudes, the
ideas, the ideals and the rationalization by which most individuals
pattern their sexual lives."

If this is so, then the incidence of exclusive homosexual behavior
and of bisexuality in India is bound to be far more than the figures
documented for the United States. In fact, we do not need an Alfred
Kinsey to discover the rich possibilities of same-sex eroticism and to
appropriate these in the form of modern gay sexuality. It's all there
in our art, culture, religion, philosophy, and sculpture.

The medical profession, in particular, is oblivious to this rich
heritage. For instance, Dr. K. Abhayambika, professor of medicine
and state AIDS programme officer, Medical College of Trivandrum,
Kerala, writes:

Even at this end of the twentieth century, the Eastern culture is untinged in its tradition of high morality, monogamous marriage system and safe sex behaviour. Our younger generation and youth still practice virginity till their nuptial day. The religious customs and god-fearing living habits are a shield of protection against many social evils. It will be difficult even for the HIV to penetrate this shield, except in certain metropolitan populations. *(Swasth Hind)*

Typically, this professor, like many others, has not cared to learn about indigenous texts, concepts, and traditions which revered and even celebrated sexual ambiguity, whether in the *Kama Sutra,* through sexual dualism, in mysticism, or in female kingdoms.

On oral congress

Kama Sutra is the first literary classic in the world on matters of sex. It was written by sage Vatsyana in the 4th–5th century A.D. The author compiled verses from Sanskrit texts several centuries old. The work contains an entire chapter, *"Auparishtaka,"* on gay sex. Lesbian activity was stated to have been observed in the *Anthapura* (harem). According to the original *Kama Sutra, Auparishtaka* (oral congress) appears to have been prevalent in some parts of India from a very ancient time. The *Shushruta,* a treatise on medicine some two thousand years old, describes the wounding of the lingam (penis) with the teeth as one of the causes of a disease treated in that work. Traces of the practice are found as far back as the eighth century, for various kinds of *Auparishtaka* are represented in the sculptures of many Shaivite temples of Bhuvaneshwar, Orissa, which were built about that period.

The *Kama Sutra* records that *Auparishtaka* is practiced by the following – male citizens who know each other well, among themselves; women, when they are amorous, do the acts of the mouth on the yonis (vaginas) of one another; some men do the same with women; male servants of some men carry on the mouth congress with their masters; eunuchs with males.

One of the original verses has been translated thus:

Young masseurs usually wearing ear ornaments do allow their friends as well as some men to have mutual oral congress. Sometimes young actors or dandies allow undersexed or elder

22

men to have oral sex with them. It is also practiced by young men who know each other well. Sometimes men who are effeminate indulge in oral sex with each other simultaneously by lying alongside one another inversely. When a man and a woman lie down in an inverted position with the head of the one towards the feet of the other and carry on oral sex with each other it is called *Kakila;* this term is also applicable to oral congress between two males as also two girls or women. (translation by Mulk Raj Anand)

Vatsyana insists that this practice is allowed by the order of the Holy Writ *(Dharam Shastras)* with just a few exceptions.

Of eunuchs, male and female

The *Kama Sutra* refers to two kinds of eunuchs – those disguised as males and those as females. Eunuchs disguised as females imitate their dress, speech, gestures, tenderness, timidity, simplicity, softness, and bashfulness; they derive their imaginative pleasure, and their livelihood from *Auparishtaka* and lead the life of courtesans.

Eunuchs disguised as males lead the life of shampooers and practice *Auparishtaka* with the males they shampoo. The following eight things are said to be done by the eunuch in sequence. At the end of each of these, the eunuch expresses his wish to stop; but when one of them is finished, the man desires him to do another and after that is done, the one that follows it, and so on:

1. When, holding the man's lingam with his hand and placing it between his lips, the eunuch moves his mouth about it, it is called "nominal congress."
2. When, covering the end of the lingam with his fingers collected together like the bud of a plant or flower, the eunuch presses the sides of it with his lips, using his teeth also, it is called "biting the sides."
3. When, being desired to proceed, the eunuch presses the end of the lingam with his lips closed together and kisses it as if he were drawing it out, it is called the "outside pressing."
4. When, being asked to go on, he puts the lingam further into his mouth and presses it with his lips and then takes it out, it is called the "inside pressing."

5. When, holding the lingam in his hand, the eunuch kisses it as if he were kissing the lower lip, it is called "pressing."
6. When, after kissing it, he touches it with his tongue everywhere, and passes his tongue over the end of it, it is called "rubbing."
7. When, in the same way, he puts the half of it into his mouth and forcibly kisses and sucks it, this is called "sucking a mango fruit."
8. And, lastly, when, with the consent of the man the eunuch puts the whole lingam into his mouth and presses it to the very end, as if he were going to swallow it up, it is called "swallowing up."

The methodology of the *Kama Sutra* seems to have been modeled on Kautilya's *Arthashastra*. According to A.A. Macdonnell, emeritus professor of Sanskrit, University of Oxford, "The contents of this work appears to us for the most part indecent, but it must be borne in mind that the Indian is much more outspoken on sexual matters than we are" *(India's Past: A Survey of Her Literatures, Religions, Languages)*. It is a shame that a Westerner has to remind us about our traditional sexual openness whereas we continue to vigorously deny it.

Sexual dualism

What modern psychologists in the twentieth century now acknowledge as sexual dualism in each individual was a principle enunciated in ancient traditions in India. *Ardhanari* (half woman) is a form in which Siva is represented as half-male and half-female, typifying the male and female energies. There are several stories accounting for this form, also called *Ardhahanarisa* and *Pavangada*.

Siva is the third deity of the Hindu triad. He is described as the destroying principle. But destruction in Hindu belief implies reproduction; he is the reproductive power which is perpetually restoring that which has been dissolved. As a restorer, he is represented by his symbol, the lingam, or phallus, typical of reproduction. It is under this form, alone or combined with the yoni, or female organ, the representative of his *shakti*, or female energy, that he is worshiped everywhere.

The idea of sexual dualism is placed before 3000 B.C. In his book *The Religions of India* (1969), A. Barth, member of the Asiatic Society of Paris, states:

> As many as an entire half of the Sivaite religions are, in fact, characterized by the culture of an androgynous or female divinity. The Shakti, such as she appears in these systems of worship, is no longer derived from the metaphysics. It has its roots far away in those ideas, as old as India itself, of a sexual dualism placed at the beginning of things (in a Brahmana of the *Yajur Veda,* for instance, Prajapati is androgynous) or a common womb in which beings are formed, which is also their tomb. It proceeds directly from the *prakriti* of the pure *Sankhaya,* from eternally fertile nature, whence issue both the sensible forms and the intellectual faculties and before which the mind, or male element, acts as a part that is featureless in character and barren of result. It is difficult to come to any precise conclusion in regard to the period when these ideas were translated into religious beliefs.

The supremacy assigned to the female divinity is affirmed in certain *Puranas* and in the literature of the Tantras.

Giti Thadani, a young independent researcher from New Delhi, elucidates on the vision of such a feminine world, "pre-patriarchal" in structure:

> Importance was not attached to the "male-female couple," but on the notion of yoni, which signifies "the womb, the infinite source," the symbol of which was the triangle. The triangle consisted of two points of "light" represented by female twins, symbols of fusion, and of a third point which was the earth. The notion of twins or *jami* also signifies, in various texts, "homosexuality." This triadic system goes back to a family structure in which importance is not attached to the notion of the "social father" or the biological mother, but in which there is a notion of multiple mothers. So, for example, families did not have the names of the biological fathers, but the names of gods; and a child could have one mother for pleasure, one for knowledge, one for art and so on. Sexuality was based on pleasure and on fertility, but not on progeny (the process of passing over the children to the man). Phallic discourse

only appeared with progenic sexuality. So, the first notion of "heterosexuality" appeared under the terminology of *a-jami,* that which is not *jami,* which is not paired, fused as it is in the notion of "homosexuality." *(Shakti Khabbar,* June–July, 1990)

The Sivaite cult

Excavations from the site of the Indus Valley civilization reveal huge stone phalli and rings corresponding to lingams and yonis, as also to prototypes of Siva. It has been suggested by some historians that this civilization was Dravidian and was destroyed by "barbarians," including invaders from northwest Iran. Some have boldly suggested their identification with the Vedic Aryans. Fierce conflicts occurred between the invaders and the Dravidians, whom the Aryans derogatorily called *dasas.* Indra, chief of the Aryan gods, became the mighty destroyer of the forts of the *dasas.* However, some Dravidian gods and goddesses, ideas, and customs were absorbed by the Aryans.

The Vedas (1000–1500 B.C.) did not countenance the worship of the lingam, but this was enjoined in the *Mahabharata* (written by Vyasa, around 500 B.C.) in two passages that appear in later editions. In *Hinduism and Buddhism: An Historical Sketch,* volume 2 (1921), Sir Charles Eliot documents that phallic worship "forms part of the private devotions of the strictest Brahmana and is not connected with low-castes, with orgies, with obscene or blood thirsty rites or with anything which can be called un-Aryan."

The appropriation of Siva without Shakti was the selective borrowing of an Aryan culture which was becoming increasingly brahmanical (some have suggested patriarchal) in structure. What were the rituals connected with the Sivaite cult which were surgically excised from the form of phallic worship that became part of mainstream Hinduism?

Tantric rituals

Describing Tantra as a school of thought that evolved the idea of universal bisexuality in human personality, Subodh Mukherjee, a gay man from Calcutta, writes:

Along with Tantra came the yogic ideas of six *chakras,* or nerve

26

centres, within the human body. According to Tantra philosophy, the basal *chakra* lies in the perineum (between the anus and the phallus/vagina) of the human body where the *kundalini,* the serpentine power of enlightenment, is said to lie (or sleep) in a coiled state. The sexo-yogic methods of Tantric discipline seek to arouse this power and make it shoot up the spine, through the six *chakras,* straight up to the cerebrum in the brain.

French Indologist Alain Danielou, in his book *Shiva and Dionysus,* explains the Tantric rite of anal penetration thus:

> There is a whole ritual connected with anal penetration through the narrow gate opening into the labyrinth (in the man the intestine). In Tantric yoga, the centre of Ganesha – the guardian of the gates – is found in the region of the rectum. The male organ, in directly penetrating the area of coiled energy, may help its brutal awakening and thus provoke a state of enlightenment and sudden perception of realities of a transcendental order.

The objective of Tantric rites is to harmonize and combine "the two polar principles, Shiva and Shakti, in one's own body"; this conception of human bisexuality elevates the homosexual to the pedestal of great sanctity (Mircea Eliade, *Méphistophélès et l'Androgyne).* "The hermaphrodite, the homosexual and the transvestite have a symbolic value and are considered privileged beings, images of Ardha-Narishwara" (Danielou).

Ardhanarishwara abroad

In sharp contrast to such celebration of sexual dualism, the official position of the Indian government on the theme of *Ardha-narishwara* can be summed up by the following description by noted Hindi writer Mrinal Pande:

> A choreographic display of the traditional Ardha-narishwara theme sent one of our venerable Indian diplomats in Moscow into a paroxysm of rage. The theme of this proposed exhibition through dance and mime illustrated beautifully how men and women house so many different capacities within male and female forms, the full range of which lies suppressed very frequently under societal taboos. But the diplomat's spluttering rage saw to

27

it that the programme was canceled. One wonders just how many musicians, dancers, and craftsmen the country must have thus lost due to this curious and intolerant obsession with body image, genitals, and "masculine" or "feminine" behaviour of a certain kind. Wouldn't it be far healthier to have a society where, without disfiguring the body, a man or a woman can, if s/he feels like it, keep house, dance, take to music or embroidery or cooking or take on a job, play, go out when s/he feels like it, if only to bum around with his/her mates, without ever feeling freaky or apologetic. *(The Independent,* quoted in *Bombay Dost,* May 1990)

Mysticism

Religious mysticism constitutes another tradition that subverts rigid male/female, masculine/feminine distinctions. Gandhi, for instance, aspired "to become God's eunuch"; many Christians seek a union of their hearts with the Sacred Heart of Jesus and the sorrowful heart of the Virgin; and many Sikhs find the intimacy of spiritual love expressed in terms of the earthly bride's wedding with the transcendental Lord. Other mystics have included Mira, the queen of Udaipur, who found her fulfillment in the love of Krishna; sixteenth-century poets Kabir, Malik Mohammed Jiyasi, Tulsidas and Eknath, poet Chandidas; Abhiram Swami and Vikramangal; and various other Sufi and Tantric mystic sects.

Radha Kamal Mukherjee in his book *The Theory and Art of Mysticism* (1960) describes a type of mystical experience –

> fervent mysticism, saturated with intense emotional satisfaction in which God appears in a concrete human pattern, and the mystic in his state of rapture can hardly distinguish between the apprehension of his unity with God and sensual and even sexually determined delight. Deep and delicate affections here blossom forth into spiritual love of which the species and types are as different as the various human relationships and the moods and temperaments of individuals.

In a recent book *The Analyst and the Mystic* (1991), psychoanalyst Sudhir Kakar explains the mysticism of Ramakrishna, one of the greatest modern mystics, thus:

Ramakrishna felt that the classical disciplines of Yoga were very difficult to follow for most human beings since the identification of the self with the body, which these disciplines seek to undo, was too deeply embedded for any easy surrendering. For those who could not get rid of the feeling of "I," it was easier to travel on the devotional path where one could instead cherish the idea that "I am God's servant" (or child, friend, mother, or lover) ... The *vairagya,* the renunciation [of the passions] can take place equally well by changing the object of these passions, directing them toward God rather than the objects of the world. "Lust for intercourse with the soul. Feel angry with those who stand in your way toward God. Be greedy to get to Him. If there is attachment, then to Him: like *my* Rama, *my* Krishna...

"The longing had to be so intense that it completely took over body and mind, eliminating any need for performing devotions, prayers, or rituals ... Devotion *(bhakti)* matures into *bhava,* followed by *mahabhava, prema,* and then attainment of God in the *unio mystica...*

"Practicing the *madhurya-bhava* of Radha towards Krishna he [Ramakrishna] dressed, behaved, and lived as a girl for six months ... When living in the motherly *bhava* of Yashoda towards Krishna, he had one disciple, who felt like a child toward him, lean against his lap as if suckling at his breast while the mystic talked or listened to the concerns of his other disciples." Ramakrishna once described how "the Divine Mother revealed to me in the Kali mother that it was She who had become everything."

Female kingdoms

Strong lesbian feelings and activities are reputed to have existed in a female kingdom during the latter part of the first century B.C. Parts of northern India had plunged into darkness at this time because of a foreign invasion. King Amlat attacked and captured Pataliputra. Atrocities were committed on local inhabitants. The attack by the Huns resulted in mass-scale tragedies. According to available records of the time:

In this dangerous war, practically all men of the nation were killed, so women had to do all the work. They ploughed the land

and protected the fields with bows and arrows. The women organized themselves. Men were so weak that on an average 10–20 women married the same man. All business in villages and cities was looked after by the women. (from the works of Gragacharya)

References to female kingdoms are also found elsewhere:

1. Kautilya (4th century B.C.), the prime minister of Chandra Gupta Maurya, has referred to such kingdoms in his monumental work *Arthashastra*. *Stri rajya* existed in various parts of India.
2. Kalidas (4th century B.C.), our national poet, refers to such kingdoms in his works.
3. Hieuen Tsang (7th century), the Chinese pilgrim, refers to two female kingdoms in his commentaries.
4. *Mahabharata* (800–500 B.C.), by Vyasa, contains references to two kingdoms, those of *Alli* and *Pavazha Kodi,* both female monarchs. A verse in the *Mahabharata* also refers to women stimulating each other's genitals and condemns them for using an artificial penis. Two references to *hijras* also occur in this work:
   a. Shikhandi (Sanskrit word for peacock, our national bird, which is also a symbol of sexual energy) was a hermaphrodite or eunuch.
   b. During their last year in exile, Yudhisthira asks Arjuna, the hero of the *Mahabharata,* what disguise and profession he will take up for the thirteenth year in order to remain undiscovered. Arjuna answers that he will hide himself in the guise of a eunuch and serve the ladies of the court. Arjuna had been cursed with the loss of manhood in a previous encounter with the goddess Urvasi, but through the grace of god Indra the curse would only hold for one year. So, Arjuna, by living for one year as a eunuch, would be fulfilling two duties at once. He describes how he shall spend the year "wearing bangles made of white conches, braiding my hair like a woman, and clothing myself in female attire, I shall engage myself in menial work in the inner apartments of the queen. I shall teach the women

singing and dancing" (Serena Nanda, "The Hijras of India, A Preliminary Report," 1984). Arjuna is said to have exclaimed in court, "Know me, O king of men to be *Vrihannal,* a son or daughter without a father or mother." (*Virata Parva,* Section 11)

Many *hijras,* including one that an ABVA member spoke to in a slum in Delhi, point to this story as the story of their origin. They also narrate the story of Ram's return from exile whereupon he found a group of *hijras* at the entrance of the jungle; they had awaited his return for fourteen years. Moved by their gesture, Ram is said to have promised that they would rule the world in the distant future.

In Valmiki's *Ramayana,* Hanuman sees women in passionate embrace in the palaces of Lanka "as if they were making love to their male lovers."

Muslim culture

As the above will have shown, homosexuality, and specifically sodomy, was not introduced into India by Muslims. Under Muslim rulers, however, homosexuality entered Indian court life. Harems of young boys were kept by Muslim *nawabs* and Hindu aristocrats in the sixteenth century. The Emperor Babar wrote romantically about his famous love affair with the boy Baburi at Andezan in the *Tuzuk-i-Babri.* Dargah Quli Khan, an important official in the principality of Hyderabad, observed important homosexual activities and homosexual love in the life and culture of Delhi on the eve of Nadir Shah's invasion. His personal diary, *Muraqqa-e-Delhi: The Mughal Capital in Muhammad Shah's Time,* contains some glimpses of gay life during his three-year stay in Delhi, between 1739 and 1741.

Azam Khan, one of the chief nobles of the empire, is described in this memoir as "a pederast [who] is fond of beautiful girls as well ... Whenever he is informed of the availability of a lad or a beautiful girl he endeavours to be the buyer." Similarly, Mirza Munnu, a man of notable birth

is also perfect in this sort of sodomy. He acts as a guide to the novices who in turn feel proud to imbibe this trade from him. He organizes *mehfils* (shows) where groups of lads are made available. His house is the palace of Shaddad (an impious king and founder of *Bagh-e-Iram,* where all the beautiful whores get together), full of fairy-like lads and lasses...

Again,

Sultana is a twelve-year-old, olive complexioned catamite, whose coquetry reflects itself in his dancing ... He is a bud who competes with flowers or the flame of the lamp facing the light of the sun. The audience wishes to hear him repeatedly and their thirst for a vision of his beauty is not easily quenched.

Mian Hinga is a fair complexioned youth and in his white dress looks fresh as the jasmine flower. He holds an assembly outside the walls of the Imperial Fort ... Many renowned people go for walks to the chowk and, under the pretense of buying rare objects, watch him perform ... he looks as fresh as dawn dipped in dew ... in spite of many invitations, he never visits anyone at their residence. His fans have to visit his house if they wish to derive pleasure from his acts. *(Muraqqa-e-Delhi,* translated by C. Shekhar and S. Chenoy)

In Islamic Sufi literature homosexual eroticism was a major metaphorical expression of the spiritual relationship between god and man, and much Persian poetry and fiction used gay relationships as examples of moral love. Although the Koran and early religious writings of Islam display mildly negative attitudes toward homosexuality, Muslim cultures treated homosexuality with indifference, if not admiration. The classic works of Arabic poetry and prose, from poet Abu Nuwas to the *Thousand and One Nights,* treat gay people and their sexuality with respect or casual acceptance. The Arabic language contains a huge vocabulary of gay erotic terminology, with dozens of words just to describe types of male prostitutes. Erotic address by one male to another is the standard convention of Arabic love poetry; even poems really written for women frequently use male pronouns and metaphors of male beauty. The association of homosexual feelings with moral looseness appears to be a comparatively recent phenomenon (John Boswell, *Christianity, Social Tolerance, and Homosexuality).*

Thus it is clear that homosexuality as a phenomenon is not new to India, and, perhaps because of the religious background of our culture, it has not been an unrelenting tale of oppression and woe. It is easy today to find the existence of the entire gamut of same-sex intimacies in India – intense friendship, romance, and companionship between people of the same sex; sexual interactions not perceived by the partners as a basis for defining their identity in terms of sexual orientation; and homosexual sex and emotional involvement self-consciously recognized as a gay identity.

Fighting back

an interview with Pratibha Parmar

Khush

Pratibha Parmar is a pioneering filmmaker whose works include *Sari Red,* a short piece that couples a lyrical narrative with haunting images and explores lethal racism in England. *Memory Pictures,* a video about gay South Asian photographer Sunil Gupta; *Flesh and Paper,* a film about poet and writer Suniti Namjoshi; and *Khush,* about gay and lesbian South Asians, are three of Pratibha's other works. In this interview, she discusses with members of Khush, a Toronto-based organization of lesbian and gay South Asians, her background, her works, and her goals.

Khush: Let's start with some background.
Pratibha: I was born in Kenya, in Nairobi. My parents left when I was eleven to go live in England. My father went first in '67, we followed in '68. We migrated, as did many Asians, because of the Africanization policies brought in by the Kenyan government. I grew up in London, went to school there, and later to a university in the north of England.

Were your parents born in Kenya or...?
No, my mother was born in Kenya – she was second-generation Indian Asian–Kenyan. My father was born in India.

When would you say that you first felt a sense of "otherness," in Kenya or in England?
I distinctly remember that sense of being an outsider in England and being made to feel that, somehow, what we were – who we were – wasn't right. Going to school in London in '68, there was a lot of

racism. Enoch Powell, this very racist MP (member of Parliament), made his famous speech about "rivers of blood," referring to future civil wars because of this alien migrant influx.

There was a lot of Paki-bashing by skinhead gangs (*Paki,* derived from Pakistani, is a pejorative used by racists in England to describe people from the Indian subcontinent). My school was in a white working-class area, and, although there were some other Indian children, we were in the minority. We were victims of Paki-bashing from skinheads in our schools. That's where I learned to fight back and struggle because you had to – if you didn't, you got crushed.

Did the experience of coming from Africa and being once again in a minority situation, albeit within a "black" context, affect your development in terms of anti-racist work? Or was the experience as an Asian more important?

I think it was much more my experience as an Asian in Britain, because I was too young to really understand what was going on in Africa. My memory of growing up in Nairobi was that of being enclosed within an Indian community, going to an Indian school, and not having much contact with African people. It was more the experience of being Asian in Britain that made me be involved in anti-racist struggles and then work with different groups in the black communities.

You mentioned [in an earlier conversation] that when you went to a conference in Kerala, it was the first time that you really became politicized.

In Kenya we were taught to think of India as home. Even in England, India was still home and was referred to as such by my parents and everyone else. So, when I was twenty or twenty-one, I took a year off from the university to go live and work in India. I went with the notion of seeing what this place I was brought up to think of as home was. In England, the image of India was somewhere with all of these starving millions. Well, I thought, that's my home and I want to do something about it.

I had these very idealistic, romantic, humanitarian notions about doing voluntary work in the villages – which I did for a year. This was in 1975, at the start of the United Nations' Decade of Women.

35

I went to some of the conferences being organized by women's organizations there. This was my first introduction to Marxism, as well as to theories of social change, in a very practical way, because it was also the year in which [Prime Minister] Indira Gandhi called an emergency (a legal order suspending a variety of civil rights). That combination really politicized me as a woman, as a feminist, but also as an Indian person. It also helped me give a language to the experiences that I had had in Britain. When I had gone to India, I didn't really have an anti-racist language and didn't even define myself as black. Only when I went to India did I get a sense in which I was an outsider in Britain and find a language for it.

Can you tell us about the sense of internal exile, the sense of being different from one's own community because of one's sexuality?

Being exiles is in many ways a problematic term. I don't think that politically I would say that we are exiled in Britain. We might feel that in some sort of a psychic or cultural way, and we may be treated as exiles, but I would assert that we are not exiles but settlers. Getting back to that sense of exile, if we are out as lesbians and gays in our communities, then we take the risk of being rejected by our families and communities. More than rejected, completely shunned and not allowed access to any of our cultural events or anything like that.

For many of us, our families are very important, as they give us a base, a refuge, from racism, and give us a sense of our own identity as Indian people. That's what I mean by internal exiles, whether we come out or not, we are exiles within our communities. If we come out, we are more often than not exiled by the community. If we don't come out, we still feel that sense of exile because we are unable to share a very real part of ourselves with them.

How do you find life now as a public figure in England with respect to the reaction of family and community?

It's frightening when you realize the level of homophobia that exists. In England there is a lot of homophobia that is given expression through actual physical abuse of lesbians and gays on the streets. I feel like I'm always coming out; it's not as if you come out once and that's it. What gives me strength to carry on doing it is

36

meeting younger South Asian lesbians and gays who say that it's very important for them to see what I'm doing and to be out saying the things that I say. They identify with the things I've written and that gives me strength and makes me feel, well, good.

Tell us how you became a filmmaker. What path did you take to get there ... did you come into it as an editor, a writer, a poet...?

As a community activist. I was a youth worker, working with young Asian women, setting up Asian girls' groups in schools and colleges. We did some work around how we were represented in the media. We made our own videos around the community. Then we worked with photography, taking photographs of each other, and explored ideas about images and self-images and how those are important in the way we think about ourselves and form our identity. Especially since from the mainstream newspapers all you consistently get is very negative images of yourself, images and stereotypes that are not true to your own experiences. Many of these young women, like myself, got very angry with that kind of depiction of us as meek and mild victims of arranged marriages and terrible parents and all of the sort of nonsense that they say about Indian culture and families.

Also, because of my academic background, I was asked to work on a series of documentaries for Channel 4 about the black communities. Two of these were about the Asian communities in Southhall and Leicester. I did research by talking to people who would have come as first migrants in the 1950s about their experiences to the present. Then I started making my own videos and films, initially by getting people to work on things for nothing because I didn't have any funds. I got people involved in my productions or produced them with small grants from independent funding bodies. It's only in the last year that I've started to do work for television and it's taken many years to get to that stage of funding.

Could you tell us about Channel 4, particularly about the program "Out on Tuesday"?

"Out on Tuesday" is a lesbian and gay magazine program which first went out on Channel 4, which is the only channel for independent work and alternative documentaries. The show is a series commissioned by Caroline Spry to try and bring in a magazine program that examined all different aspects of the lesbian and gay experience in England and internationally on a regular basis. One of the show's premises was not to explain lesbians and gays to a straight audience. It was very much on the terms that lesbians and gays would do it for themselves and for their communities.

For the first series there were over one million viewers, and that ran at eleven p.m. The first series ran for eight weeks and the second series this year for ten weeks. That's really an achievement, especially in a climate like the last few years, where Clause 28, an anti-lesbian and -gay act, was passed through Parliament, and because of the crisis around AIDS, which has really compounded all of the prejudice.

What kind of feedback have you had from the program so far?

In the first series I directed a twenty-minute item on lesbians and gays adopting children. This involved talking to both white and black communities. Then I worked as a researcher for a program about two gay political activists in South Africa, Simon Nkoli and Ivan Toms. I've also worked with Sunil Gupta on a four-minute video postcard about gay men in India. Really great response.

What you've done is pretty broad ranging, so that it appeals to anyone, and that's important.

Yes, especially for TV because you have such a mixed audience.

It's good that the premise is not educational, otherwise there would be a constant going over of the same ground. Freedom is being able to develop an idea as an idea, rather than having to assume that your audience is going to want to be educated about homosexuality. As you said in *Flesh and Paper*, it was simply a fact in the film that Suniti [Namjoshi] was a lesbian and her work was lesbian. But it was not an educational thing. If the viewer does not know in the beginning that Suniti is a lesbian, it somehow takes away the sensationalism and "normalizes" it.

That's exactly what I wanted to do in *Flesh and Paper*. I think it was a level of maturity to come to that, to say for ourselves, well, here is this woman who is a writer, a poet, and she's lesbian. This is her writing and this is her story. That's a fact of her existence. We are lesbians and gays and it's not a problem for us. If it's a problem for others, they have to look at or read our work on our terms; we don't have to be apologetic about who we are or try to explain it.

How would you feel about having your work shown in India?

I would like my work shown in India. I'm going to plug into some of the film festivals that are going on there, which is one way to get them shown to a lot of people. I don't really know how they will respond. But I think it would be a fruitful exchange for people in India to see some of the kind of experiences of Asians living outside of India. They know racism exists, but they don't really know the extent of it. But also, for a lot of middle-class Indians in India who are sort of scathing about Indians in Britain, it's almost a class thing; they see us as migrants who are ruining the name of Indians abroad, in the West.

Gaze into your crystal ball and tell us what you see happening in the next five years.

[*Laughing*] Where, happening where, and with who?

In London, in England, with South Asian gays and lesbians.

I could answer that in terms of saying what has happened in the last few years. When I first came out twelve years ago, there were very few South Asian lesbians and gays around. We knew we were around and would travel hundreds of miles to meet. Now, twelve years later, we have Shakti, a very strong, over-1,000-member gay and lesbian group with a newsletter, regular meetings, and socials.

Because of Shakti, we have a lot of younger lesbians and gays who are able to come out into a supportive environment. They know that there are people they can go and talk to. There's a group of men and women in Shakti working on a housing project for young people forced to leave home because they have come out to their families. Projects like these are positive and they make me feel good and, at times, envious. I wish that was around when I was coming out, instead of being one of the ones who had to build the base, the groundwork.

Now there are programs on TV. Not that many, and some are pretty awful because they still problematize us and make us into victims who don't have control of their sexuality, but it is talked about. We are beginning to exist as a visible group within our communities. I think a lot has happened, is happening, and I'm sure in the next five years will continue to happen.

What are your plans? Where do you see yourself in five years, doing what things? Call it a wish list.

Right. I would like to be living on an island where it's sunny year-round, with a group of friends and you know...

To be more realistic, I guess I really want to continue to make films. With filmmaking, I really feel I have found a medium in a way that's most fulfilling for me personally and politically, where I can be creative at the same time as making work that I hope is meaningful. Work that is actually going to help bring about change, no matter how small. I hope to adopt a child and to be parenting by that time.

Would you want to go live in India?

No. No, I did think about that at one time, when I went in '75. Since then, I go back every three years. I don't want to go back and live there because, as a woman and as an out lesbian, I'd find it very difficult. That is the sad reality, especially having talked to lesbians living in India and hearing of the ways in which their lives are circumscribed. It is bad enough in England.

Toward a global network of Asian lesbians

Sharmeen Islam*

Since the mid-1980s, a number of exciting events have heralded the emergence of the Asian lesbian and gay movement, both in the United States and in Asia. The formation of AMALGM (Alliance of Massachusetts Asian Lesbians and Gay Men), Trikone (gay and lesbian South Asians), and Shamakami (a forum for South Asian feminist lesbians and bisexual women) has added new and welcome diversity to the voice of the lesbian and gay movement worldwide. An immensely successful 1989 conference/retreat of Asian lesbians in Santa Cruz, California, which drew participants from the United States, Britain, Canada, and numerous countries in Asia, is another sign of our awakening. Conferences of Asian lesbians convened in Asia, the first held in Bangkok, Thailand, in 1990, and a second to be held in Tokyo, Japan, in 1992, serve further notice that the time for the mobilization of lesbian and gay Asians has arrived. These groups and events provide us Asians with badly needed support and give us a forum to address the issues that are not always addressed adequately in both the Asian and lesbian and gay communities.

One of the issues that has begun to be addressed is the oppression of racism in the gay and lesbian mainstream. In the United States, our history has been excluded from lesbian history, our literature from gay and lesbian literature, and our images from our community's media. The evidence of lesbianism in Asian cultures predates the days of Sappho, yet this history is not known, read, taught, or researched in the mainstream lesbian and gay context. The gay culture in the West marginalizes our experience and lumps all nonwhite women under the umbrella term "lesbians of color," thus denying our diversity. Recently, a renowned gay defense organization, Lambda, chose to use *Miss Saigon,* a racist, sexist play with Asian stereotypes, as a means for fundraising in New York City. These are just some examples of the oppressions on which we, Asian-American and immigrant women, spent much energy in the last decade. We fought to educate, to make room for ourselves, to make our voices heard in an oppressed community's social, literary, and political spheres.

In many Asian countries the desire to create a positive identity and existence as lesbians entails obstacles above and beyond those faced by our sisters in the West. In Iran, perhaps the most extreme example, gays have been stoned to death simply for being themselves. Such problems of oppression and persecution render the West an attractive haven for many Asian gays and lesbians. In a real sense, many of them are sexual refugees who, in the extreme example, may be escaping summary execution. Yet when they turn to the West, they face another brand of oppression: being gay is reason enough for denial to enter or immigrate into the United States. If they do somehow make it into the country and perhaps gain some residency status, they are silenced and inhibited by immigration problems and threats of deportation. The fears and persecution accompanying this status severely limit our mobility, our choice of living an openly gay life, and our desire to be politically active.

Along with these fears, Asian lesbians often face a loss of cultural, familial, and spiritual support in the alien culture that they "choose" to embrace as a refuge. Others rarely understand that a choice between being a lesbian and leaving one's native country for good is not a choice free of cost. Asian lesbians who grow up in the United States and women of mixed heritage face still other problems. They grow up with negative stereotypes about themselves and their cultures; both overt and subtle racism dwell in the land their parents or grandparents emigrated to in the hope of finding a better life.

As numerous as the negative consequences of our oppression are, there is a brighter side; some positive experiences result, however unintentional, from the oppression. The emergence of the identities "lesbian of color" in the U.S. and "black lesbian" in the U.K., while denying our diversity, have enabled us to move toward unity and to network with many lesbians of color worldwide. This sisterhood through shared oppression and experience is unique and has opened many doors and dialogues between us, connections that may not have been possible otherwise. The creative art form in our exhibits, poetry, anthologies, films, music, and journals have combined our experiences of pain and exile into culturally positive art with progressive themes on sexuality and feminism. Two examples that immediately come to mind are the films *Khush,* by Pratibha Parmar, and *Khush Refugees,* by Nidhi Singh.

The potential and the responsibilities of the Asian lesbian and gay movement extend beyond a response to white racism and homophobia. It is necessary that we collaborate in the liberation of gays and lesbians in Asia; we must take in hand the reins of our destiny and determine our sexuality and politics in our own cultural context. We must pull together a global community that empowers Asian lesbians and gays everywhere.

In order to achieve these objectives, the various Asian lesbian and gay communities, in the West and in the East, need to network with one another. The formation of the South Asian lesbian organization Shamakami, which I founded in 1990, illustrates this process of networking. The word *shamakami* is from my native Bengali language and it means "love for your equal or same." As I stated in the first editorial for this organization's newsletter, I personally feel very good about the word *lesbian.* It is a powerful word, yet I think it's important to convey the same meaning and power in our own language. We women who love other women are not untouchable, nor are we invisible; we are nameless only for as long as we choose not to name ourselves. We are unique, we are courageous and beautiful, we are pioneering women. We are *shamakami* and we need to show that we are proud of our existence.

Shamakami was formed with two visions in mind: the creation of a structured way of networking for South Asian lesbians and the creation of a forum in which we can express our sexuality and feminism in our own cultural context. In 1990, Shamakami had no funds, an initial membership list of about 40, and a collective of about nine women. Today the organization provides free circulation of newsletters in South Asia, has a membership of 230, and has an active collective of about twenty women. This year, a woman from Assam, one of the more remote parts of India, connected with two lesbians in different parts of India through Shamakami and thus broke her isolation. In June 1991, a contingent of South Asian lesbians participated in a gay parade, marching joyously behind the Shamakami banner during the gay pride festivities in San Francisco.

Shamakami is one example of how an organization for Asian lesbians in the U.S. can contribute to not only the lives of those of us here, but to the lives of our sisters worldwide. However, we need to build a much more powerful network if we are to address the serious issues facing Asian lesbians across this planet.

The challenges confronting Asian lesbians today include the need for visible and powerful lesbian and gay organizations in Asian countries. These organizations have begun to form slowly in some countries, such as Japan, India, and Hong Kong. We Asian lesbians in the West need to be supportive of these nascent groups and to serve as a resource to these networks based outside the Western world.

At this point lesbian invisibility is the norm, not the exception, even in these gay organizations in Asia. This is due in large part to the economic and political discrimination that women face in Asian societies; this oppression makes it nearly impossible for a "single" woman to survive. There are also the familial pressures; women who want to live without the "benefit" of a man's presence and protection are considered aberrant and thus suspect.

Overt violence against lesbians and gays in the international arena is routine. As mentioned earlier, over ninety people were executed last year for being gay in Iran; in India, two policewomen who chose to undergo a marriage ceremony together were persecuted and jailed by the authorities; in China, electric shock is administered as a form of torture to lesbians; in Mexico, the ILGA (International Lesbian and Gay Alliance) conference was threatened and had to be moved to a different location. To compound the problem, the information about these incidents and follow-up reports and lobbying efforts have been minimal or nonexistent.

Perhaps the biggest problem faced by the average lesbian in Asia today is an extreme isolation which stems from a lack of community; there is a dearth of native literature on gay and lesbian lifestyles, few "out" role models, and little in the way of organizations. And, of course, there are the oppressive legal codes and the lack of anti-discrimination laws.

As we Asian lesbians in the West become aware of these and other problems faced by our sisters in Asia, we must recognize that many of us have economic, academic, intellectual, personal, lifestyle, and political freedom and privilege that is not available to the same degree to lesbians in the East. Conversely, lesbians in Asia must acknowledge that Asian women who live in the West face a set of unique and important daily issues: racism, exile, immigration and deportation threats, cultural isolation, and Western hybridization.

In coming together and creating organizations, conferences, and networks, Asian lesbians have made an immeasurable leap forward in gaining visibility and empowerment. However, we can work toward improving the existence of Asian lesbians and gays across this world in many other ways.

We can publicize ourselves, our viewpoint, and our lifestyle to Amnesty International and similar organizations. We can lobby to have these organizations intervene in situations where lesbians and gays are being imprisoned, raped, and killed or are being persecuted for being politically active. We can also publicize our existence to the United Nations for concrete recognition as an oppressed group in need of economic and political assistance, and refugee status.

We can publicize our news in the media of the Western countries. Information about persecution and victories pertaining to gays and lesbians internationally could be disseminated in the United States. Additionally, we can help keep the lesbian and gay community informed about and involved in international issues, whether this entails the selection of statesmen and women or the determination of foreign policy. Similarly, we can also make the governments and media of Asian countries aware of our existence and struggle.

By taking such actions, by forming organizations in and between our respective countries that are organized, efficient, and egalitarian, and by accepting one another for who we are, without judgment, we stand to achieve so much in our struggle to be acknowledged and accepted on an equal footing with other human beings.

We must define and promote Asian gay and lesbian culture, celebrate our survival and progress, and be committed to making social and political changes that are necessary for all oppressed communities to succeed. We must move towards globalizing issues. We must break our geographic and cultural barriers and reach out to other Asian sisters everywhere. We must continue to move forward in deconstructing sexism, classism, and homophobia. Together we are strong and powerful, not just in numbers but in our diversity.

Feminism and men

Rakesh Ratti

"The word *gay* should be good enough for all of us," my friend said with characteristic sincerity. "Using *gay* to describe men and *lesbian* to describe women is much too divisive."

"Each one of us should have the right to label ourselves as we please," another responded.

"But there aren't that many of us to begin with. We undercut our own power when we fractionate into smaller groups."

"We are all men. How dare we presume to decide what is good for all of us, when half of 'us' in this world are women!"

"We" at that moment consisted of four gay Indian men. It was one of the initial meetings of Trikone, and we had run into unforeseen problems over the designation of our organization. Should we describe ourselves as an organization of gay South Asians or should we also add *lesbian* to the title?

All of us desired to be as inclusive as possible; calling ourselves South Asians rather than Indians, and thus tangibly welcoming Sri Lankans, Pakistanis, Bangladeshis, Nepalis, and Bhutanis, had been the first step. The question of gay and lesbian brought more debate. On the one hand, people like my well-meaning friend thought that the word *gay* would be more unifying. Some lesbians, not self-identified as a part of Trikone, thought it presumptuous of us to speak for women when we had no female members, and they did not want the word *lesbian* included. In the middle were a few of us who felt that both words, *gay* and *lesbian,* should be used, not because we spoke for both, rather because we hoped for a mixed group void of patriarchal exclusivity.

The Trikone incident was not the first time that I had encountered the issue of feminism among men and, more specifically, gay men. Years before, when I had been one of the organizers of a gay and lesbian pride parade in Sacramento, California, a number of us had anguished over the same argument. We live in a world that has been continually defined by men, a world in which men have zealously protected their position of power. As women assert their right to share in that power, this issue is bound to come to the forefront. Too often it is framed along gender lines, as if only women are or should be conscious of gender inequality. Too often we as men buy into this view and lose sight of the fact that gender inequality is an important topic not only because it oppresses half of the human race, but also because this same inequity oppresses us as men and confines us to a small segment of the spectrum.

My reasons for having strong feminist beliefs are purely personal. Like most South Asian men, I was raised to uphold a clearly defined separation of the sexes; a glaring double standard existed in my household. Father was an autocrat, though a gentle one for me, while Mother was the archetypal co-dependent Indian woman – tremendously nurturing, submissive, suffering in silence. My father's attitude toward his sons and daughters was like night and day; the boys were the light of his eyes, especially me, as the youngest, but he had few kind words for my sisters. Just as my mother had to be subservient to my father, the daughters in the family were expected to cater to the sons.

As an adolescent, I became a mouthpiece for my mother and my one sister who was still living at home. It might have been out of guilt, it might have been a budding feeling of outrage at injustice in the world around me, but whatever gave birth to my early activism led me into many a battle with my father over his attitude toward women. I suppose that, in some sense, when I lend my voice to the chorus demanding a just standard for women now, I am still fighting for my sisters and my mother.

My family, because of its rural roots, may be a bit more conservative than most South Asian families, yet the dynamic that operated in our household is not atypical. To understand this dynamic, and the ideas and attitudes it gives rise to, one must understand some of the religious and familial influences within which it operates.

The religious foundations of South Asia, based largely in the Hindu and Islamic faiths, institutionalize an inferior status for females. Women are largely viewed as the property of men (as are children). A good Moslem woman is required to keep herself covered at all times, is expected to walk a few paces behind her husband, and can be divorced by him if he simply utters, "I divorce you," a requisite number of times. A Hindu woman is encouraged to look at her husband as *pati-parmeshvar,* a representation of God. She must be subservient not only to her husband, but also to his family. Hinduism gave rise to the ritual of *sati* (widow burning); whatever its roots and frequency, this act is the most blatant and brutal symbol of the idea that a woman becomes worthless when she loses her man.

Paradoxically, this same culture that forces a woman to seek status through her relationships with men (as mother, daughter, wife, etc.) also provides increased flexibility in sex roles for males. In South Asia, the individuation process of the male child, as defined by psychoanalytic psychology, also does not follow the pattern more common in the West. In Euro-American families the primary dyad is that of husband and wife; the male child eventually must break with the mother, for his connection with her is seen as a threat to the father, which in turn threatens the child. In the South Asian family the primary dyad is that of mother and son; there is a societal expectation that this connection will be maintained. The connection between the mother and a male child undergoes modification, but the child individuates without severing this bond. (This connection is not that of day-to-day contact or a necessarily deeper emotional sharing, but rather one of psychological dependence.) The end result is that the mother, and other females in his life, play a more influential role in the life of the South Asian male, and for a longer period of time.

As a result, a South Asian man is likely to have a sensibility that incorporates more of the "feminine" than his Western counterpart. Unfortunately, this does not necessarily change his view of gender roles. Because of religious and historic influences and an entrenched power structure based on gender, he is still likely to restrict women to roles based on tradition and on women's relationships with men. It is such an oppressive paradox that men who allow themselves to experience more of their "feminine" self continue to undervalue women and thus perpetuate their oppression.

A wide variety of experiences may sensitize a man, gay or straight, South Asian or other, to the inequality women face. These experiences may be formal or informal, political or personal. I think that the experience of dealing with the world as a marginalized "other" can open a man's eyes to the added obstacles women face. I know that as a gay man, I have suffered at the hands of this same sexist system that renders the double standard for women; the mistreatment of women and of gays and lesbians springs from the same source. Our patriarchal systems, be they American or South Asian, have much vested in keeping the sexes as well defined and far apart as possible; only with this separation can their power structure be maintained. Feminist women, who want to share the power, are seen as a threat. Lesbians and gays, who threaten to blur the distinctions between traditional ideas of masculinity and femininity, pose a similar danger.

In the time that I have been active in issues of interest to gay and lesbian South Asians, I have encountered many more men than women from our subcontinent. This may be because, as a man, my circle of friends is likely to be more male. On the other hand, it also crystallizes the fact that South Asian lesbians face added obstacles in coming to terms with their identity. They must liberate themselves not only as lesbians in a straight society, but also as women in a patriarchal culture. In a world that tries to keep them tied to the home, to children, and to the concept of male-identified status, they are given less support and fewer opportunities, by both family and society, to strive for independence; the South Asian system has pragmatic reasons to keep them dependent.

Unfortunately, South Asian lesbians also receive little under-standing from South Asian gay men and are faced with the task of educating on yet another front. So many of us reflect the hierarchical gender attitudes of our fathers. While we demand that our cultures treat gay men equitably, we undervalue our lesbians sisters in relationship to ourselves. I have heard many South Asian gay men complain that some women's organizations, such as radicalesbian

50

groups, are separatist, divisive, and therefore pose a threat to unity in our community. Is it really that difficult to understand the purpose of these organizations? There is nothing complicated about wanting to put distance between you and a system that has oppressed you. We, as gay and lesbian people, have formed our own organizations to gain some identity; separation from the larger system and self-labeling are both necessary for any group to unite. As South Asian lesbians and gays, we have gone through a similar process. Why should it be difficult to understand when some women choose to disengage themselves from the male presence and construct a totally woman-identified persona?

On what basis do gay men react adversely to this choice? Is it merely that we don't want to divide our ranks any further? Or is it that we, as males, are threatened by the idea of being superfluous to the lives of certain women? Either way, we need to examine our line of thinking. We cannot blame lesbians for our lack of unity because, as beautiful a concept as unity is, it can only be actualized once we approach gender parity. As long as gay men harbor the sexist views passed down by their forefathers, these will manifest themselves and continue to alienate the very people with whom we are trying to build unity: our lesbian sisters.

Being a feminist man can mean different things. For me, it means being aware that my Indian culture embraces a double standard validated by the economic, legal, and religious components of the system, and that I carry the seed of these ideas in my subconscious. It also means being aware that my gay culture is a microcosm of the surrounding Euro-American society and possessed of all of its biases regarding gender issues.

On a more personal level, being a feminist man means being aware that being gay does not make me immune to sexist, patriarchal ideas. It means being conscious of what my thoughts and feelings reflect about women; I cannot decry the injustice around me without acknowledging and addressing it within myself. It also means being aware of the attitudes around me, especially those of other gay men. Being a feminist means taking issue with terms like "fish" (a gay men's pejorative term for women) and not using sexist everyday language that is gender-exclusive, like mailman, police-man, chairman, and mankind. It means taking a firm stand against

51

exclusionary policies, such as gay bars that exclude women, and making clear my support of women-identified issues, such as reproductive rights and general gender equality.

Being a feminist man also means acknowledging that I can be supportive of women's struggles but cannot paint myself as some sort of savior; that would be presumptuous and a perpetuation of the male-in-power thinking. Just as people of color must empower themselves and not be "rescued" by Euro-Americans, it must be acknowledged that women possess the power to liberate themselves. As a feminist man, I can serve only an auxiliary purpose, and I must be satisfied with that role.

Another facet of being a feminist man requires that I acknowledge the value of traits that have long been devalued as feminine. In our world, a woman may dress in pants and a shirt, but a man who wears a dress, skirt, or a sari will be ridiculed. Our patriarchal system understands why a woman would aspire to be a man but cannot fathom why a man would aspire to be a woman, since it regards this behavior as a loss of status. Men are taught to stifle their "feminine" urges, and to exaggerate "masculine" attitudes such as aggressiveness or combativeness. Being warm, nurturing, and understanding is anathema to the traditional masculine concept.

In some ways, we South Asian men experience a milder version of this dichotomy, since our culture leaves room for men to be gentle. But being a feminist man means going beyond these stereotypes and allowing expression to the qualities that are inherent to us as human beings, regardless of their labels. It also means being supportive of women who give expression to their "masculine" traits and not feeling threatened when they do so.

I have often encountered reactions ranging from mild discomfort to outright disapproval from some South Asian gay males on the issue of androgyny. Many of us are so intent on integrating into the gay mainstream of America that we forget it is not perfect, that much more is possible than is now available. To seek out more, be it through androgynous clothes, styles, attitudes, or sociopolitical beliefs, is to court the disapproval of our own gay mainstream, which is trying so hard to prove that it is "no different" than the heterosexual mainstream. We gay South Asians, in our search for community, can fall squarely into this trap.

I am saddened when we stumble this way; there is something so freeing about androgyny, about shattering the masculine-feminine polarity. If we, as men, can come to express the "feminine" traits inherent to each of us, we can then vest them with the value they deserve. Once we start to value these traits, then perhaps we can go a step further and see that, once the distinction between what is a man and what is a woman is blurred and each is seen as a human being, there is no basis left for any sort of sexist, misogynistic beliefs. This is not to say that everyone must attempt to be androgynous, for some people by nature possess more "masculine" or "feminine" traits; rather, each one of us should be free to explore the masculine-feminine continuum as we see fit.

Thus, if I am to be a feminist gay South Asian man, I must acknowledge and address the sexism in myself and in the world around me, be it the gay subculture, the South Asian environment, or combinations thereof, such as Trikone. And how was the discussion about semantics resolved in Trikone? The word *lesbian* was included in a description of the organization, just as it had been years before at the parade in Sacramento.

Some thoughts on bisexuality

Kamini Chaudhary*

I hate labels. I find them limiting and don't care to oppress myself with their weight whenever possible. The world around me does not appear to share this distaste, however. People seem to want desperately to label anyone and anything, as if this process of identification is going to somehow increase their security and render their world more understandable. Many people question me on the issue of sexuality. Am I lesbian? Am I straight? For those folks who are dying to label me, I tell them that I am bisexual. I am not crazy about this label, but for me it is preferable and more appropriate than the other two.

I have not always labeled myself as bisexual. I once had a lesbian identity, which seemed appropriate at the time and served a purpose for me. That was a very politically conscious, feminist-focused period; I was beginning to explore sexuality and had found myself in love with a woman. Eventually I broke up with her, and I went out with a number of other women. Before long, lesbianism became a central part of my identity.

I did not simply wake up one day and stop identifying myself as a lesbian, nor did I do it by choice. I gave up the label because of the bullshit in the lesbian community around me regarding sexual orientation issues. I was sleeping with a man at the time; I was attracted to him and being intimate with him was no different than being in bed with a woman. It turned out to be a problem for some of my friends, however. Most of my women friends were lesbian and many saw my relationship with a man as betrayal; nearly all of them pulled away.

When they turned away from me, I had no one to talk to, no one to understand my feelings. My few straight friends didn't understand, and I did not really know any bisexual women. It's ironic; I had thought that lesbians, of all people, would understand a difference in sexual orientation, but they just freaked out. What were they enraged about or afraid of? In my angrier moods, I felt that it was just a basic insecurity about their own lovers, perhaps even about their own validity as sexual partners. I thought that they were just projecting and it was a heavy psychological trip.

Although it was a difficult time, I'm glad that through it I stopped identifying myself as a lesbian. I still find women sexually and romantically attractive, but the label was very restrictive. It made sexuality the central component of identity, which was too narrow an approach for me. My thinking was becoming wider with experience, and I was beginning to feel that the lesbian community did not understand or include me. Still, I did not run joyously and embrace a bisexual identity; I chose not to label myself at all, unless absolutely necessary.

I suppose that, beyond general distaste for labels, there are other reasons for my hesitation in adopting the identification of bisexuality unconditionally. On issues of community and politics, it presents a barrier, though not an inherent one: there is distrust of bisexuality in both the lesbian and straight communities. The mainstream society focuses on our gay aspects and is thus suspicious of us, while the lesbian community takes issue with our straight side and sees us as either suspect or uncommitted.

I must admit that I probably expect more from my relationships with women than I do from my male partners. Perhaps this is because women are not different entities but more like me. It may also be that my expectations are based on cultural variables. In India, I had such strong friendships with women on so many levels, so much closeness, commitment, and sharing. I keep searching for that and expect that it can more likely be found with women.

What is bisexuality, anyway? Many people seem to think that bisexuals are just interested in fucking around and will grab anything that moves. Others think that bisexuals are confused, cannot make up their minds regarding sexual orientation. Still others think that being bisexual means you haven't been able to come out as gay or lesbian yet; they are likely to think that you are screwing around with the minds and hearts of lesbians with no respect for the individuals. I think all of these "explanations" are simply ignorant bullshit.

For me, being bisexual has not meant being open to the whole world sexually. It means being open to only certain people that I have a chemistry with; these people may be male or female, but they are few. The idea that if I, as a bisexual, am involved with a woman I will still screw around with guys on the side to satisfy some heterosexual part of me is ludicrous. Bisexuals do not walk around with a need at all times to satisfy themselves both heterosexually and homosexually; it's a question of attraction to an individual, regardless of gender. Besides, I'm so co-dependent and have such a difficult time hurting people or breaking up with them that I could not even think of deceiving them.

The suspicion that some lesbians have of bisexual women, that they had of me as a bisexual woman, may also have to do with a reaction to the oppression of the patriarchal, heterosexual system we live in. They seem to see any sexual and romantic connection with men as capitulation to this system, and, since they distrust this system so much, anyone who is identified with it becomes suspect. It is almost as if the bisexual is a potential spy who must be scrutinized.

There is also at times too much intellectualization at work in the lesbian community. Rigid definitions of what is politically correct and appropriate exist or dominate. How one behaves or dresses, what one says and how it is said are all scrutinized. Whatever happened to emotions? Why is it not okay to follow your feelings, wherever they might lead? Why is it not okay to be different, to not have to burden yourself with an unmovable label?

The consequences of this intellectualization are illustrated by one of the more bizarre experiences I had when I made my break from the lesbian community. A number of lesbians came to me during this time and confessed that they were also attracted to men. They were not disavowing their love for women; they were expressing a part of themselves that they had not felt free in expressing before. It was as if I, as an ostracized member of their community, represented safe ground. They couldn't spill their guts to a woman of the lesbian community because that would be politically incorrect. They were feeling such pressure to be 'pure' lesbians.

One woman I know is in a committed, two-year-old relationship with another woman but has fantasies about men and would like to check them out at some point. This is not a rejection of her lover, but only an acknowledgment of another part of herself. Still she feels terribly guilty. It is dreadful that she and other people like her should feel pressured to suppress the desire to explore another aspect of themselves.

Another woman I know mentioned that she is attracted to a gay male friend. When she was younger and living a straight life, she used to dress up and wear makeup, what is sometimes labeled as "femme drag." When she came out as a lesbian, she went to the casual extreme, trying to avoid any emphasis on her looks. One day she decided to go out with a group of us. Just for fun, she dressed up and put on makeup. She had a blast! Now she dresses up more often, something I have always enjoyed doing. Why should that be seen as catering to any sort of heterosexual stereotype when it is only an expression of oneself, no less valid than the jeans-and-shirt "natural" look?

Last year, while marching in the gay pride parade in San Francisco, I was dressed in traditional Indian clothes. I enjoyed how I looked. An Indian lesbian feminist came up to me and started describing feminism to me, as if I must be totally ignorant. Because of the way I was dressed, she assumed that I must be some bimbo. I could not believe it! What a stereotype! I was too nice, too codependent to reveal that I could tell her a thing or two about feminism.

In my relationships with women, sexual toys have also been an issue. Some women won't use them because they are politically incorrect or reek of surrogate maleness. What the bloody hell! No matter who you are with, you should be able to use what makes the two of you feel good. Exploration of any kind is fine if it is consensual and should not be burdened by political expectations. Intellectualization strikes once again, this time in the sexual arena rather than the emotional.

When people take roles too seriously, they oppress themselves and the person they are with. You have to free yourself to express all aspects of self. It is healthy to loosen up from your politically correct posture, at least when it becomes oppressive. Pressure to be butch, femme, or androgynous becomes a burden when one loses sight of one's own preferences and needs. Identity itself is rather free-flowing, forever changing shape. The clothes you like today, the look you adopt, the views that you hold are all subject to change over time. It's not about being lesbian, straight, or bisexual, it's not about being politically correct or incorrect; it is about being human.

I try to see the issue from the point of view of lesbian friends, especially from a South Asian context. One Indian lesbian told me of all the women in India who are married, have families but have female lovers on the side. The lovers have a difficult time since they can never really have these women. It becomes a waiting game for them, and I can understand their anger, as well as that of the lesbian community, over situations like this. Yet it is not fair to generalize from these situations and paint all bisexuals as sexual opportunists with no respect for other people's feelings.

I have had a hard time liberating my straight side. As a lesbian-identified woman, a part of me was a closet straight. Isn't that pathetic, to go through the whole closet/identity confusion/self-acceptance process a second time? It was made more difficult by my holding the label of lesbian, and by the unwillingness of my lesbian community to allow for a bisexual reality within its parameters.

Lately, I have heard the bisexual issue discussed more openly, and I think it's great. There needs to be dialogue between lesbian and bisexual women. If we can drop our politically correct expectations, our intellectualizations, our suspicions that are based on insecurities, and come to see one another as people at various points on the same continuum, we can work to free ourselves of the oppression that is common to us all.

No apologies

Kaushalya Bannerji

I began "coming out" when I was nineteen, yet it seems as though the journey has only begun. My first encounters and relationships with women were not the results of choice, but rather of being overwhelmed by what appeared to be a startling awakening of sexual feelings. At that time these feelings appeared right to me, but they were not always acceptable to the world I lived in. Being comfortable with homosexuality in societies that view your life as being not only abnormal, but in fundamental opposition to patriarchal notions of the family, love, and heterosexual norms of desire is never an easy process, no matter where one lives.

Like so many other lesbian and gay people, I felt that calling myself a lesbian amounted to reducing my whole being to my sexual preference, while in reality many other aspects of my personality remained unnoticed. I wanted the world to see me as human, generic and transcendent of sexuality, so for a period I fought defining myself as a lesbian. Yet relationships with women continued to attract me and, moving beyond my feelings for women, I began to realize that these attractions were not purely physical but also contained an active emotional involvement. I drifted into the politically and culturally active lesbian community, started to see that self-acceptance and social acceptance were connected. However, being "out" in the lesbian community raised may other issues, both personal and political.

While we in this community were challenging a number of oppressive norms as lesbians, some of us were being defined in social and cultural terms that were just as destructive and politically rooted as sexism and heterosexism. Racism permeated the bars, dances, meetings, collectives, and stereotypes that were a part of my life. The exoticism and patronization I had experienced as a "nonwhite" woman in the North American left reappeared as an element of my interactions with white dykes; now it took the form of my being a "lesbian of color" or a "South Asian lesbian."

In those early days of sexual discovery, not many faces like mine were out in the lesbian scene. I was almost seduced into believing that I could not be an Indian and a lesbian without betraying either the culture of my birth and family, or the culture I had chosen as a lesbian and a feminist. Just as men had silenced me in the solidarity committees and meetings of the left, so too I found white lesbians talking for me and about me as though I was not present. Although I had been active in anti-racist work since high school, I could not accept the blinding racism and assumptions about my mind, body, and culture that prevailed in the white lesbian community. Living in permanent opposition to the heterosexist world, many white lesbians felt that they had a monopoly on a rebellious victimhood; they were defensive and uncomfortable about confronting racism in their glorification of sisterhood.

As a lesbian of Indian origin with an active relationship to India and to my family, I was struck by the conformity to androgyny that appeared to be the norm of white lesbian beauty. Having grown up with a body and an aesthetic value system that was utterly different than this white androgyny, I struggled to accept my Indian woman's body against all white heterosexist odds. My breasts, hips, and long hair were not seen by everyone as symbols integral to my identity as an Indian woman; they were reinterpreted by white lesbians as manifestations of my being a "femme." It was difficult to fight against the white feminist canon of androgyny, particularly as my coming out was a recognition of the fact that I loved flesh-and-blood women, not symbols. I saw androgyny as a symbolic statement being made on an ideological and cultural level.

As I acknowledged my lesbianism more and more, at least to myself, I began to define my own self-image. Growing up in Canada,

I had never fit in as a child. Racism was everywhere and the absence of nonwhite men and women was conspicuous in the classroom and the media. I began to feel that in my particular situation, sexual liberation and anti-racism were linked by the internalization of compulsive heterosexism on the one hand and the values of white supremacy on the other. Because both of these processes have profound psychosocial ramifications, re-examining my sexual identity led me to take pride in being Indian. Strangely enough, I have found that the process of integrating my heritage, of my countries and my choices, has freed me from the need for the white lesbian community's approval.

The long-term psychological price that we pay as we go through both coping and healing processes sometimes forces us to deal with the erosion of self. I know of no more corrosive abuse than racism. Under its tentacles, we have been abused sexually, exploited economically, and we have been forced to internalize our colonizers' value systems and aesthetics. What is even more frightening is that men and women are differently, but nevertheless thoroughly, re-constructed within a racist framework in which all nationalities are perceived as being within the fundamental categories of master and slave.

Much of the experience of racism is constructed through gender. As a child and adolescent, I not only yearned to be a white girl, I also saw white femaleness through white men's eyes. Indeed, the first women to whom I was attracted reflected the white male gaze that I had obediently eroticized. Conversely, I found nothing sensual about my own body nor of the bodies of black and Indian girls around me.

I began to re-evaluate the relationships I had to sex, power, and race only when I experienced the blatant racism of some white lesbians. I began to ask myself what kind of messages I was giving out to white women. As an Indian woman with a fondness for jewelry, bright colors, dresses, and makeup, I became aware that many women tried to categorize me as a "femme" – a repository of sexist eroticism totally devoid of reality.

In choosing to move away from such an image, I found myself moving toward an image deliberately open to a definition as a lesbian on North American terms. As time passes, I see that the life

I live has placed me squarely in the front lines of the battle for liberation from racist and sexist oppression. Coming out has enabled me to come in from the margins of patriarchal colonialism and allowed me to begin recreating an identity that rejects the mystification of Indianness and the glorification of white supremacy.

I was fortunate that my immediate family was able to come to terms with my lesbianism. As I lived at home for a number of years after being involved with women, my initial problem was explaining to white lesbians that my living situation was not "Eastern patriarchal oppression," but instead reflected my family's attempt to integrate my lesbianism into their overall acceptance of me as a young woman. Of course, this process has not been easy and I don't wish to glorify it, but it has been valuable for me.

Living at home as a South Asian lesbian daughter has been a complex and sometimes contradictory process for both myself and my parents. Yet it is rewarding and moving to see my parents at Lesbian and Gay Pride Day. Their presence is an acknowledgment, also, of the many lesbians and gay men they consider to be their friends.

On the other hand, in some ways my gradual transition to open lesbianism reflects my caution regarding both real and perceived notions that being "obviously" lesbian might alienate me from my family. Hence, only after living away from my parents' home was I able to integrate clearly and unashamedly a lesbian world view into my personal consciousness.

To some extent, being comfortable with my sexuality has also helped me to gain my sense of dignity as an Indian immigrant woman. As with my color and cultural origin, I am "stuck" with being a dyke. I deal daily with the racist sexism of the straight and gay white world and often confront the homophobia of my Indian reality.

Living in two overlapping worlds, I find a need to create social spaces in which aspects of my personality are not censored and silenced. This can mean socializing with lesbians from India and the Indian diaspora or with other women of Third World or Southern Hemisphere origins. In this way, I have found some similarities in how we all look at notions of family, womanhood, and patriarchy, as well as class and race oppression.

When I realized that any discomfort I felt was not due to my personal inability to cope with all the mixed messages the world gives me, I began to look for the reasons for my isolation from both the Indian and lesbian and gay communities. This sense of not belonging in either culture seems to be a form of exile. Perhaps it is not the exile our parents experience, but it is nonetheless a fundamental fear of not having a real sense of community or country. Perhaps my holding onto my Indian lesbianism through a variety of methods is a way of dealing with this sense of exile. Sometimes it is just the ability to speak up in a room full of white lesbians without any self-censorship. At other times it involves talking to my family about the feelings I have for my lovers without a sense of shame. It is also asserting myself and pointing out to my classes at the University that not all Third World women are passive or heterosexual and that we are not weak in our daily struggles to live with economic and personal dignity.

On a more private level, I see that being a lesbian forces me to take responsibility for my own sexual desires, actions, and fantasies. This is something that few heterosexual women have to confront, since our societies encourage the sexual availability of straight women without providing the support that women need to become accountable to themselves. Because most teenagers are assumed to be heterosexual, it is common to feel that your sexuality just "happened," without any sense of active participation in sexual choices and behavior. This laissez-faire attitude is fairly unusual for lesbians, since we must confront the displeasure of family and society, not to mention our own internalized homophobia.

As a South Asian woman, I feel that being proud and healthy in my own sexuality and that of my lovers is a necessary and fundamental step in integrating my history into my present circumstances. To be a lesbian is not, as I used to think, a Westernized rejection of our Indian identities. We can look to our own societies and cultures for examples of strong female friendships and of the heroic rebellion of all women dealing with aspects of patriarchy, including sexual and economic degradation.

I would like to end with something that I have learned through many difficult and painful experiences. Like many other lesbians of Third World origin in North America, I'm realizing that community is what we make daily when we go to work, school, bars, and demonstrations, and when we support and hang out with each other. We may grow up in exile, but we make our victories and our homes through surviving as who we are — with no apologies.

An/other country

Ian Rashid

All this new love of my parents' country:
We have bought the videotapes together,
bought the magazines and books,
all the advertisements,
each other's responses.
We watch the slides of your visit.
Your handsome face tanned, surrounded by mango trees,
planted above the poverty,
the moist beauty
(which you think of blowing up and then framing,
building into your walls),
majesty imposed upon majesty.

Now I watch you watch Sergeant Merrick watch poor Hari Kumar.
And follow as the white man's desire is twisted, manipulated into
    a brutal beating.
You are affected by the actor's brown sweating
body supple under punishment. What moves you?
The pain within the geometry of the body bent?
The dignity willed in the motions of refusal?
A private fantasy promised, exploding
within every bead of sweat?
Or is it the knowledge of later:
how my body will become supple

for you, will curve and bow to your wishes
as yours can never quite bend to mine.
What moves you then?

My beauty is branded into the color of my skin,
my strands of hair thick as snakes,
damp with the lushness of all the tropics.
My humble penis cheated by the imperial wealth of yours.
Hari's corporal punishment, mine corporeal:
yet this is also part of my desire.
Even stroking myself against your absence
I must close my eyes and think of England.

Krishna

Rakesh Ratti

To you I sing,
my sweet androgyne,
an often hidden truth.
I dance my nakedness
before your round hips
and waist-length hair.
You float above the altar,
float above my life,
seduce me with an impish grin.
Dark-skinned,
filled with light,
forever dancing your youth.

You with the exquisite Indian eyes,
mischief overflowing,
looking coyly
at Radha by your side,
unfaithful to her,
for you are the lover of all.
Sweet Radha,
whom my heart envies.
It is not the fullness of her breasts
that I yearn for,
the curve of her supple body

does not draw.
She shares your altar,
for this I envy her.
It is images of you I crave,
my own form,
hard flesh against hard flesh,
heart against heart.

A world of love flows
from the flute
cradled by your hands.
I adorn myself with the bamboo notes,
for they offer all the covering
I need and want.
Your seductive omniscient smile
does not flee my altar
as I dance the joy of my truth.
So it should be,
for the world may lay claim to you,
but you are still my God.

Metamorphosis

ShivOm

I was a heart
sinking into the bottomless gray of London sky,
searching for a reflection of my mocha sweetness
in the blighted bland mugs of the Britishers.
I longed for the affirmation that I was
beautiful   desirable   wanted.
Wanting my enemy to want me,
I tried to charm my oppressor.

I am Ardhanarishwara
as I dance my Kathak,
half-male   half-female   all-human.
I am a kick in your sexual pants,
a gender terrorist,
outstripping the Bowies and Boy Georges,
challenging the body that doesn't
feel   kiss   hug   stroke
for fear of being too sensual.

I am a whirlwind of dazzling color
in the city of plurality by the bay.
Music   acting   painting
give me a pattern for existence,
free me from convention.

In their chaos I design my liberty,
choreograph my dreams.
I blaze with inventions,
an unending metamorphosis,
each winged creation more beautiful than the one before,
the Dance of Shiva
forever altering the balance of the universe.

Narman

Ifti Nasim

So many lies I believed in,
so many sermons I heard
and took as an ultimate truth.

But when I finished
the seven circles of reincarnation
and came out of the hearth of my thoughts,
opened my third eye,
I found out that I had given birth
to myself.
I bore the pain of being the man and the woman.
I enjoyed fully
being a creator and creation.

My intuition
is that a woman completes a woman,
and a man is the other half of a man.

I know I am different from the majority;
if you cut me in half,
I am a complete person.
I am above the controversy
of a male or female.
I am a person of today's world.

I am a human
I am a god
I am Narman.

Home seekers

Zariamma Harat

Varied are the interests
  of a phoren returned traveler
She can be anything
  can't quite place her
but you know
  you know
she's from some/one/where

      here
This is a big country hard to keep
           track of
Drifters in and drifters out
Out-speaking the British at their
           rubbery tongue
Her ease at contempt and she's dark

     God is she!
She's so sure and we're worried
Where'd she learn it
In America? In Europe? Is she married
  to a European?
Something like that I am sure
  Who orders about like this when we want
    to ignore

that she's the color/features of my dhobi
What Indian would marry so arrogant
    of a curly plump fairy
Friend, I don't know.

The sun's been out these past two hours
and I'm amused. It's all amusing
    these returners of Darkness.

Turquoise Lady

Zariamma Harat

In borrowed rooms
Turquoise Lady   poses
stringing jasmine-fated flowers
to persons
looking beneath
inner-cripple smile
who   say   yes   laugh
                 indulge
with her
Turquoise Lady
    is
all colors
no colors
    as
no one
Turquoise Lady has
    no title
You cannot contain
    this Tamil vase
in starch-stiffened
    tailored chic
She's cloud
      free
watch her whirl

unafraid
    watch her dance
dawn woman
   giving birth on open   sky   sand
No one to intrude
No being to chase titles or tampones
         up
cloud-holes
Turquoise Lady
is on all of the temporary
    hold in our
Social Service/Unemployed Divisions
Her eyes. Her   eyes   her
       voice
Wet.

The flame

S.D.G.

People stare at us.
Your muscles, my slightness.
My hand round your waist.
Your earring glints softly in the sun
as we stop sometimes
to gaze or touch lips.
Their minds whir on—
cocksucker assfucker faggot freak—
how little they know,
so much to learn,
hiding in the safety of prejudice and scorn,
they point fingers and give labels.
Their inner flame long extinguished—
parents and teachers saw to that.
One day that spark will spurt
into a lick of fire
and all people will feel,
love, live
with hearts unbridled
with the rules of religion, society, elders.
I hope
that's all there is...

Fabled territories

Ian Rashid

for Sunil Gupta

I.

Where I am when he looks at me?
  Uncertain
if what he sees
is as fable territoried
as what I have myself
claimed a place where planted
upside-down in an earth so red-red rich
– Rajasthani red? – so
I(t) can't quite be believed

and sometimes fear(ed)

II.

Where I am when you look at me
is the certainty of complete
worlds pictures-perfect, not jewel-like,
but messy – shoved in my mailbox

and the relief of music
-scapes that can't be danced to
familiarity of a language
that modulates

my life maps
gravity, knowing location,
the familiarity of a language I cannot speak

III.

Where I look when I look at me
is down and what I see
are feet marching through
a muddy uncertainty
no chart for this journey
no Berlitz phrases
just a sliding, spongy
familiarity in comfort
warm between my toes
again-familiar
again I am in shit.

Beta

Rakesh Ratti

Mummy keeps her jewels
in a box full of dreams,
dreams that will be realized
in the echoes of my screams.

Father waits for the day
I bring a crimson bride
yet if I sit on a white horse
it'll be an empty ride.

Every chapter of my life
written by their hands,
if I now reach for the pen
will they understand?

Should I listen to my heart
and wrestle with this guilt?
Should I lock myself inside
the walls they would build?

I want to fill their eyes with joy,
yet let my spirit run wild.
How can I find the love I seek
and still remain their child?

Inverting tradition: The marriage of Lila and Urmila

Anu* and Giti

In December of 1987, policewomen Lila Namdeo and Urmila Srivastava of the Twenty-Third Battalion, stationed in the outskirts of Bhopal, India, capped their year-long close friendship by marrying each other. The wedding consisted of a simple ritual of exchanging garlands, a *gandharva vivah,* conducted by a Brahman in a Hindu temple at Sagar. Their parents, who had consented to the wedding, were also present at the ceremony. However, the news was not received well at the barracks. The women were discharged without a show of cause or notice and dumped at the Bhopal railway station in the dead of the night. According to Lila and Urmila, they had been kept in isolation and not given food for forty-eight hours. They were also coerced into signing papers they had not read. The news caused an uproar in the media, but much of the debate around their marriage skirted the issue of sexuality in general and homosexuality in particular. In the following article, Anu and Giti of Anamika analyze the varying public responses to the unusual marriage, which served to bring the taboo of sexuality out of the closet.

Urmila and Lila's affirmation of their relationship in marriage represents a courageous step in a society which is willing to condone any measure, however violent, to ensure the myth that all women are heterosexual, and that heterosexual marriage is the only viable form of long-term commitment between two people. Their marriage has challenged the self-righteous insistence of conservatives and progressives alike that there are no lesbians or gay men in India. It has thus placed the issue of sexuality squarely in the public arena.

But what is the response to their decision and subsequent harassment? First, bewilderment and, then, anxiety that women can imagine a life together. This anxiety is manifest in the elaborate apparatus of explication that is being developed to "explain" the women's decision. Thus we are told that Lila is a widow, and Urmila a child bride who refused to accept her husband. Their status as marginal women outside the institution of heterosexual marriage is offered as rationale both for their decision to join the police force and for their sexist treatment within it.

This discrimination is said to have drawn them to each other and to marriage. In short, society's misogynistic treatment of women is held responsible for their decision to be together. Thus it is that an affirmative decision by two courageous women is rewritten as the desperate option of victims hounded by society.

Not only are the reports anxious to present the women's actions as wholly overdetermined by a cruel society, but there is also a concerted effort to deny the possibility that their relationship might be sexual. It is clarified that the women "pleaded ignorance of the word lesbian," that their solace in each other is strictly emotional and that, in fact, their marriage "was a protest against the system."

Concern with the real nature of the women's relationship is certainly voyeuristic, but only partly so. Far more important than the event's value as sensationalism is its implicit challenge to patriarchy and to heterosexuality. Lila and Urmila's decision to marry and support each other, financially and otherwise, questions the prevailing notion that only heterosexual marriage can provide women with security and pleasure. It raises the possibility that men could be redundant, that the roles they have hitherto claimed as naturally and exclusively theirs need not be so. In this sense, the marriage poses a fundamental challenge to masculinity in its current form.

No wonder, then, that the inspector general of police, Narendra Virmani, finds their conduct unbecoming. "It could lead to indiscipline and, what is more, others could learn from their example, too. It could lead to problems in the battalion, too. They would want to sleep in the same bed, share food from the same plate, and things like that which cannot be allowed" *(The Sunday Observer,* February 21, 1988).

Although Virmani articulates the problem in terms of discipline in the police force, a problem of disciplining women's bodies is really at stake. No wonder, then, that it becomes even more critical to deny any sexual connection and to belittle the relationship.

In this context we must understand the sudden re-entry on the scene of a "husband" whom Urmila had rejected upon coming of age. He is reported as attributing their separation to Urmila's reluctance to live in a joint family and as having consented only a few months back to move to Bhopal if she were allotted quarters. (Note it is no longer desertion but their separation.) Urmila's family is also quoted as claiming responsibility for her. These "facts" serve to question whether the women's relationship with each other is primary. They also reinstate the family's claim on her as prior and authentic and last, but by no means least, they resurrect and legitimize the husband's masculinity.

Interviews with Lila and Urmila make it clear that there is an explicit contradiction between the way they see themselves and the representation of their action by others. They speak of their marriage with a frank dignity and are clearly angry with the treatment meted out to them by the police force. It is reported that they "seemed puzzled over the fuss of their so-called [*sic*] marriage!" They are also unequivocal that their relationship is neither indecent — "We would not have got ourselves photographed in such postures, if it were indecent or immoral" — or unusual — "There are ninety women in our company and usually a woman will be more friendly with someone. Then we would say 'Joda bana liya' ('they are now a couple')" *(The Times of India,* February 23, 1988).

As for the claim that their marriage was a gesture of protest, it is important to note that it is indeed conceived by them as protest, but not in the way suggested by the news reports. Their interview clearly indicates that the object of their protest was not a society that had left them single [*sic*] and lonely, but one which had harassed them for their relationship with each other: "Constant teasing irritated them and they got themselves photographed garlanding each other" *(The Times of India,* February 23, 1988).

Such harassment provoked them into breaching the iron curtain between the public and private realism of society, to bring to visibility what many would prefer to ignore or decry. To portray such clearheaded and articulate survivors as pathetic victims of society is to do them grave injustice. Worse, an analysis that sees them not as victimized but as victims functions to contain the broader critique implied in their actions.

The response to Urmila and Lila graphically illustrates that our society sanctions only certain representations of women's sexuality, predominantly those that serve the interest of patriarchy and heterosexuality. Women's commitments to each other outside heterosexual marriage are clearly dangerous and are to be tolerated only so long as they are seen to be secondary friendships. These women's actions have implicitly called into question a heterosexual definition of marriage and a patriarchal conception of the male as provider. They've also challenged heterosexuality's exclusive occupation of the public sphere. It is in this context that we must locate the enactment of their commitment in marriage, at a temple, and in the presence of four people. It is the event itself that is significant, not its legality.

Given the kind of questions implicitly raised by Lila and Urmila's marriage, is it any wonder that there is an attempt to construct these women as victims and to place the onus on society? What are the politics of such an analysis? Should we not be suspicious of the sharp contrast between the ready and uncomplicated apportioning of blame on society in a case of marriage between two women, and the reluctance and difficulty many have shown in taking a similar stand against the current romanticization of *sati* (widow burning)? Will these and other issues that connect the struggle for women's rights and lesbian and gay rights be confronted in the future? Or will there be an embarrassed silence and failure of political will to support the actions of these pioneering women?

Hijras: Challenging gender dichotomies

Arvind Kumar

A couple of women dressed in bright *salvars* and *kameezes* bang on the gate, then slip into the courtyard without waiting for a reply. Two musicians trail after them. The various members of the host family watch the visitors with equal parts of amusement and annoyance. The musicians settle on the ground, lift their instruments, and begin to play. The women respond to the music, sway in the style of the *mujrah* dancers, borrow moves from Hindi films best forgotten. Upon closer scrutiny, the "women" reveal rather masculine faces better suited for drag queens. A crowd of villagers gathers in the courtyard, uninvited, unimpeded. The "women" lift a month-old baby out of his grandmother's arms, coo to him as they murmur blessings. They tease the father, sing songs that border on the bawdy as the villagers laugh and clap their hands. The father slips ten rupees into the "women's" hands, coaxes them into finishing their show, then directs them to the door.

These "women" are actually *hijras,* enigmatic transgender individuals who are often talked about but rarely understood. They inspire questioning of the idea of gender as a dichotomy and they also attest to the brutal fate that some homosexual men experience when their attempts to live out their nature are severely limited.

A number of gay South Asians I know have mentioned the occasional use of the word *hijra* as a pejorative for homosexual men in India. A few Western writers have also confused the concepts of homosexuality and *hijras* and at times attempted to equate them. A closer look at the reality of the *hijras,* however, makes it clear that they have a rather complex relationship to homosexuality, spirituality, and mainstream society. *Hijras* and other individuals who undergo gender transformation, be it nominal or surgical, may seem bizarre, unreal to a Westerner, yet they have existed and continue to exist in varying forms, under a host of names, and in a number of different cultures.

Among Native American tribes, transgender persons were variously known as *winkte* (among the Lakota tribes), *hemanch* (Cheyenne), and *nadle* (Navajo); the French settlers and explorers referred to them as *berdache*. In the country of Oman, they are called *xanith* and inhabit a niche between those of men and women. Among the Muslims of Mombasa, Kenya, such individuals are called *washoga,* and the Polynesians refer to them as *mahu*. In many of these cultures, as with the *hijras* of India, special powers are attributed to the gender-transformed people (Mihalik, 1989).

Hijras have traditionally been a north Indian phenomenon, although they are found in smaller numbers in the southern regions of the country. Rural Indians often define the *hijra* as a hermaphrodite, a person with the genitals of both a man and a woman. Others maintain that *hijras* are mostly transsexuals who give up their male genitals in homage to their goddess, Bahuchara Mata, in a quest for spiritual transcendence (Nanda, 1990). There are also those who believe that *hijras* are homosexual men who undergo sexual surgery, or simply dress in drag, in order to have sex with other men.

In the villages of Punjab, Haryana, Uttar Pradesh, and other states, *hijras* are well-known, though in Punjabi they are often called *kusras*. Visually many of them are somewhat masculine-looking, though some, like a few transvestites in the West, can pass for quite pretty women. *Hijras* always dress in women's clothes; they wear the *saris* that are ubiquitous to India, or the *salvar-kameez* that is favored by north Indian and Pakistani women. Like many a Western transvestite, they often exaggerate feminine manners of speech and movement, and their use of makeup and sense of fashion can similarly present an exaggeratedly traditional image of women. Unlike cross-dressers or transsexuals in Western countries, *hijras* have a sanctioned niche in the Indian culture, if at best near the fringes of society. They are despised, feared, and ridiculed – yet also respected. These contradictory attitudes on the part of the general populace have their source in the seemingly asexual condition of the *hijra*. Whether they think that *hijras* are hermaphrodites or transsexuals, Indians believe that such individuals derive a special power from their familiarity with both genders. This power is thought to manifest itself in the ability of the *hijras* to lay both blessings and curses on others. Thus, no matter how they might be reviled or ridiculed, it is considered wise to stay in their good graces.

A group of *hijras* will make the rounds of the villages in its territory and visit the houses in which births (of male children) and weddings have occurred. To an outsider they can seem to appear out of nowhere, but they have their own network for such communication. The visiting group usually consists of two or three *hijras* and a like number of musicians on the *tablas* and other instruments. Invariably, a crowd forms to watch them. The *hijras* will dance and sing, tease the onlookers, and bestow blessings of good health and fertility. It is considered bad luck to turn them away, and the *hijras* will not leave until they have been "paid" for their performance. If they are paid an amount they consider inadequate, they will resort to teasing that gets progressively more crude; most often the host family gladly pays what is asked simply to have them depart on good terms.

Hijras live in small groups and in each of these groups there is a kinship hierarchy. Each group consists of a guru and her disciples *(hijras* always refer to themselves in the feminine). These gurus in turn answer to other gurus and, ultimately, all *hijras* come under the auspices of a handful of top gurus. Within each small group the members may adopt kinship ties with one another; thus one may refer to another as her "sister," a second might be a "mother" or "daughter." Similarly, all of the groups within the hierarchy under one top guru may treat one another as extended family (Nanda, 1990). In some ways, these groups and kinship ties are not dissimilar to the relationships adopted by the various "houses" of Harlem transvestites in the 1991 documentary *Paris Is Burning.* Social scientists assert that the loyalty of a member to his or her group is directly proportional to the price exacted for entry into the group; thus one can safely assume that the power of the bond that emasculation creates among *hijras* must be quite great.

One of the difficulties in trying to define *hijras* is their own varying descriptions of themselves. Some speak proudly of their sex change and see their emasculation as a tribute to their patron goddess, Bahuchara Mata. This operation takes place in the group's home and is performed by another *hijra,* without the assistance of anesthesia. There is little guarantee of the client surviving the surgery. When the male genitals are removed, no female organs are constructed in their place; thus the survivors become truly asexual. Many of these individuals speak of a history of feelings incongruent with their gender, similar to the experience of transsexuals in the West. It is something of a paradox that those who can neither father nor give birth to children are attributed the power to give blessings of fertility.

Many *hijras* do not speak of this sacrifice but rather insist that they were born hermaphrodites. It is difficult to ascertain the truth about these claims, yet stories of such births are stuff of village lore in most rural areas. In parts of north India many people believe that all children born with the genitals of both genders are the property of the *hijras,* to be raised by them into their caste, and there are numerous stories of *hijras* claiming these children. In reality, most, if not all, *hijras* choose to join the ranks of this community as adolescents or adults. Still, it is not unusual to hear a *hijra* recount in song of how from her birth as a hermaphrodite she was shielded by her parents, raised as a girl, married off to a man who, upon discovering her dual genitals on the wedding night, threw her out of the house and left her with no choice but to join other *hijras* in earning a living. Questions of veracity notwithstanding, these songs certainly lend drama to the performance.

Both the self-proclaimed hermaphrodites and the transsexual *hijras* frown upon transvestites in their midst. These latter individuals are anatomically male and have never undergone the ritual emasculation; they simply adopt female garb and join the groups for pragmatic reasons, the opportunity to have sex with men being one of these. It is not uncommon for groups to expect new members to prove their status (they may join the group as preoperatives but must undergo the ritual to remain members). Some of this disdain may be due to the need of the *hijras* to project an image of asexuality and thus preserve their status in society. Despite claims of asexuality, however, many *hijras* engage in prostitution to support themselves; this may be due to economics, but the pursuit of pleasure as an objective cannot be ruled out (Nanda, 1990).

Given the status of homosexuality in Indian society (being denied, hidden, or condemned), many homosexual men have found, and still do find, their way into the *hijra* community. As *hijras,* they at least have sanction to exist within society; as homosexuals they are not given even this marginal validation. As *hijras,* they are also allowed to adopt an identity and become part of a community of similar others; as homosexuals, they are likely to be isolated and have fleeting interaction with others like themselves. Some researchers, like G.M. Carstairs, have asserted that *hijras* merely serve as an institutionalized option of homosexuality; eunuchs and transvestites have had acknowledged roles in sexuality since the days of the *Kama Sutra* (Nanda, 1990).

Individuals like Carstairs attempt to simplify the rather complex role of *hijras.* They also seem to have a peculiar definition of homosexuality. Once a *hijra* has been emasculated, does his having sex with a man constitute homosexuality? In light of the fact that we define a man as such primarily by his genitals, and given that homosexuality is defined as sex between two individuals of the same gender, sex between a *hijra* and a man could hardly be labeled homosexual behavior. This is not to say that one or both do not get pleasure out of their interaction and that this pleasure is not their main objective. The *hijra,* however, is merely serving as a surrogate and is playing the role of a woman both in the sexual act and in visual appearance. Of course, if the *hijra* is an anatomically male transvestite, "her" sexual activity with men would certainly constitute homosexual behavior.

In the case of the hermaphrodite, the scenario becomes more complex. These between-gender individuals come in a variety of forms: they may have functioning genitals of both genders, they may have functional female sexual and reproductive organs and non-functioning, vestigial male organs, or their male organs may be fully functional while their female genitals are merely vestigial. In the latter case, an argument could be made that such a *hijra* having sex with a man constitutes homosexual behavior. In the other two cases, however, such a claim would be specious. In the first instance, a label of heterosexual or homosexual behavior would be equally accurate, while in the second a heterosexual label would constitute a more accurate characterization.

❖

The percentage of *hijras* who are true hermaphrodites is estimated to be very small (Nanda, 1990); emasculated men thus probably constitute a large majority of this community. This majority can be further divided into those who have felt cross-gendered throughout their lives and thus are really transsexuals, and those who are homosexual and turn to the *hijra* community because no other paths of acceptance and sexual expression are available to them.

In the case of homosexuals who become *hijras,* this writer cannot help but feel a deep sense of sadness and anger. Sadness because of the physical pain and mutilation these individuals go through in seeking an avenue for sexual self-expression. Anger at the society, at the world, that withholds validation from so many man-loving men and compels them to mutilate themselves in an attempt to achieve some of the pleasure intrinsic to their nature.

Perhaps these feelings of anger and sadness are rooted in the influence of the Western gay culture. I suppose a counterargument could be that the status, validation, and community offered by a *hijra* identity is preferable to the shame, isolation, and fear that a clandestine homosexual identity would entail. But in the end, the transformation of a homosexual man into a *hijra* is an act of desperation, born out of a lack of self-acceptance and a dearth of alternative ways of being true to one's nature. It may bring a sense of community to the individual involved on one rather limited level, but it also stigmatizes the person deeply and forecloses his participation in many facets of the surrounding society. For those individuals who are true transsexuals, emasculation and the status of a *hijra* may provide partial relief from their gender confusion; for homosexuals, however, it is a brutal fate that strips them of their identity and robs them of finding pleasure and love with other men as men. Perhaps as awareness of homosexuality increases in India, as the possibility of loving and being with other men becomes more of a reality, the number of homosexual men, potential gay men, lost to ritual emasculation will change inversely.

References

Mihalik, Gary J. (1989). "More Than Two: Anthropological Perspectives on Gender." *Journal of Gay and Lesbian Psychotherapy* 1(1): 105–117.

Nanda, Serena (1990). *Neither Man nor Woman: The Hijras of India.* Belmont, Calif.: Wadsworth.

They aren't that primitive back home

Kim

I would love to get back home to the gay scene in India and get away from the clinical isolation of the U.S. scene. Even gay Indians settled in the U.S. are surprised that there is a massive, vibrant, and exciting gay scene in India, primarily in metropolises like Bombay, Delhi, Madras, Calcutta, and Bangalore. Of course I speak of the scene as it prevailed over a year ago – I have been in the U.S. for a year and a half now. I have stayed in regular contact with my friends back home, however, and the scene in India seems to have progressed and developed even more.

I had been actively gay in India since 1980, when I first returned home from engineering college. No, I did not turn gay, nor was I coerced into being gay at my hostel. That history runs further into my past, but I shall not delve into that now; that subject deserves an entire book! When I say "gay," I refer to open cruising and attending gay parties. I have had gay experiences and encounters both before and after "coming to terms with my gayness."

India lives up to the theory of 10 percent, underscores it, validates it emphatically, and, I should say, stretches it more than a wee bit. In India there are gays everywhere, just as it is in the U.S. They don't simply shop and commute, they cruise unabashedly in ways that would make an American bathhouse seem demure and conservative. Cruising in overcrowded buses and trains, in parks, in movie theaters, in restrooms, in lobbies of hotels, on beaches, in colleges and health clubs, under flyovers, in open fields, during religious festivals when millions throng together and rub shoulders and crotches as they carry a multitude of Indian gods for immersion in holy water ... I could go on and give you a detailed list of where all you could unearth pink triangles on the Indian subcontinent.

To begin with, there are no rules. Unlike here in the U.S., where gays, gayness, and all the luggage that comes with it have clear labels and are pigeonholed into clearly defined slots, a virgin continuum exists in India. A yawning abyss. At one level, "gays don't exist"; "homosexuality is a social and psychological aberration"; "homosexuality is a Western phenomenon." Indian men are "real men," and the ones who sit on the fence, if they exist, are *hijras*. This is, fortunately and unfortunately, the broad opinion held by the masses and, surprisingly, by many of the intellectuals.

The prevalence of this opinion is unfortunate because enlightenment could bring with it a certain broadening of outlook that would possibly benefit Indian gays. On the other hand, we gays are not bothered too much by the world around us, because straights tend to either dismiss our existence or deem us as being inconsequential. Without being militant like American gays, we manage to live a life of unbridled joy and virtual bliss. So what if we don't have gay churches, gay bars, and a score of societies and magazines in India? We don't draw undue attention to ourselves, for with attention come rednecks, homophobia, and everything else that gays do not want in the first place.

Now, now, I can see you falling off your seats, livid. I can hear you saying, "Something needs to be done for our poor brethren out there"; "This is outrageous"; "You mean that gays have no rights and are persecuted." Before we start casting value judgments, picketing, and dragging out all the other cute props of expressing one's political awareness, let's hit the brakes. For once, let's not impose our templates of what a blissful society should be on those halfway around the world. Let us endeavor to become aware of the situation there, try our utmost to comprehend how affairs evolved to their current point, and give consideration to the thought that

93

maybe the gays in India are actually better off than we are!

I know that I must be shocking a few of you politically aware, conscientious, and active gays who belong to more organizations than are in existence and who walk in more parades than the cause warrants. I seek here to allow you a window into the exotic world of gays in India. Hopefully this will clear a few misconceptions and misgivings and prevent the typical American reaction of "We must do something about this."

In the Indian cities mentioned earlier, and to a certain extent in the other cities, towns, and villages, there are not hundreds but thousands of gays. One only needs to do a bit of math to work out that for a country of nearly a billion people a conservative gay estimate of 10 percent would amount to a whopping 100,000,000 people! Is it any surprise then that in India you run into bellboys at hotels, men on crowded local trains, the guys in the seats next to you at the movies, all of whom are more than adequately interested in fondling your penis?

India has no gay movement and perhaps never will. There are no gay magazines; perhaps they don't need them. There are no gay bars *per se;* again, perhaps they are not necessary.

Really, I don't consider myself any more creative, intelligent, or oversexed than my next-door neighbor Jerry. But bedding someone back home was far easier than over here. The cultural differences or the fact that I'm brown and hence may appeal less to gay white males than I would to fellow Indians back home does not account for this drop in frequency. Simply, there are more gay men in India than in the United States. You find them anywhere and everywhere. When I referred to the gay scene in the U.S. as being one of clinical isolation earlier, I was alluding to the fact that you primarily go to a gay bar or a bathhouse to pick someone up.

Within the U.S. is a world that is well developed. There are shoes for the sophisticate who loves partying. There is wallpaper meant for kids who need a Disney environment and ought not to be able to permanently disfigure the walls. There are candyless aisles in supermarkets and magazines that talk only to computer game hackers. There is cereal for those who are prone to heartburn, who love raisins but not calories. There are "I miss you" cards from a pining lover to his butch ex.

In this wondrous world of specializations, separate bars for straights and gays are no surprise. Our American free enterprise and overzealous marketing prowess by no means stops there. We have gay bars that the young gay white males frequent. There are the Asian ghettos and separate bars for both blacks and Latinos. Of course it goes without saying that those who frequent any one of these specialty bars don't need to conform to the house color. What is more critical is what makes their gonads tick. If you are a rice queen (slang for those who prefer East Asians), you hit Faces; if you love nachos (slang for Latinos), you let your hair down at Circus; if blacks make you sweat, then you can catch them at Catch One.

When I was in Bombay, we used to have gay parties each month; often one had a choice of three or four parties on a Saturday. People kept their networks alive this way. This was of course a chance for gays to socialize, meet their friends, have a rip-roaring time, dance, bitch, and pick up partners for torrid sex. When we felt the need to have a gay bar or two, we converted a few straight bars. We accomplished this by simply spreading the word. Each Saturday, for instance, we would meet after nine at Amigo or Gokul's. Soon the straights would stop visiting these bars. The owners would be only too pleased, for their revenues would actually skyrocket. It was a wondrous state of affairs. In fact, I met my lover, whom I was with for two years, at one such bar that I had converted.

There is considerable concern about contracting AIDS back home. Not that there are too many AIDS cases; in fact, there have not been more than 100 cases detected in India. (This may be due to the fact that not all gays get tested, testing facilities are not easily available, and there is fear of social ostracism and persecution for those who test positive.) Gays use condoms very widely in Bombay, and it is not unusual to pick up a tart in a park, go behind a tree, and have "her" quickly extract a condom and lubricant from "her" pocket.

There are instances of gay bashing; groups of straights may suddenly appear in public toilets frequented by gays and beat them up. These incidents are few and far between and they tend to make gays cautious, but they never serve to dampen their spirit. Police also engage in such sweeps, but only with the intent of extorting money through intimidation. Hardly anyone gets arrested, though being caught partaking in homosexual activity is illegal. In practice more than a few of the cops are gay or bisexual, and it is not unusual for some queens to be surprised by cops who then proceed to sodomize them.

Indian society is a miasma of contradictions. In the land of the *Kama Sutra* and Khajuraho − a city whose ancient temples are covered with postures that rival the most ingenious hard-core pornography − the policymakers are prudes. Kissing is taboo on the Indian screen, and pornography is banned. But that in no way limits the attitudes of the people. Unlike China and the Far East, where people are loathe to show affection in public, Indians are usually rather permissive. Gays are not chastised or socially ostracized. They may not be praised, but neither are they outcast. It is a fact of life that people have grown to live with. However, people (gay and straight) are confused about homosexuality. Ignorance is so prevalent that gay men are often classified as *hijras,* the rationale being that they must want to be women.

In more educated circles of major cities, a few men have even undergone sex-change operations. The transition seems to have been made without too much effort, at least as far as their acceptance by society is concerned. In Bombay, the best-known Western music critic of the largest national newspaper, who was known to be gay, had a sex-change operation; Faroukh Rustom became Farah Rustom. A national sportsman named Radhakrishnan became Radha and continues to participate in sports, though now she competes in the women's events.

Among the plethora of Indian gods, the apex consists of a trinity. Out of this trinity, Shiva is widely revered and worshiped. Nearly all Hindus − and they constitute eighty percent of India's nearly one billion people − worship the Shiva lingam (which in fact is Shiva's penis!). So in the heart of the Shiva temples, in the sanctum sanctorum, jutting out of the floor, is an erect penis! The reasons behind this are several. Women worship it, pour milk over it to evoke fertility for themselves. Men worship it as well; could it be a sanctification of their own gayness? Anyway, there it is, sticking out of the ground, with the entire congregation chanting praise around it.

The only reason I have delved into the vicissitudes of Indian religion is to give you a brief idea of the complex environment the Indian psyche operates within. Religion is terribly important, for Indians are very god-fearing people in a fatalistic way. Their thought process is too intricate, however, for me to attempt an explanation of it in this short piece.

I am not trying to imply in this article that any one system is better than any other. I am merely trying to compare and contrast the gay scenes of India and the United States. I am urging you to comprehend the differing scenarios and take each for what it is. There is a world of joy in savoring the cuisine of each country, but try to serve a Big Mac with curry, and you get more than just indigestion.

A question of color

Rakesh Ratti

My newly arrived Indian guest was all eyes as I led him through the Mother Lode, one of the hotter gay bars in West Hollywood. Ismael was nervous, but not too nervous to stare as pretty faces streamed by.

"They are all so tall and fair, so handsome," he whispered to me later as we headed for the door.

I was amused by Ismael's reaction, touched by the awe the bar's mundane scene had evoked. In some ways it was like watching myself ten years before, when I was nineteen, so green, and the whole gay scene was so new and impressive.

"You liked the blonds in there, didn't you?" I asked wryly.

"They were handsome," he answered, "but I don't think they like Indians. They looked at me strangely. I don't like it when they think they are better because they are white."

"I agree," I responded. "But I don't think they were being rude about skin color. People in that place, and in most bars, just have a lot of attitude toward everyone."

A few minutes later, after a clarification of the word *attitude,* we sat talking in a coffee shop on Santa Monica Boulevard. I mentioned to Ismael that there are also bars that cater only to women, to blacks, Latinos, and East Asians.

"I don't like blacks," he commented, scrunching up his face in distaste. "I don't find them handsome."

It took effort for me to stifle a scream. Ismael is new to this country, I reminded myself; his words are coming out of ignorance. But that wasn't explanation enough, not for my militant soul. I had to say something; I could not escape the feeling that if I said nothing, I would be validating his double standard.

Ismael's reaction to skin color, though lamentable, is not all that atypical among the gay South Asian men I've met. (The South Asian lesbians I know seem to have a greater awareness of color issues.) We, as Indians who have been raised in the West, or have chosen to live here, have been exposed to a double dose of a racial hierarchy that is ages old. As we struggle with this racism inside of ourselves, we also find ourselves made the target of other groups' racist ideas and hatred. Thus we find ours a doubly challenging dilemma, one in which resolution comes neither easily nor without pain.

In India (and, in a more informal manner, in other South Asian countries), the caste system was originally set up by the light-skinned invaders, known as Aryans, who conquered the dark-skinned Dravidian natives more than three thousand years ago. As the victors, they secured the upper castes for themselves. Even today, the color of an Indian's skin is a fairly good indicator of his or her caste. And though the Indian government has followed the lead of Mahatma Gandhi and tried to dismantle the caste system, it is too old and omnipresent to fall away easily. We Indians of today are suckled on many of the same unjust, hurtful, and demeaning aspects of this structure that have kept many of our brothers and sisters in bondage for centuries.

As much as we may rail against the injustice of this hierarchy, even when we see the inequity it engenders and the pain it causes, the seed of this system is nevertheless a part of us. We Indians who come to the West, be we old or young, male or female, gay or straight, bring the baggage of this hierarchy with us. Sometimes we begin to grip these attitudes even more strongly as we cling to something familiar in the face of the new and the strange.

Most of us who come to the West are faced with an abundance of prejudice. In language, dress, culture, and way of being we are quite alien to our host countries. Many of our new neighbors are unwilling to see commonalities we share with them, and they do not celebrate the diversity we bring. So often we are called names, our customs are ridiculed, and our skin color is branded inferior. We resent this injustice and fight its effects as best we can.

Paradoxically, we face our new, multiracial and multicultural home clutching the divisive ideas and attitudes we learned as children. Too often the caste system is unconsciously applied to the new faces we encounter, an action that has troubling consequences in a pluralistic society like that of the United States.

One result of this transference is that, because light-colored skin has been at the top of the Indian caste system, we flirt with the danger of endowing white Westerners with an undeserved superiority over ourselves. They too often become the sought-after prize, and we risk being disrespectful to ourselves in putting them on a pedestal. This can be especially harmful given the legacy of colonialism that has already left its scars on people of color.

On the flip side of our caste-transference, we may also relegate dark-skinned African-Americans to the bottom of the caste hierarchy in our minds, as is the case in our native country. African-Americans, who have already been sensitized to issues of marginality by their history and encounters with white America, sense and resent this implication of inferiority laid upon them. Certainly they have every right to object to a system that establishes whites as the *Brahmins* (upper castes), blacks as the *harijans* (untouchables).

This sort of a mind set is not the harbinger of a peaceful transition to immigrant South Asians. To further complicate matters, the inherent racism of American society reinforces our conscious and unconscious application of the caste system. We are fed the blond-haired, blue-eyed ideal. This ideal seduces us to hate ourselves when we don't match up with it and invites us to join in the deprecation of those who reflect it even less. Even as we are shouting our outrage at being treated unfairly, we may be subjecting our new black countrymen to the same prejudice. The hypocrisy of it all would be laughable if it did not cause so much pain, if it did not disrupt the possibility of achieving harmonious coexistence with the marginalized as well as those in power.

Our gay culture is but a microcosm of the American mainstream, and as such, it reflects all of the latter's prejudice and pain. To anyone who disagrees with this assessment, please remember the

"Wetback Night," with swimming lessons as a prize, at one gay bar in Texas, as well as the "Aunt Jemima" look-alike contest another establishment staged, complete with a watermelon-eating competition. We gay men, who have experienced so much pain in asserting our right to live and love as our nature dictates, have learned little if we turn around and wound our brothers and sisters on the basis of skin color.

More than once I have heard my African-American friends complain that they sometimes feel invisible at gay bars; people of other races too often ignore their presence. How can I doubt the validity of their protest? How many times have I heard someone say "He's good-looking, for a black man"? Much too often, and a few times it has flowed from the mouths of my South Asian friends. Yet some of these same friends have, at other times, voiced their resentment against the white standard of beauty in this country and complained of being overlooked by whites because of culture and skin color.

For obvious reasons, I am especially troubled when I hear such racist comments coming from other gay South Asians. This attitude is reflected in the conscious effort some individuals make to cultivate friendships with white men and women and avoid associating with other people of color. It is reflected in the unwillingness of many South Asians to spend much time out in the sun, lest their skin turn too dark. I might expect such an attitude from my minimally educated, seventy-year-old mother (who is a saint in every other way), but not from educated people my age.

Do we want to create a hierarchy in which we are subservient to those with white skin? I would think not, and yet we find ourselves doing just this when we make choices in friendship, association, and love based on skin color. When dealing with sexual or romantic relationships, there might be a mitigating and excusable difference; hearts are so idiosyncratic and such willful entities that who is and isn't our "type" can come to seem purely beyond our control. In terms of friends and acquaintances, however, no excuse exists. Our choices based on a white standard evidence a subtle form of self-hatred. When we give greater credence and value to someone who is light-skinned, we are necessarily downgrading our own worth as well as that of other people of color.

It is not easy to let go of ideas and attitudes that have been taught to us from the time that we lay in our mothers' laps. By virtue of being human and thus being ultimately open to social influence, none of us is immune to these blatantly unfair ideas. Somewhere along the way, however, a choice must be made between following them blindly or seeing the hypocrisy inherent in these attitudes and actions. The caste system has been ultimately hurtful and unjust in its original framework in India; it will continue to be so in any context. We gay and lesbian South Asians must lay it aside, and we must struggle actively against its more subtle Western counterparts. Perhaps it is in this manner that we, the Ismaels of this world, can begin to unlearn our prejudices and stop subjecting others to the pain we ourselves have experienced.

As for Ismael, I'm afraid that my inability to avoid engaging him in dialogue over the question of color proved too much for him; I never heard from him again.

Working together

An interview with Urvashi Vaid

Meera*

As executive director of the National Gay and Lesbian
Task Force in Washington, D.C., at the time of this interview,
Urvashi Vaid held one of the most influential and visible jobs in
the gay and lesbian community in the United States. Born in
New Delhi, Vaid came to the United States with her family at the
age of eight. A graduate of Vassar College and the Northeastern
University School of Law, she has lived in Washington,
D.C., since 1983. In this interview with Meera,
Urvashi talks about her life, work, and future goals.

**Meera: I want to start by asking you about your personal history —
your background and childhood.**
Urvashi: I was born in New Delhi, India. We moved to the United
States when I was eight, where I grew up in a small town in upstate
New York called Potsdam. My father taught English at the state
university — he is also a writer of novels and short stories. My
mother had been a teacher in India. I have two older sisters who still
live in the U.S.

I am one of the millions of immigrant children whose parents
came to the U.S. for jobs and educational opportunities and ended
up staying. I have the experience that so many Indians and South
Asians who live in this country have — of being part of a family that
very much identifies as being Indian. At the same time, you grow up
in this culture and assimilate quite dramatically. I think that's a
tension that a lot of children who grew up in Indian families go
through.

What was it like being ethnically different, outside the family?

Even in that little college town, there was an Indian community of graduate students and families of faculty members. There was an India Association. It was very good. It really helped foster a sense of community.

The experience of being Indian in America is probably the same as being any kind of immigrant ethnic group. You feel like an outsider all the time. I'm not even talking about overt acts of racism or discrimination, but just the general sense of not being from that place, not speaking the same language, speaking with an accent – all those things that you are very conscious of as a child.

Did you face any discrimination?

I don't think I did. There were examples of discrimination that other Indians encountered – in employment, or just comments from people in the street. My family was very Indian-identified culturally and tried to convey that to me to the best of its ability. I think I am quite Indian, yet I feel very blended into this society.

I don't think Indians as a whole identify with black people or people of color very much. I think we try to create for ourselves some kind of special status. We identify more with British white colonialists than with other people of color.

A lot of it has to do with associations people make with us, like our coming from a spiritual culture. I hate carrying that burden, but it does happen. I think that it sets us apart. We are still perceived as exotic.

It's absolutely true. What that does, though, is that the Indian community doesn't ever integrate fully with other minorities in this country. Therefore, we have a disproportionately small amount of political power compared to what we could have. There is a lot of money in the Indian community, and politics is all about money.

We don't come together as a distinct ethnic group in a political way. There are some that do – I have become aware of some Indian democratic clubs, South Asian groups that are very active in mainstream party politics – but in terms of working in a local community where people live, one rarely sees the India Associations develop a political or communitywide visibility.

Why do you think we shy away from politics?

That's a good question. I don't know. I will say that in my own personal experience, while my parents and my sisters are quite politically aware, there is disdain for politics. You do your work and have your family and that's the most important thing in the world. You have certain obligations to contribute to the world outside of that, but it's not something that we as Indians are trained to take responsibility for.

When did your involvement in politics begin?

I always felt politically interested. Ever since I was a kid, I read the papers and had opinions about everything. I was too young for any kind of activism in the peace movement, but I remember marching with my sisters and friends of the family during demonstrations.

My first organizing involvement began in college in the mid-seventies in the feminist movement, working on issues like violence against women and reproductive rights. The women's movement in this country at that time was very exciting and active. There were lots of new books and organizing efforts. Feminist bookstores were flourishing. It was a real cultural renaissance.

I also worked in that first wave of divestment – getting colleges and universities to divest their funds from corporations that did business in South Africa. It really began in 1976 or '77 in some universities, and now in the last five years has become very effective again.

How did you get involved with gay and lesbian issues?

Before I went to college, I had not thought of myself as gay or lesbian. When I look back on my life, I can see that I was always lesbian, though I didn't know it at the time.

To me, it was just a matter of exposure and recognition. Until college, I had not met people who acknowledged themselves to be openly gay. I just hadn't. Growing up in a fairly protective Indian family, I certainly didn't have a lot of the same experiences of being sexually adventurous that my American friends had. It was a very different kind of family situation. Dating was out ... you just didn't do it.

It is certainly true of Indian families in other parts of the world.

I grew up in a very traditional family as far as sexuality went.

When was your first date?

I don't know. I don't think I had an official date – maybe the senior prom or something like that. [*Laughs*] In high school, we went out in groups, with girlfriends and a bunch of boys. You just went to the movies or whatever.

In college, you were on you own and you made choices. I dated men but I just didn't feel the same with them. In college I also learned the labels and the theory, and came to some understandings. I realized that, gee, I think I'm gay. It was not a traumatic realization. It was just a matter of acknowledgment and acceptance of something that was very deep in me. I started to come out in college. By the time I graduated, I was truly, fully comfortable with being a lesbian.

Where did you go after college?

I moved to Boston, which for many years has had a very strong feminist community. I got involved with a lot of different projects again – issues of violence against women, neighborhood and community organizing like food co-ops.

I believe – I believe this for myself, and I am a little moralistic when it comes to others – that people have a responsibility to contribute to the society that they live in. You shouldn't be a passive participant in your own community, whatever you find that to be. Whether it is the community of Indians living in a certain place, the community of gay people, the community of women, or the community of a city, you have an obligation to contribute.

Boston is also where I started to get involved with gay and lesbian issues in a major way. Because of this, I realized I had to tell my parents. And so, in the early eighties, I came out to them. My parents' reaction has changed over the years, but even in the beginning it was "We don't understand what you are doing, but we love you and you'll always be loved. You're our daughter." It was not this hysterical family scene from some awful Hindi movie with the trauma and uproar and people being banished from the family. [*Laughs*]

I've heard the same thing happen with other Indian families. There is some reaction at first, but family bonds override the homophobia.

We have to put that message, that experience out to others who are scared of their families finding out. One thing we have going for us Indians is that there is a very strong commitment to the family. I feel very committed to my parents and my sisters. It doesn't matter if I am gay. I know I am going to be a part of their lives. Of course, there are moments of awkwardness and pain, but you have to go through that.

What is it like being an Indian lesbian?

In my conversations with the handful of Indian lesbians I've met, I've found my experience has been different from theirs. My experience is that people are fascinated by India. There is this exotic element that you mentioned earlier. They ask you all sorts of questions. They are curious.

But again, there is a certain element of men in the gay community who have a problem with women, period. They are not open to women's leadership or participation in organizations. I've certainly encountered that as a woman. There are also people who have a problem with people of color. I know I have experiences of racism in my life and work in the gay and lesbian community. But I don't think it's anywhere near the extent that some of my black lesbian and gay friends have.

How did you come to be working for the National Gay and Lesbian Task Force?

In terms of political organizing, I was really active in the Boston area community efforts. I wrote for *Gay Community News,* a weekly newspaper. I was also on their board. I worked for the Boston Lesbian and Gay Political Alliance, a number of feminist groups, and legal groups.

I began law school in Boston and graduated in 1983. I moved to Washington, D.C., to take a legal job, working for the American Civil Liberties Union (ACLU), doing prisoners' rights litigation. The goal is to improve the quality of conditions of confinement, and make sure that they are constitutional in the sense of not being cruel.

I also did a lot of work on AIDS in prisons among inmates. I saw from letters I got that HIV-positive inmates were getting absolutely no treatment. They were, in fact, being isolated and confined. Others were just terrified of AIDS and were getting no education. The AIDS education program we began continues today.

All along, I was also doing a lot of gay and lesbian community organizing. I finally decided that it was too schizophrenic to have a nine-to-five job and then from 5 p.m. to 9 a.m. do all the things that I wanted to do. I began to think about and look for a full-time job in the gay and lesbian movement.

I got the job at the National Gay and Lesbian Task Force in September 1986 as the public information director. It was my job to get the mainstream press to cover gay and lesbian issues in a fair manner. It was a great, great experience.

Tell us about the NGLTF.

The NGLTF is a grass-roots political organization. It works for gay and lesbian civil rights through political lobbying, grass-roots organizing, public education, acting as resource center, and direct action. We worked very hard on the big civil disobedience action that happened at the Food and Drug Administration a year ago that had a major impact on the federal government's policies about releasing experimental AIDS drugs at earlier stages of development.

We are a membership organization – I stress that because that's how we are funded. People join at $30 per year. Many of them give a lot more. Membership and individual donations account for over 90 percent of our income. Our budget for 1989 is about $950,000. And we really need to grow, frankly.

The foundation world has not supported gay and lesbian organizations. The corporate world doesn't come near us. The government is overtly hostile. The conservative wisdom is that the government exists to fund the military and the police. In my view, the government exists to fund and support social service programs. I think the government should be funding gay organizations, especially community centers, hotlines, programs for the elderly, the youth, etc.

The threat to us from the organized right wing is quite great. People date the birth of the gay liberation movement back to the

Stonewall Rebellion twenty years ago. In this time, our community has become much better organized and more visible. But concurrent to our efforts has been the growth and emergence of a very strong fundamentalist right wing that is better organized, better funded.

The annual budget of just one of their organizations – $11 million for the Heritage Foundation – is more than the combined annual budgets of four gay and lesbian national groups. Our four organizations – NGLTF, National Gay Rights Advocates, Lambda Legal Defense Fund, Human Rights Campaign Fund – collectively have less than $6 million.

The other pieces of the landscape for gay politics are that across this country there are no strong statewide gay organizations. They just don't exist, by and large. It really hurts us to not have sister organizations to turn to in the state of North Dakota, Alabama, or other places. Not only do legislators from those states say and do outrageous things because they know they are not accountable to the gay communities in their states, but when we want to do something – when we want to reach our own people – it makes it harder for us when there is no mechanism.

I come to the movement very much as a grass-roots organizer. I really believe in a ground-up model for political change, which starts where people live, rather than a top-down elitist model where you have an in-club that has a lot of power, makes decisions, and imposes them on people.

How do you plan to increase membership?

By informing people about the work we do, by telling them you don't have to be out to support the movement that can be out for you. You don't have to take all of the risk. All you need to do is sign that $30 or $50 check every year, and we'll do the rest. But my hope is that when people start getting involved and start receiving the newsletter in the mail, they'll realize that there is a lot they can do.

I want to energize people to not be apathetic, to not see politics as something that happens in an abstract way that doesn't affect them. What happens in Washington affects gay people all the time. Every single day this September our lobbyists were facing anti-gay amendments to a variety of bills. We were able to modify, block, and defeat most of those. We're still working on the ones we lost.

They're on the floor of Congress debating whether homosexuals are natural, normal, or healthy. I thought we resolved this debate in the 1970s when the American Psychiatric Association removed homosexuality from its list of disorders. There is a lot going on here every day that affects ordinary gay people. We have to communicate to people that their involvement is critical.

What are the laws affecting immigration for gay individuals and partners?

Right now, if a visitor declares herself or himself to be gay, she or he can be turned away at the border. This has happened. It happens each year to Canadian women who are trying to come to the Michigan Womyn's Music Festival. It happens to European visitors who come with gay books.

There is certainly a restriction on immigrants – those who are applying for permanent residence or citizenship. It's an old law codified in the early 1950s that classifies homosexuals as "psychopathic personalities." It is outdated scientifically and in every way. A new revision of the Immigration Act has been drafted and we're working to get it passed.

For people who want to immigrate, if you openly acknowledge being gay or lesbian, you are going to be precluded from immigration. Although there is one very good recent case – a lesbian from the Soviet Union who applied for citizenship as a lesbian and got it – it may be unique because she was a political refugee.

I'm a lawyer, so I don't advise people to engage in illegal activities like marrying (for immigration). The Immigration and Naturalization Service does scrutinize marriages quite carefully. It's not that easy. The best way to come to this country is through regular channels like educational opportunity, being sponsored, working in a job. Indians have a lot of professional training, and many people do qualify for these categories.

Are there no laws allowing partners of gay U.S. citizens to immigrate, as in Denmark or Australia?

No. In this country there is absolutely no recognition of gay marriage. There are a couple of cities that have extended health benefits for married employees to unmarried employees, gay or heterosexual.

I read with great interest the case of the two women in India who got married. I think a lot of gay people in this country have commitment ceremonies and get married. But the issue of the legal recognition of that marriage is another case. The best way to protect our relationships at this point in this country seems to be through contracts and legal documents which will at least assure that your partner's and your wishes are carried out.

There are many examples right now because of the AIDS health crisis of families being unable to deal with the homosexuality of their son who has died and just cutting out the lover in every way, from attending the funeral to disposing of the property. There are just a lot of sad stories like that, and that's just an example of homophobia.

Are there issues that the gay and lesbian community has not addressed, that you would like to see addressed?

Our community has to see itself as a movement for social change and take that mandate very seriously. What I mean by that is that it is not a single-issue movement, that gay and lesbian rights aren't the only issue on our agenda. It's a pretty major issue, obviously, but our gay and lesbian civil rights movement should continue even beyond the passage of a particular piece of legislation. We must work until we have a society where women and people of color and gay people and poor people can be treated fairly and justly.

For example, AIDS has taught us that the health care system of this country is a joke. People were saying that all along, but the AIDS health crisis has brought it home. It has affected a lot of people very personally — over 100,000 diagnosed — and brought home the fact that health insurance doesn't cover everything. Ten years ago, if you had said at a gay meeting, gee, we should really be thinking about national health insurance, people would have looked at you as if you were crazy. Today, everybody looks at you and says, absolutely, let's join those unions and those coalitions working on health care issues. And we are. Health care is now on the gay and lesbian agenda.

That's what I'm talking about. On the one hand, our position in society is affected by our sexual orientation – totally. We are hated and despised and discredited and defamed at every turn because others can't stand what we do. But at the same time, we are also people who live in society. We are very diverse people – we are women, we are people of color, we are poor and rich, we are American and we are from other countries – we are all sorts of things, and that kind of diversity must also infuse our political agenda.

Sexuality, identity, and the uses of history

Nayan Shah

"**tri-kon** *n. (tri* as in *trim, kon* as in *cone)* Sanskrit for triangle. Pink triangles were first used in Nazi concentration camps to identify gay prisoners. Today the sign is embraced by gay men and women not only as a reminder of injustices of the past, but also as a symbol of gay pride." –Savir and Arvind, "Our First Time..." *Trikon*[1]

"Words invent the world" –Suniti Namjoshi and Gillian Hanscombe, *Flesh and Paper*[2]

In 1986 Savir and Arvind invented the word *trikon* to break silence and to create a sense of identity for themselves. The lead story for the first issue of the *Trikon*[3] newsletter opened with a dictionary-style definition of the new name, a definition which attempted to translate the symbols of North American and European gay politics into a South Asian language. This definition invokes a particular history of oppression and the transformation of that history into a symbol of gay political assertion.

Trikon was one of the first of a half dozen South Asian lesbian and gay newsletters and support groups that emerged after the mid-1980s in North America, Britain, and India. *Anamika* (U.S.) started a year before *Trikon* (U.S.); *Khush Khayal* (Canada), *Shakti Khabar* (U.K.), *Freedom* (India), *Shamakami* (U.S.), and *Bombay Dost* (India) followed fast on its heels. These newsletters mix politics and desire. They have served as forums for articulating identities, shaping community, and sharing the cultural products of South Asian lesbians and gay men. Following the first issue of *Trikon,* they have presumed the existence of an audience which shares a distinctive yet global identity, a sexual identity which binds the concerns and needs of gay men in Patna with those in Pittsburgh, with lesbians in London and Lahore. The desire for community has led to the creation of a global South Asian queer identity, an identity that has fought silence and invisibility to emerge.

Silenced in both South Asian patriarchal societies and the white queer communities in North America and Europe, South Asian gays and lesbians have had to invent themselves, often with new words and names of identification. They have appropriated the Hindi and Urdu word *khush,* which means "happy"; some have reconfigured it to mean "gay," while others define it as "ecstatic pleasure." In 1985, a lesbian collective in the United States used the Sanskrit word *anamika,* meaning "nameless," to address the lack of names in South Asian languages for relationships between two women. The *Anamika* newsletter folded in 1987. By the time a new lesbian collective formed in 1990, the editors had created a name for their newsletter which affirmed their relationships – *Shamakami,* which in Bengali means "desiring one's equal." The appropriation of language has been integral to the invention of identity for South Asian men and women who feel marginalized in dominant South Asian societies. They have used language to name themselves and also to address heterosexist oppression.

Many of the essays, stories, poems, and letters that have appeared in these newsletters and other publications have engaged in this politics of assertion. Many self-identified South Asian lesbians and gay men have struggled for representation in both dominant South Asian worlds and dominant white queer worlds. In this struggle they have enlisted history – personal, archaeological, and social – to attain visibility and voice. The uses of history have complicated assumptions about the construction of identities and about the project of reclaiming history.

The formation of South Asian queer communities has inspired me to claim an identity, that of a South Asian gay man living in the United States. The narratives, testimonies, and histories produced by self-identified South Asian lesbians and gay men often resonate with my own struggle for identity and desire for community. These powerful resonances have also generated sharp doubts and raised questions about the nature of identity and the creation of culture and community.

Marking sexual differences

Identity is about belonging. At its most basic level identity marks what we have in common with some people and what differentiates us from others. Jeffrey Weeks reminds us that

> each of us lives with a variety of potentially contradictory identities ... Behind the quest for identity are different and often conflicting values. By saying who we are, we are also striving to express what we are, what we believe, and what we desire. The problem is that these beliefs, needs, and desires are often patently in conflict, not only between different communities but within individuals themselves.[4]

The cultural production of South Asian lesbians and gay men charts these conflicting identities.

The South Asian queers, like other gays and lesbians in North America and Europe, have used coming-out narratives to make sense of their feelings of difference from mainstream society. These narratives follow two general patterns which seek to explain the process of developing a queer identity. The first explains sexual orientation as originating in adolescence with an awareness of attraction to members of the same sex. The second narrative pattern shows desire developing out of politics.

The first set of narratives often dwell on a first crush or sexual experience. Emotional relationships and sexual experiences often drive self-knowledge and the assumption of a gay or lesbian identity. In a typical narrative strategy, Rahul recalls feelings of tenderness for another boy which he now interprets as sexual. He describes his feelings for his classmate Ali Askar at age nine, "I experienced a warm rush through my body and felt an urgent desire to feel his body close to mine. I wasn't even aware that my feelings were sexual at that time..." Later, after recounting several high school love affairs with boys, Rahul explains, "I have been gay as long as I can remember. It seems quite immaterial to me to find a reason for homosexuality."[5] Shilpa Mehta experienced a similar sense of same-sex attraction: "Around puberty, I got real conscious that I was attracted to women, not men. Men were my buddies ... [but] It was women I wanted."[6] Shilpa did not act on her desires and have sexual relationships with women until she left Bombay for college in the United States.

In the first set of narratives, both men and women define sexual identities through reflections on their objects of desire. However, women alone seem to participate in the second set of narratives, which describes the movement from political consciousness to sexual identification. Feminism spurs many self-identified lesbians to articulate their sexual desires. Uma, a New Zealander of Indian descent, fashioned a sexual identity after engaging in battles against discrimination and racism in Australia:

> At the university in 1975, I discovered more about sexual discrimination, and felt myself validated at last about this form of oppression ... I could read and find out what women around the world were writing − that women who were fighting against sexism called themselves "feminist." I then became a "black feminist" ... I think that my sexuality came more through my politics than anything else. And, of course, because I am a political person, I made my sexuality a political act and came out as publicly as possible.[7]

Kamini Chaudhary also became aware of lesbian relationships and identities through exploring feminism: "I wonder if I had not heard about lesbianism through the women's/feminist literature I was reading, or if I wasn't close friends with a lesbian couple, would I have discovered that loving a woman can be sexual. Was that what was undiscovered with Nazreen?"[8] Kamini's reflections on her intimate adolescent friendship with Nazreen suggests that "politics" alone does not explicate the difference involved in marking identities. Kamini's choice is one of both pleasure and politics. Kamini and Uma's narratives suggest that sexual identities and expression are a choice − a pleasure choice − not something prescribed by biology and certainly not by the hypothalamus.[9]

Kamini's knowledge of lesbian relationships informs her reflections about the intimacy between women in India:

> I have always loved women. Women friendships in India weren't

116

sexual, but they were like love affairs. Drama, trauma, jealousy, intimacy, hugging, holding, touching, and involvement far more intense and complete than any I have experienced in a friendship or relationship with an American.[10]

While she marks the romance with Indian women as "more intense and complete" than those she experienced with American women, Kamini is able to name friendships between women in India "romances" through a language of lesbian relationships learned in the United States.

In most of these coming-out narratives, knowledge of relationships and identities as gay men and lesbians were acquired by South Asians living in North America, Britain, and Australia. Men and women who have never left South Asia have also developed a sensitivity to gay relationships through European publications, American films, and now through newsletters such as *Trikone, Shamakami,* and *Shakti Khabar,* which are distributed through personal networks and subscriptions at college campuses and in major South Asian cities among the English literate middle and elite classes. While sexual experiences may have occurred in Bangladesh or Sri Lanka, the framework to understand and celebrate these experiences as gay and lesbian identities developed in white societies.

These coming-out narratives reveal a shared strategy of reframing the past with present knowledge. Many times these narratives attempt to show a linear progression or the origination of an identity, but often the straight lines tumble into spirals or tangle into webs. In one narrative, memory and desire mix so often with denial and flashes of awareness that the processes of desire and self-understanding can be read in a number of different ways. A woman recounts:

> I had my first lesbian relationship when I was twelve years old. I had a crush on a girl in my boarding school which developed into a deep emotional involvement. We would spend hours together, kissing and touching, we had no words to describe what was happening but I remember Rita often saying, "We love each other but we're not lesbians, are we?" There were all these negative connotations to lesbianism – that it was bad and wrong and that as long as we weren't lesbians, it was okay.[11]

Even at age twelve there were words to name their experiences, but perhaps no meanings that celebrated and affirmed their affection; "bad" and "wrong" seemed unlikely adjectives to match their delight. Years later, when she left India for studies in the U.S., she became a feminist:

> Suddenly I had a framework to explain a lot of feelings and frustrations I had been experiencing ... I also began to meet women who called themselves lesbians, and it was comforting to find that I was not alone, that I wasn't abnormal or weird or crazy ... the term "lesbian" began to acquire many new dimensions for me. It wasn't just about sleeping with women; it was the way in which I defined myself as a woman in relation to other women...[12]

Lesbianism no longer meant "bad" sexual acts. To identify as a lesbian was an attempt to claim a community, to share needs and values.

Resisting silence

Despite the affirmation that may develop from a lesbian and gay identity, many self-identified South Asian lesbians and gay men fear rejection from their families. A South African graduate student in New York writes of the alienation he feels from his family: "I'm an outsider, an outcast in my natural community, a hidden silenced nonperson. To participate in the life of my family, I bury my sexuality, my politics, my anger as deeply as possible; I suspect there is a secret dread in my family that I might ultimately shame them horribly."[13] This dependence on family and South Asian communities for affirmation has paralyzed may gays and lesbians in South Asian immigrant communities. These communities and families act as a nurturing refuge in environments of racial hostility and cultural misunderstanding. Members of Khush have "discovered that the greatest obstacle to our members' coming out is the fear of losing our ties to our families and communities. We are people whose sense of identity is constructed in a very large part by these institutions."[14]

Lesbians and gay men have felt invisible in the South Asian subcontinent as well. Many have felt as helpless as the poet Suniti Namjoshi: "what could we uncover? / the history not for taking: /

the family not for joining: / the cause not for naming:"[15] Entangled in the feeling of alienation is an acute sense of bewilderment. How does one justify one's own existence when one cannot summon the history or utter a name that describes one's identity? Names creatively appropriated, such as Khush and Shamakami, are not always enough:

I know not any word for myself
　　　but Khush
　　　and even that is a mocking translation
I cannot envision
　　　living in India
　　　persevering in my "American" individualism
　　　loving a woman
　　　building a home with her
　　　defying family, friends
　　　ignoring disapproval, silence
　　　and still speaking, still fighting
　　　to prevent silence.[16]

In trying to speak and live, we confront the contradictions of our identities. South Asian heterosexists have often denied the authenticity of queer-identified South Asians by labeling homosexual relationships a white disease, insinuating that our presence in the U.S. or Britain has "contaminated our minds and desires."[17] These heterosexists attempt to use the politics of race to condemn lesbians and gay men. They perceive queer identities as a threat to the cultural integrity of South Asian immigrants. The rhetoric is lethal and well understood by immigrants and their children, who are unceasingly chastised for shedding their "culture" and acquiring the degenerate and destructive values of white societies. The notion of culture here is like a fossil – solid and petrified. The conservative ideologies of heterosexist South Asians equate queer sexualities with an already well-defined yet adaptable arsenal of "Western evils" – divorce, drinking alcohol, eating meat, or drug abuse. Any unfavorable value is displaced onto a non–South Asian source. Ironically, these heterosexists unquestioningly accept the "Western" notion that heterosexuality is natural, normal, and biologically correct and that homosexuality is unnatural and perverse.

Arvind Kumar, the editor of *Trikone,* has attempted to address this pervasive argument that homosexuality is a "Western disease" and nonexistent in South Asia. He writes that "the Trikon Archives are an attempt to prove the perception false. This effort is to validate our existence not only in the minds of others but also our own. We were present in Ancient India. We were there in Moghul India. And we are very much here in South Asia now."[18] *Shakti Khabar* has also solicited references to "homosexuals in the history of the subcontinent, particularly in the various religions, .i.e., Sikh, Muslim, Hindu, so that we can prove that homosexuality has nothing to do with the color of one's skin."[19] Both organizations have begun to create archives and libraries as an act of representation, validation, and recovery of the past.

Whatever happened to the Vedic dyke?

To resolve the conflict between national and racial identity and sexual identity, several South Asian queers have searched for "our very own gay tradition." Shivananda Khan, editor of *Shakti Khabar,* describes the historical presence of homosexuality in South Asia: "Within the history of the subcontinent there has always been homosexuality. Sex between those of the same gender is discussed in many Hindu texts and sex manuals. Homosexual activity was also depicted in religious statues..."[20] Subodh Mukherjee of Calcutta explores descriptions of Tantric initiation rites, Hindu festivals and sects which celebrated homosexual acts, the descriptions of sodomy in *Kama Sutra,* the court customs of Babar, and references to women loving women in the *Mahabharata* and *Ramayana.*[21]

Giti Thadani, a lesbian living in New Delhi, has embarked on an archaeological project which substantiates Shivananda's claims. Giti's work began with a study of Sanskrit texts: "I set out to read ancient texts, looking for traces of visions of a feminine world which pre-dated patriarchal society. Then I travelled all over India for three years, taking photographs of sculptures, temples, and vestiges from those times." Her photographs and summaries of her interpretations are frequently published in South Asian queer newsletters. She interprets the texts such as the *Rig Veda* and sculptures which depict sexual acts between women as revelations of a feminine world prior to 1500 B.C. where sexuality was based on pleasure and fertility.[22]

Giti's analysis begs the question, "So, whatever happened to the Vedic dyke?"[23] Giti claims that Aryan invasions dating to 1500 B.C. first began to suppress homosexuality through the emerging dominance of patriarchy. Both sexual systems coexisted, despite fluctuations in relative repression and freedom, until British colonialism when the destruction of images of homosexual expression and sexual expression in general became more systematic and blatant. Giti argues that Indian middle-class acceptance of Western "homophobia" has encouraged destruction of ancient temple images.[24]

Subodh Mukherjee also envisions a golden age of sexual tolerance, but he dates the onset of the repression to the thirteenth century during Moghul rule. Since then there has been a gradual erosion of liberal attitudes toward sexuality, "damaging Indian gay culture and forcing it underground." He insists that

> by coming out to society as gays, we will thus be only reviving our ancient and varied culture and freeing it from the shackles of unnatural prudery and nauseating morality ... For our movement to be successful in India, Indian gays must discard disruptive Western models. In light of our own tradition, we must build a new movement for acceptance of gay love by our society.[25]

The irony in Subodh's observations is that while he finds Western models of gay identity disruptive, he still relies on the notion of an "Indian gay" movement which is itself a Western construct.[26]

This concern about reclaiming the past, this search for the Vedic dyke, makes me think about what I consider history. History is about interpreting the past. We are writing history by producing new interpretations of the past and the formation of cultural identities is dynamically related to the project of writing history. The past is not a thing waiting to be discovered and recovered. A "recovered past" cannot secure or fix an identity for eternity. The relationships between identities and histories are fluid and constantly shifting. As Stuart Hall reminds us, "identities are the names we give to the different ways we are positioned by, and position ourselves within, the narratives of the past."[27] Implicit, then, in the writing of history are the politics of knowledge and the politics of position.

The politics of the South Asian gay and lesbian history are refreshingly self-conscious. Shivananda Khan writes that we can use

121

the past to buttress our claims, our identities in the present. We are not then producing a history of Vedic times. We are at best using ancient text and sculpture to shade today's meanings of sexual practices:

> As we, living toward the end of the twentieth century, fight for our rights to be lesbian or gay, we need to reclaim our historical antecedents, to reconstruct our history, to reinvent the social and philosophical basis that preceded our historical times. If we are to reclaim our own invisible history ... then we need to explore our temples, our religious sites, reread our Sanskrit texts, truly explore our history with open eyes and go out here and record our history. We must not leave it to the dominant heterosexuals to construct our own history for us.[28]

This is precisely where Giti's work, and historical narratives like hers, are the most exciting. They reconstruct and revise the master narratives of the past which have sought to erase differences and ignore contested values. The alternative vision they provide can empower us to reclaim and remake both our present world and the understanding of historical contexts which shaped it.

Shivananda, however, goes too far when he interprets Giti Thadani's work as follows: "If we define a lesbian and gay culture as a legitimate space to form same biological gender sexual/emotional relationships that were *socially acceptable* as well as having *high esteem* ... it seems therefore that pre-Aryan India had a strong lesbian and gay culture" (my emphasis). Giti Thadani's work does not prove that same-sex relationships were "socially acceptable" and "highly esteemed" several thousand years ago in some parts of South Asia. The presumption here is that sexuality is a definable and universal activity, ignoring the variety of cultural patterns and meanings.[29] How do we know that a representation of two women embracing meant sex for historical actors? And even if they did refer to sex; does sex have the same meaning as it does for us today?

How does one go about proving that some social practices are acceptable and highly esteemed? What kind of evidence does one need to make those kinds of claims? It is necessary to understand the context, the map of social reality at the time. Trying to reconstruct the context of second-century India is difficult. Yet we can begin by reading legal texts, religious documents, court texts, and even the placement of the sculpture within architectural complexes. These texts, of course, are usually prescriptive; they provide ideals. They cannot be used to understand attitudes, actual behavior, or motives. We can use these texts and materials to speculate about how people lived and thought. Perhaps, though, the only people we will know anything about are the elite men who wrote and were written about, who endowed temples and who designed law. These are the conditions of our knowledge of the past. They influence my own skepticism about how much we can know about ancient India.

While the project of reclaiming and reconstructing the past is critical for present political and cultural struggles, let us not read too much of "us" today into the past. We may trap ourselves in the need of a history to sanction our existence. South Asian lesbians and gay men are present now. On that alone we demand acknowledgment and acceptance.

Sharpening our present political struggles demands an understanding of our current historical context. We can begin by acknowledging that while there may have been homosexual acts in the past, "what is perhaps relatively new is the idea and development of a 'gay relationship.'" Gay relationships are not limited to "emotional and sexual bonds akin to marriage between heterosexual couples."[30] Over the past several decades, lesbians and gay men have developed a range of social arrangements and relationships, relationships which have, at moments, allowed some women and men to break out of conventional gender relations and identities.

Recovering histories both of the ancient and recent past challenges us all to understand the possibilities of alternative sexualities and social arrangements. Through mobilizing histories, reappropriating languages, and other cultural strategies, we may be able to gain affirmation and support within South Asian immigrant communities for queer desires and relationships. Simultaneously, these cultural strategies may unexpectedly destabilize the self-definitions of South Asian lesbian and gay communities.

Desiring community

Claims that lesbians and gay men who can trace their origins to the subcontinent share a common social history and identity has shaped the politics of South Asian queer organizations. While social support groups like Khush have a local focus – for gay men in Toronto – the newsletters presume an international audience. *Shamakami*'s editorial mission is typical of this perspective: "While *Shamakami* will be based in the United States of America, it will strive to promote international networking among South Asian feminist lesbians."[31]

Yet, it is the migration from the subcontinent that generated a distinctive South Asian queer identity. The formation of South Asian queer communities has been structured by the post-Stonewall gay liberation movement, experiences of racism, and the development of racial minority identities in North America and Britain. The experiences that spurred the creation of *Shakti* are typical:

> The main reason for forming a South Asian lesbian and gay group is because of racism and cultural marginalization. Many white organizations and individuals do not see us as people but as exotic creatures. We want to define our own agenda within a racist climate and not have an agenda imposed by white people.[32]

The social organizations and networks like *Shakti* which emerged in the second half of the 1980s developed a self-conscious policy of developing contact internationally with other South Asian lesbians and gay men. The newsletters consistently provided information, addresses, and frequent news of the other organizations. These groups distribute their newsletters and focus coverage on lesbian and gay experiences and histories on the subcontinent. Increasingly, gay and lesbian organizations drawing their membership from the urban middle class and elite of India have adopted this international South Asian queer identity. In *Bombay Dost*'s first official issue, the editors reprinted a December 1990 article from the *Advocate* which proclaimed Urvashi Vaid, executive director of the National Gay and Lesbian Task Force of the U.S., "woman of the year." The editors served notice that Urvashi Vaid's "presence alone does a great deal for us here in India."[33]

Despite its fluid application, the construction of this identity has been problematic. In 1989, Khush organized a cultural program called "Salaam Toronto." One of the organizers, Ian Rashid, reflects on the problems of self-representation and coalition building:

As a fledgling organization, Khush had wanted to use Salaam Toronto to introduce ourselves to the larger gay and lesbian and South Asian communities. But in many ways, the event was primarily for Khush. The members of the group, coming from different parts of the world, wanted to reconcile and reclaim our various ties to our notions of South Asia ... Very few of Khush's members are actually South Asian born, the majority coming from East Africa, the Caribbean, Britain, and North America. Constructed around individual memories, mythologies, and histories, Salaam Toronto was trying in some ways to link all of us to a collective sense of source. There seemed a need within Khush to justify the existence of the group beyond our sexual orientation; to develop a sense of collective as opposed to individual identity.[34]

Ian describes a collective identity that is mitigated by individual memories and histories, an identity which must be molded from individual particularities and differences to provide some sense of collective "source." Ian points to how we not only presume community and identity, but also create it. This presumed queer South Asian identity is not singular or static. The organizers of "Salaam Toronto" form a coalition of people with different identities, politics, and positions. The debates, disputes, and labor involved in the process of organizing the event produce new political practices and identities. Since "Salaam Toronto" in 1989, South Asian feminists, lesbians, and gay men in Toronto have organized two other cultural festivals: "Desh/Pradesh 1990" and "Desh/Pradesh 1991." Events such as these are transformative; they can constitute new identities.[35]

Liberating identity politics

Although identity emerges from an awareness of difference, articulating an identity can also serve to mask differences. By presuming a global South Asian queer identity, what do these organizations, newsletters, and individuals lose or deny? What complexities, diversities, and contradictions are tensely bound in this collective identity? The differences in experiences and understanding that Ian describes do more than simply complicate the notion of a global South Asian queer identity, they draw into question the assumption that these "imagined political communities" are ideal democracies.[36] These inequalities – often analyzed through categories of gender, class, and race – within our communities must be addressed.

Some South Asian lesbians have called attention to the way gender inequalities structure organizations like Khush and Trikone, which are dominated by men. Lesbians in North America have often developed their own networks through the newsletters *Shamakami* and *Anamika,* or affiliated themselves with Asian or black lesbians in order to establish more supportive communities. Recently, these structural inequalities have been challenged in the pages of *Trikone.* Mita Radhakrishnan wrote:

> You, Trikone men, have to talk about violence against women and what you can do, as gay South Asian males, to stop it. You have to talk about lesbian invisibility. You have to talk about sexism, and how you as males are privileged in comparison to us, your South Asian lesbian sisters ... When you say that women have been "underrepresented in Trikone" you have to realize and take *responsibility* for the fact that "underrepresentation" of women doesn't just "happen" passively. It is the direct result of sexism within the organization and within individual men. Make *the ending of sexism one of Trikone's reasons for being...*[37]

The editor, Arvind Kumar, responded by changing *Trikone's* editorial statement to include a commitment to "ending sexism and discrimination against women in all forms" and specific encouragement of women to "develop [editorial] policy guidelines and co-edit issues."[38] These changes in policy and purpose pleased Mita Radhakrishnan, and she encouraged the readers of *Trikone* to "continue the hard but wonderful work of confronting sexism and other oppressions."[39] Although women continue to contribute to *Trikone,* none of the four issues since Mita's original letter have had a female co-editor.

There has, though, been even less conversation about class differences and inequalities. Often the subjects of South Asian gay and lesbian discourse see themselves as undifferentiated, as profoundly middle class and educated. There are sometimes nostalgic stories of young men and women having sex with servants in their households in South Asia. Sharmeen Islam relates how she "found women who worked as domestic help in our house to be a lot [more] comfortable with me physically than educated women."[40]

However, once in Britain or the United States, there is less awareness that South Asian lesbians and gay men may experience differences in class positions and origins. An explanation is perhaps that race structures so much of our experience here. In a society where South Asians are rendered either invisible or alien, South Asian queer organizations have developed to create safe spaces. These spaces are defined by race and often displace class differences. Curiously, even racism is not always acknowledged. Sunil Gupta criticizes *Shakti* for having a curious lack of self-conscious politicization despite the fact that the group itself is defined by race. He writes that "the pain and anger of daily living the race problem has to be recognized."[41]

Race not only structures organizations and communities from the outside, but from within as well. Aziz Ahmed sees the presence of racial consciousness within South Asian communities when he notes that every South Asian "wants to be as white as possible, or at least wants to be looked on as being fair. Whiteness has become the criterion for beauty. We are defining ourselves from the perspective of white people. We need to challenge racism not only from white people, but also from our own people."[42]

I share with Sunil Gupta the belief that talking about the "inherent contradictions and subtle differentiations of color and background"[43] within queer communities will help us acknowledge and celebrate differences. We need not fear that differences or a lack of predetermined "unity" will produce irreconcilable divisions. It will help us develop communities which are stronger and more self-affirming. A global South Asian queer identity does not have to presume a singular set of experiences. It can be about building coalitions and networks of support and understanding.

South Asian lesbian and gay newsletters have served as forums for articulating identities, establishing communities, and have demonstrated the necessity of identity politics as an important stage in the liberation process. The gathering of solidarity and support is critical for any struggle. In a 1986 issue of *Anamika,* Anu wrote that the individual strategies "deshi dykes" had developed to deal with the pressures of inhabiting contradictory and fragmentary lives were

127

not enough. "For it seems clear to me that any advance will have to be collectively imagined, if we are to escape the stealthy and fugitive-like existence whereby we only dare come out to the tried-and-trusted few."[44] Forums like *Anamika* provided a safe space where one no longer has to fear judgment or retribution. For many these organizations and networks have transformed their social landscape. Pratibha Parmar recalls that when she first came out living in Britain in 1976 "there were very few South Asian lesbians and gays around. We knew we were around and would travel hundreds of miles to meet. Now [in 1990] we have Shakti, a very strong, over-1,000-member lesbian and gay group with a newsletter, regular meetings, and socials."[45]

However, the practice of everyday life will not automatically be transformed by the existence of safe spaces, no matter how strong. Parents and relatives, employers and strangers, friends and acquaintances may respond to our lives with hostility, misunderstanding, or indifference. But the creation of safe spaces and communities has made a difference. As Ravi relates in a 1987 issue of *Trikone,* "no South Asian will have to embark on this journey of self-discovery and self-affirmation in isolation, but will be able to draw upon a supportive South Asian gay and lesbian *community.*"[46] These imagined communities serve a real purpose. They allow us to engage in struggle and self-discovery without feeling alone or alienated.

In inventing identities, creating new subjectivities, and imagining communities, we embark in forms of "empowerment political consciousness."[47] These personal, social, and archaeological histories are engaged in the act of self-representation. bell hooks explains that the process of becoming subjects "emerges as one comes to understand how structures of domination work in one's own life, as one develops critical thinking and critical consciousness, as one invents new, alternative habits of being."[48] For South Asian lesbians and gay men, as with other silenced groups, self-representation alone cannot liberate us, but breaking silence is the first step in resisting conventional expectations and challenging domination. In 1991 Jigne Desai of California tantalizes us with the transformations in her own life. She says, "Being Indian and queer, I felt I was the only one. I've always looked at myself as not fitting in. That's changing. Now I'm not afraid to say who I am and what I believe in."[49]

Notes

1. "Our First Time," *Trikon,* January 1986, p. 1.

2. Suniti Namjoshi and Gillian Hanscombe, *Flesh and Paper* (Charlottetown, Prince Edward Island: Ragweed Press, 1986), p. 1.

3. Trikon changed the spelling of its name to Trikone in 1987 in order to be incorporated as a nonprofit organization in California *(Trikone,* vol. 2, no. 4 [November 1987], p. 2). I have used "Trikon" to refer to the newsletter and support group prior to November 1987 and "Trikone" for the November 1987 issue to the present.

4. Jeffrey Weeks, "The Value of Difference," in *Identity: Community, Culture, Difference,* edited by Jonathan Rutherford (London: Lawrence & Wisehart, 1990), pp. 88–89.

5. Rahul Mukhopadhyay, "Transplanting Roots from India to America," *Trikone,* vol. 4, no. 3 (May–June 1989), pp. 1–2.

6. "Silent No More: A Talk with Shilpa Mehta," *Trikone,* vol. 4, no. 2 (March–April, 1989), p. 3.

7. "Uma," *Connexions,* Fall 1983, p. 5. A different version written by Uma, entitled "Don't Open Those Lips," was published in the British Asian Women's Journal, *Mukti,* no. 3 (Spring 1985), pp. 7–10.

8. Kamini Chaudhary, "The Scent of Roses: Developing a Sexual Identity," *Trikone,* vol. 4, no. 3 (May–June, 1989), pp. 1–2.

9. The latest development in deducing a biological basis for sexuality is Simon LeVay's hypothesis that differences in the structure of the hypothalamus determine sexual object choice. Like straight women, gay men purportedly have a smaller hypothalamus than straight men. Scientists and journalists have speculated that lesbians might have a hypothalamus structure similar to straight men's. LeVay's research follows more than a century of European and American scientific inquiry which has persistently tried to fix a biological cause or measure to putative differences in race, gender, and sexuality. This kind of research has attempted to naturalize social inequalities as the result of differences in human biology and genetics. See Simon LeVay, "A Difference in Hypothalamic Structure between Heterosexual and Homosexual Men," *Science* 253 (30 August 1991): 956–957, and Ann Gibbons, "The Brain as a Sexual Organ," *Science* 253 (30 August 1991): 959–960.

10. Kamini Chaudhary, p. 2.

11. Anonymous, "khayal," *Anamika,* vol. 1, no. 2 (March 1986), p. 9.

12. Ibid.

13. Letter by R.S., "South African, Indian and Gay," *Trikone,* vol. 2, no. 4 (November 1987), p. 2.

14. Ian Rashid, "Out of Home: The Contradictions of Identity. Creating A South Asian Gayness in Toronto," *Rites,* vol. 7, no. 3 (July–August 1990), p. 9.

15. Suniti Namjoshi and Gillian Hanscombe, "Because of India," in *Flesh and Paper* (Charlottetown, Prince Edward Island: Ragweed Press, 1986), p. 62.

16. A.V., "A Response to 'A Room of One's Own,'" *Shamakami,* vol. 2, no. 1 (January 1991), pp. 4–5.

17. "A White Disease," *Shakti Khabar,* no. 3 (August–September 1989), p. 1.

18. "The Trikon Archives," *Trikon,* March 1986, p. 7.

19. Shivananda Khan, "Networking in London," *Trikone,* vol. 3, no. 4 (July 1988), p. 4.

20. "A White Disease," *Shakti Khabar,* p. 1.

21. Subodh Mukherjee, "Homosexuality in India: A Personal Quest for Historical Perspective," *Trikone,* vol. 5, no. 1 (January–February 1990), pp. 1, 3.

22. Interview with Giti Thadani reprinted from *Lesbia Magazine,* January 1991, in *Shakti Khabar,* no. 14 (June–July 1991), p. 3.

23. This question is a paraphrase of the question raised by feminist historian Uma Chakravarti, "Whatever Happened to the Vedic *Dasi?* Orientalism, Nationalism and a Script of the Past," in *Recasting Women: Essays in Indian Colonial History,* edited by Kumkum Sangari and Sudesh Vaid (New Brunswick, N.J.: Rutgers University Press, 1990), pp. 27–87.

24. Shivananda Khan, "Giti Thadani: Sexuality and Gender in Ancient India," *Shakti Khabar,* no. 15 (August–September 1991), p. 12.

25. Subodh Mukherjee, "Homosexuality in India," pp. 1, 3.

26. Subodh Mukherjee's investigation of ancient sexual practices also relies on the work of Orientalist scholars, particularly the work of French scholar Alain Danielou. Subodh fails to consider the pervasiveness of the assumptions of Orientalist scholars that India was more primitive, sensual, and eroticized than repressed, and that civilized Western Europe may have shaped Danielou's expectations and interpretations of ancient Indian sexuality. For an examination of Orientalism, see Ronald Inden, *Imagining India* (London: Basil Blackwell, 1990).

27. Stuart Hall, "Cultural Identity and Diaspora," in *Identity: Community, Culture, Difference,* edited by Jonathan Rutherford (London: Lawrence & Wischart, 1990), p. 225.

28. Shivananda Khan, "Giti Thadani," p. 13.

29. For an elaboration of this argument about sexuality as socially constructed and historically constituted, see David Halperin, "Sex before Sexuality: Pederasty, Politics and Power in Classical Athens," in *Hidden from History: Reclaiming the Gay and Lesbian Past,* edited by Martin Duberman, Martha Vicinus, and George Chauncey, Jr. (New York: New American Library, 1989), pp. 37–53, and Jeffrey Weeks, *Sex Politics and Society: The Regulation of Sexuality since 1800* (London: Longman, 1981).

30. "A White Disease," *Shakti Khabar,* p. 1.

31. "Shamakami Editorial Policy," *Shamakami,* vol. 1, no. 1 (June 1, 1990), p. 3.

32. Editor's response to letter from L.N. in *Shakti Khabar,* no. 11 (December 1990–January 1991), p. 13.

33. "Being Legit: Event or Process!" *Bombay Dost,* vol. 1, no. 1 (July–September 1991), p. 3.

34. Ian Rashid, "Out of Home," *Rites,* p. 9.

35. Judith Butler writes about how coalitional politics need not assume that "identity" is a premise or "unity" has been reached in advance to proceed with political action. Coalitions then can develop and identities can emerge or dissolve depending on the concrete political practices which constitute them. See Judith Butler, *Gender Trouble: Feminism and the Subversion of Identity* (New York: Routledge, 1990), pp. 14–16.

36. Benedict Anderson, *Imagined Communities: Reflections on the Origin and Spread of Nationalism* (London: Verso, 1983), pp. 15–16.

37. Mita Radhakrishnan, "An Open Letter from a South Asian Lesbian to Trikone Men," *Trikone,* vol. 5, no. 3 (May–June 1990), pp. 1–2.

38. "Trikone," *Trikone,* vol. 5, no. 3 (May–June 1990), p. 2.

39. Mita Radhakrishnan, "Letter from Delhi," *Trikone,* vol. 5, no. 4 (July–August 1990), pp. 1–2.

40. Aziz Ahmed and Sharmeen Islam, "Breaking the Silence," *Trikone,* vol. 3, no. 5 (September 1988), p. 2.

41. Sunil Gupta, "Correct Singularities," *Gay Times,* August 1989, pp. 40–41.

42. Aziz Ahmed, "Breaking Silence," p. 5.

43. Sunil Gupta, "Correct Singularities," pp. 40–41.

44. Anu, "notes from an indian diary," *Anamika,* vol. 1, no. 2 (March 1986), p. 8.

45. Nelson Carvahlo, "Pratibha Parmar: Fight Back and Struggle (Because You Have To)," *Khush Khayal,* vol. 2, no. 2 (June 1990), p. 7.

46. Ravi, "Bits and Pieces," *Trikon,* September 1987, p. 7.

47. Pratibha Parmar interview in Lloyd Wong, "Fuck You: This Is Our Home. Claiming South Asian Identity in Britain," *Fuse,* Summer 1990, p. 10.

48. bell hooks, "The Politics of Radical Black Subjectivity," in *Yearning: Race, Gender, and Cultural Politics* (Boston: South End Press, 1990), p. 15.

49. Jigne Desai interview in "Out in America," *Outweek* 105 (3 July 1991).

Awakenings

Painting of a hermaphroditic figure. (India, period and locale unknown)

Mummy's darling

Ankur*

She pauses for a moment. A lifetime of experience makes me feel apprehensive.

"I can see that you are taking pride in being a man, " my mother says, fixing me with her disarming green eyes. "Are you going to get married?"

I should have known. So much distance, so many difficult memories that bind us to one another. For a lifetime I've loved and hated her, at times with equal intensity. Now she sits on a sofa, my sofa, thousands of miles from our home. I am twenty-six years old, and yet some part of me shrinks into the child she found so difficult to comprehend. A child whose eyes were always seeking understanding, too often full of pain.

She sits sipping tea now, and I think back to the moment when so much of my pain began. I was seven years old, the second son of a middle-class New Delhi family whose roots lay in the Indian state of Punjab. My brother, Rajiv, who is two years older, was being allowed to go away to boarding school. Having one child away was all that my parents could bear, so I was being kept at home. I resented my brother so much; he had always been my parent's favorite, that was painfully clear to me. He was the athlete who got all of the attention, while I was reserved, timid. He had always bullied me, and though I had my own friends, I felt quite intimidated by Rajiv and his pals.

135

After enrolling in the boys-only boarding school, Rajiv began to bully me even more. At school the older boys bullied the younger ones, in keeping with a tradition common to schools in the British mold, and he was starting out near the bottom of the ladder. When he came on holiday, he would take his frustration out on me. To make matters worse, my parents would make a fuss over him during his visits while I, being home all the time, would be taken for granted.

When Rajiv was fourteen, my mother persuaded him to switch to a day school and come home for good. I thought this might improve my lot a bit in the family, but my parents began to favor him even more. I felt like an outsider by comparison and resented my brother even more.

To make matters worse, I was experiencing similar feelings at school. I was a gentle, soft-spoken child and found myself the object of much teasing, from teachers as well as other students. One of my teachers in Delhi started calling me "mummy's darling" because I was rather sheltered and dependent. She did this in front of my classmates, who quickly picked up on it. "Mummy's darling! Mummy's darling!" they would shout. Their taunts cut deeply and the name followed me into every class. I became even more reserved, but I never told my parents about it; I was not only ashamed, but also afraid of their reaction.

One teacher, a Jewish Indian named Rebecca Sudan, helped me a great deal. Ms. Sudan was my elocution instructor and in her class, as in all others, I was very soft-spoken. Instead of ridiculing me, she tried her best to get me to speak more loudly. The first time she asked me to read something I, of course, did so very softly. The other boys started pointing at me and shouting, "Mummy's darling." She was furious.

"Shut up, you silly cows!" she screamed at them.

Ms. Sudan was the first person to stand up for me. In a way she really made me the class project; the whole class seemed to revolve around me. She would encourage other boys to coax me to shout louder and be more assertive during break time. They got caught up in her enthusiasm as well and tried their best. When it came time to stage our class play, she gave me the leading part. She tried her best to instill confidence in me, and in many ways, she succeeded. I had never had so much positive attention. I even became popular with a group of boys and made many new friends. It was a happy time for me; little did I know that the next few years would chip away at my newfound confidence. I did not know that when my friend's thoughts began to turn to girls, mine would turn to boys.

I can recall being attracted to other boys from the age of five or six. Many of them were my brother's friends, and I wove fantasies around them. Not fantasies of sex, mind you, but of being with them. I had no idea what it meant back then; I just knew that it felt nice when one of them touched me, especially when I was wrestling with them. I got an impression that they had power over me. I enjoyed that as much as the physical contact, but I never labeled any of these feelings.

As I entered puberty, I developed strong feelings for many other boys. Like my brother, I attended an all-boys school, and I became physically involved with several of my classmates. There was no all-out sex, but plenty of playing around. When I realized that what I felt for them was emotional and romantic, I became confused. It seemed strange that I should have these feelings for other boys; I had no idea of the existence of homosexuality. Trying to be rational, I figured that if I had these feelings for a boy, then I should be a girl. Soon I began to manifest some of the behavior one would associate with a girl. My friends and I would stage our own versions of plays and, inevitably, I would play the woman's role.

There was one boy I spent much time with. We played around a lot — feeling each other, kissing, and sitting together romantically. One day my mother caught us sitting in an embrace. God! was she angry.

"Why don't you go outside and play ball or something instead of sitting in here all day?" she demanded.

I had no answer.

"What were you two doing?"

"Nothing," I replied.

She left it at that. I don't think she was too anxious to deal with it directly. She and my father sensed that something was wrong, but I think they regarded it as just another phase in my growing up.

As I continued to become involved with other boys, I invariably found myself playing the passive, so-called woman's part. I would become emotionally attached while they kept things on a physical plane. I must be a girl, I would think; that's why I get so involved. It was less abnormal and threatening to think of myself as a girl than to face the thought of being a boy who wanted other boys. I began to play the feminine role even more.

At the age of thirteen I was visited by the secondary male characteristics: hair appeared on my face and thickened on my legs. I hated the change. This proof of my masculinity didn't seem fair, and I thought it bizarre in my case. My parents would comment on what a nice mustache I was sprouting and I would resent my facial hair and their words. Since I hated the changes in my body, I began to suppress them. One day I got my mother's hair-removing cream and applied it to my mustache. She was furious with me and told my grandparents. They all screamed at me. For my mum it was probably just one more indication that I didn't have the "proper" behavior and attitude for a boy.

My mustache eventually grew back, and the memory of my mother's lecture did not lessen my hatred for it. One night, while I was lying in my bed, I pulled out much of the hair above my upper lip. In the morning it looked quite scraggly so I located my mother's tweezers and pulled out the remainder. Realizing what I had done, she was even more angry, but I continued to do it on a regular basis. I remember my grandmother saying that I was abnormal, that a normal boy wouldn't act like that.

"What do you want me to do with him, finish him off?" my mother shouted back. "Do you want to give him a drug and kill him?"

This scene was played out right before my eyes and it humiliated me. It seemed that no one understood the feelings growing inside of me. This feeling of being alone hurt so much, yet I did not stop using my mother's tweezers. This behavior became the source of continuous conflict. Each time I plucked my facial hair, she would scream at me, sometimes hit me, but I would do it again.

Soon I took the next logical step in my war on my secondary male characteristics: I started shaving the hair on my legs. I showed it to the boys at school – I suppose to convince them that I was not a boy – but they took to teasing me about it. Word soon spread, and people once again began to whisper about me, to point at me.

Around this time I also found out what "homo" meant. I became even more depressed when I realized that it applied to me.

My mother soon realized that I was shaving my legs.

"What are you becoming?" she screamed at me.

"He is becoming a *hijra,*" my grandparents would say to her.

Disapproval continued at both home and school, but no amount of conflict could make me change my actions. I soon began to pluck my eyebrows, then all of my facial hair. Eventually I was even shaving my arms. It became an obsession. By the age of fifteen I even tried putting on a bit of my mother's makeup, in private. The older I got, the more she freaked out. I suppose my actions made it difficult for her to rationalize my behavior as being just a phase. She and my father were now extremely irritable with me. My brother was getting more attention than ever, and I felt worthless. At school I went from being one of the best students to one of the worst. I was becoming dangerously depressed.

I continued to have secret physical relationships with many of the boys at school. Playing the part of the girl to the hilt, I would refuse to undress. I even went so far as to tell them I did not have a penis, hoping this would convince them that I was not a boy. They were convinced all right; they started calling me a *hijra. Hijra,* pansy, mummy's darling, homo. There were many names. The same boys who had sex with me in private would ridicule me in public. It hurt a lot, yet I continued to see them.

My depression was deepening. School was painful, home was no better. I was getting tired of fighting the feelings that seemed to cause all of this misery. I didn't want to grow up to be a homosexual; the very thought frightened me. It would have been more acceptable to be a woman, but that was not an option. I concluded that my future would be bleak, and I did not want to deal with it.

One day, when all of my family had gone out of the house, I found twelve sleeping pills and popped them in my mouth. I remember going next door and telling my friend Ravi what I had done and making him swear not to tell anyone. The last thing I recall before waking up in the hospital is playing with our dogs. Apparently, I was very drowsy and unresponsive when my parents came home, and my mother realized something was up. She sent my brother to Ravi's house and Rajiv forced my friend to talk. I was rushed to the hospital, and my stomach was pumped. I was in the hospital for four days and stayed home from school for an additional four weeks.

Ravi told someone at school of what had happened, and soon it spread across the campus. When I finally went back to school, people had another reason to point their fingers at me. They added "sissy criminal" to the long list of names. I was angry with Ravi for opening his mouth and told him I never wanted to speak to him again. My mom heard of what was going on at school; she told me I deserved their ridicule.

"You have been given everything," she told me, "that's why you do these bizarre things – out of boredom. It is time that you got a grip on life and stopped feeling sorry for yourself."

Needless to say, I became even more withdrawn, so my mother took me to a psychologist. She filled him in on everything about me. The two of them sat facing me, and he asked me how I felt about my growing into a young man. I said nothing. My mother tried to get me to talk, but I refused. The doctor then sent me to have my cheek scraped to determine if I was biologically your average boy. I was petrified of the whole thing.

"You see, you are normal," my mother shouted at me on the way home; the test had come back normal. She pointed to a *hijra* walking beside the road and said, "That's what you are becoming. Have you seen any boy or girl who is like you? You're a freak."

Worthless doesn't begin to describe how I felt sitting next to her at that moment. There was nothing I could say that would change her opinion or my feelings.

Things did not change, however. When I was sixteen, I developed a serious crush on a guy at school named Sanjay. He seemed to be attracted to me and was quite nice. He would take me to the movies, hold my hand, and embrace me. We did not have sex, but I became very infatuated with him. I talked about him a great deal, and my mum began to grow suspicious. By this time she was suspicious of many of my activities, and she considered Sanjay a bad influence on me.

My love affair with Sanjay, if I may call it that, was quite private. In public he ridiculed me like all the others. Soon we began to go to the movies only with a group; the other boys would call me pansy and *rundi* (whore). Eventually these boys, including Sanjay, stopped talking to me. They wouldn't even answer me. It hurt like hell, but there was nothing I could do. While everyone went outside during break time at school, I would lay my head upon my desk and try to shut the world out. At home I began to sleep way too much and cry a great deal.

These boys, and others, used me in many ways, only to turn around and treat me cruelly. My parents used to send me to school in a chauffeur-driven car. These guys would get the driver to drop them off all over town, then call me names the next chance they got. It was humiliating and just pushed me further into myself. I felt powerless in the face of all of this and, at the age of sixteen, I tried to kill myself a second time. Again I took a bottle of pills, but this time my mother caught on more quickly. She rushed me to our doctor, who made me drink salt water and black coffee to induce vomiting. My mom told the family doctor what was going on with me; he suggested that she introduce me to more girls.

My mother dealt with this second suicide attempt much more appropriately than with the first one. She sat down and had a long talk with me.

"What is wrong? Why do you have no confidence in yourself?" she asked. "All these people you are running after, they will be running after you if you become a success."

"I'm unhappy because I'm a pansy," I told her. "I accept who I am and I know that there is no hope in life for me."

"No," she said, "if tomorrow you are successful, these people will chase you. The main thing is to have confidence in yourself."

That talk help me a lot. I desperately wanted to win my parents' approval, so I decided to stop doing the things they found so objectionable. The attention wasn't worth the pain. If I was going to grow into a man who loved other men, I would just learn to suppress the feelings. I stopped removing my body hair and began to shave my face properly. I focused totally on schoolwork and let my social life fade away. Thus I improved academically but continued to become more introverted.

The next year I applied for a scholarship to a college in England. I was very surprised when I received word that it was mine. I think they wanted a well-rounded Indian youth, and the fact that I had learned to play the *tabla* and sing was instrumental in their decision. My parents were very happy with this turn of events; they figured this would give my confidence the boost it needed.

Being so sheltered, I had difficulty leaving home. England was nothing like New Delhi. It presented me with a chance to make a fresh start, but the scars from my past made me very fearful. Hiding my feelings was perhaps my biggest challenge. In the beginning I was able to maintain my resolve without too much problem. As the months passed, however, I became quite frustrated and lonely. All around me I saw love sprouting, always with a heterosexual face but love all the same, and yet it never came for me.

At least some of my sadness and anger came out as rebellion toward my parents. I refused to accept their authority and decided that I did not need their approval. I was learning to be assertive, aggressive, and they bore the brunt of this change. I showed no respect when they came to visit, and they were very shocked and hurt by my behavior. They assumed that I had been corrupted by Western society.

I was celibate during my first year. In my frustration I would be nasty to the boys I found attractive. I lost a lot of friends that way, but it seemed to be my only means of suppressing the feelings. When it came time for the final exams, I became ill and was not able to take them. My parents were very unhappy and put much pressure on me to take the exams the next year. I did finish out, at another school in England, and did very well. There was a big sacrifice, however; I had no social life whatsoever. How could I, when I was so busy running from myself?

I could have contacted a gay students group on my campus at this college, but I was too afraid. In desperation, I called a gay switchboard in town. The guy I reached was part of a couple, and the two of them very sweetly came to the campus. They took me to a bar, not at all what I was expecting. The two of them played rather rigid roles; one was definitely the "man" while the other played the traditional woman's role. I was put off by this. I was also intimidated by the bar they took me to; it was fairly rough and made me feel insecure. I left the bar pretty quickly and vowed never to return.

I had many infatuations during this period and, since I suppressed everything, I invariably fell into depressions. The worst one was in my senior year when I nearly screwed up my exams again. That is the closest I have come to having a nervous breakdown. People would ask me questions in public, and I would not know what to say. My hands shook, I lost weight and had difficulty sleeping.

When my parents visited me, I reapproached the topic of my sexuality. I had previously told a woman friend and my roommate, and both had reacted fairly well. So I told my mother that I still had homosexual feelings but that I did not intend to act on them. She and my father suggested that I concentrate on my college degree and expressed their concern about diseases going around. That was that.

After I got my B.A., I came to the United States for graduate work. I started out at a college on the East Coast, still in the same mode of focusing totally on my work and suppressing my feelings. One day, at a friend's suggestion, I worked up the courage to go to a gay students meeting and met a guy who seemed quite friendly. I wasn't that interested in him romantically, but Paul came onto me pretty strongly. I had not been kissed for eight years now, and I decided that I wanted to see how it would feel. I was nervous, but it felt great. As I saw him again and we spent more time together, I became romantically attached and thought that I had met the man of my dreams. It turned out that Paul was involved with someone else. I found myself depressed once again and decided to seek out a counselor.

My visit to this counselor was pivotal for me. He was the first person to tell me that I had to stop living against my nature. It was time for me to forget the responsibilities that dominated my life; I should be giving expression to every aspect of myself. I needed to open up, make new friends, and search for happiness. I took his advice and began to go out much more.

In the last three years I've met many people, made many friends, had many affairs, and watched my confidence grow. I've blossomed. My attitude toward life is much more positive, and I'm excited about so many things. I've had my disappointments, especially when love hasn't worked out, but that's okay; those are the sort of things I can deal with, for they are a part of everyone's life.

I wish I could have come to these realizations about myself earlier and spared myself so much pain and confusion. If only my family, especially my mother, had understood what I was going through and given me a bit of support, I would not have done all of the bizarre things that turned them against me. But that is an item on some wish list. The reality I must deal with is my mother, sitting in my apartment, asking a question that undermines my commitment to myself.

"No, I'm not getting married," I answer her. "I'm not heterosexual."

"But you see that you can function as a man!" She sounds exasperated.

"Yes, I can, but not with women; only with men," I respond.

I am still dealing with my anger toward her, toward my whole family, but I tell her everything that is going on in my life to help her understand. She has her doubts, and yet she has changed her attitude toward me in many ways. She seems to respect me more and actually favors me over my brother Rajiv, something that I thought would never happen. She will not give approval to my lifestyle overnight, but I think that over time she will come to accept me as a man who loves other men. Perhaps then "mummy's darling" will take on a whole new definition for me.

The scent of roses

Kamini Chaudhary*

"*K*amini ... *I need you*" – *and I'd be off on my trusty Atlas bicycle, pedaling furiously, narrowly missing rickshaws and pedestrians, undeterred by catcalls from the* paanwallahs *(sellers of betel nut leaves).* "Jaaneman, jaaneman, tere chaar nain...," *roadside Romeos serenading me as I whizzed by, incongruous in my middle-class attire – Lee jeans, a local brand that never quite passed for Levi's, and my special Janpath shirt, bespectacled eyes blinking as I swerved left and right, avoiding lecherous, grasping hands, raucous vendors, and full-hipped, heavy-bosomed ladies in maroon lipstick and matching* bindis. *The weekly* paintth bazaar *(sidewalk sale) was on, and my eyes were drawn, as always, to the stalls with pointed brassieres flying like beige, black, and white banners from poles, surrounded by women eagerly fingering the thick, nylon padding, poking the stiff, pointed nipples and laughing as they sprang back up again.*

I would sail from the overlit sea of glass lanterns into a darker street – Mom's voice echoing over the last strains of "Yeh hotel hai kya – kabhi to ghar rahna chahiye – aaj nahin jaa sakte" *("Is this a hotel? Shouldn't you stay home sometimes? You can't go today").*

I would smile, all parental battles forgotten. One thought was music to my ears: Nazreen needs me.

It would have been easy then to die for her. How I loved those nights of talking, talking, holding her in my sleep. Waking, eating, playing. "If you were only a boy..."

Then one day she didn't want to be with me. That was not the death I was prepared to die for her. I recall walking with tears streaming from my eyes down some forgotten dusty Delhi street. That was so long ago. I was fifteen years old. I had never dreamt of being lovers with a woman in the physical sense, but I loved Nazreen with the passion of Laila and Majnu (famous star-crossed lovers of Indian lore).

Five years later, studying for a B.A. in the United States, I was to find myself holding the hand of a woman with gray-green cat eyes and red fire in her hair. I knew from the way my fingers twisted, grasping hers, that I wanted her passionately. I wanted her heart, her mind, her body, her very breath. Romance was an old feeling, but sexual desire was new. I had gone for four years with a man and never felt that I wanted him in the way that I wanted to at once devour and be devoured by this woman.

I wonder if I had not heard about lesbianism through the women's literature I was reading, or if I wasn't close friends with a lesbian couple, would I have discovered that loving a woman can be sexual? Was that what was undiscovered and unexpressed with Nazreen?

For two weeks my fire-maned lover and I drowned in each other. Passion and tenderness enveloped us like a summer cloud; we basked in its warmth, and whenever we moved, it followed us, surrounding us with the scent of roses. Loving her was like holding a scarlet rosebud till it bloomed, then gently tugging off each of its soft, open petals with my teeth, slowly savoring the feel of each smooth, curved, pink-red petal on and around my tongue, and then deliberately chewing all of them, one by one, squeezing out every drop of nectar before swallowing them, ready for more. I don't think that I have loved a woman or a man that way since.

Unfortunately, it didn't last very long. The thorns began to prick within a couple of weeks. There was a meeting, melting of bodies and spirits, but our minds fought each other all the way. She, thirty-three, white, a product of her environment, open to difference but very set in her ways, essentially an individualist, very much a woman, a witch – tender and bewitching in one breath, cruel as a whiplash in the next. She sought independence fiercely, feared the dependence of a relationship, did not want a lover but wanted an affair.

I was twenty, open, naive, soft. Her hardness scared me as much as my emotional intensity scared her. I was willing to live my whole

146

life with her, to cast off everything for her – community, family – if she loved me enough. But with our cultural differences it could never be enough. To me her frankness sounded grossly selfish and individualistic. Her desire for space was a way to shut me out. I had, after all, grown up on a rich diet of Hindi films with Lata's lyrics still ringing in my ears – *"Yeh zindagi usi ki hai, jo kisi ka ho gaya"* ("This life belongs only to the one who belongs to another"). Her personality was in complete conflict with my Sita/Savitri all-for-the-one-I-love personality.

She was so much more powerful than I was in the relationship. Her whiteness, her age, and her Westernness were all pieces of her armor that I felt repelled by. She may or may not have used this power deliberately, but she had no way to understand my insecurities about these things. Despite the differences, our connection was always intense, and so we went on and off for a long time. Two years passed before I finally disentangled myself from her web, pushing her pain and beauty into the past.

Disappointment at imagined promises. Cynicism at egalitarian relationships. Was I expecting the feminist utopia of my mind to suddenly manifest itself just because I had found a woman lover? Fortunately or unfortunately, the real world is the real world and fantasy soon fades.

I violently discarded the dream to assuage my heart. I decided to try out the way the other ninety percent of the world lives. Nothing prepared me for the indeliberate violence of that encounter. It's one thing to deal with conscious, deliberate violence; you can blame the perpetrator. But how do you deal with the violence perpetrated by ignorance? And your own complicity due to your ignorance? I guess one can only blame this sexist society that promotes violence in sex as romantic. This, coupled with the lack of education imparted to men and women about women's bodies, often makes the first heterosexual act one of rape.

The wounds are healed, the blood has dried, the scars are hidden deep within me...

An aunt once said to me, "You kids are lucky you know everything about these things – we did not know anything. When we were married, we were set up for rape." The only difference was that I was not committed by marriage to this man, I could leave. Which I did.

147

The expatriate Indian community had started gossiping about me. I was close friends with a young Indian girl whose family, on finding out about my "lifestyle," kicked me out of their house, abusing me and accusing me of making passes at their daughter. Sarcasm, snide remarks, over-gleeful grins, icy-cold snubs were all signs of gossip traveling like a whirlwind. A new female student from India looked intimidated and scared at our first meeting. I realized later that she had probably been warned to keep away from me – a dreadful, raging lesbian who might ravage her.

Word went all the way to my father in India. He was upset but knew it useless to try to change me. "If two women want to live with each other, fine, but so long as they are not yelling it on the streets!" followed by "You will make it impossible for me to live in public one day." Blackmail, guilt, pain, disappointment, distance, despairing acceptance – we are still going through the gamut.

I had told my mother and my sister as soon as I knew that I wanted to be with women. I was happy about it and I expected that they would understand. I felt no shame. I knew that if I felt this way then it was right. I knew I was good and sincere, and I trusted my feelings. My sister understood. My mother didn't quite understand but accepted it.

I have always loved women. Women's friendships in India weren't sexual, but they were like love affairs. Drama, trauma, jealousy, intimacy, hugging, holding hands, touching – an involvement far more intense and complete than any I have experienced in a friendship or relationship with an American.

I was dejected and disappointed, still carrying a torch for my ex-girlfriend, unsure of my place in a society that works so much more from the head than the heart. Missing home, desperately missing all of the smallest details about home, missing even the people and things I disliked.

The universe is great – it takes away with one hand and gives with the other. Two people walked into my life within the space of a few months: Neeru, an immigrant of thirteen years, the first South Asian lesbian I ever met, and Rahul, who had just arrived at my university and become a friend before he told me that he was gay. Slowly my support network was beginning to grow. Soon I heard about Anamika, an organization of South Asian lesbians, and Trikone, which was for both gay men and lesbians.

It's taken me two years to move closer to some of the people from Trikone who are now friends of mine. Still, I feel as if I kind of fit and kind of don't. There is such a separatist attitude about sexuality – people expect it to fall into two neat bundles of homosexuality and heterosexuality. My belief is that human beings are innately bisexual and they get socialized to varying degrees of sexual orientation. That is, sexuality is a spectrum that ranges from nongay to gay. I consider myself bisexual. I've had other relationships with both men and women along with those that I have described earlier.

Because of the attitude of both gays and nongays toward bisexuals, I often feel socially like a *dhobi ka kuta – na ghar ka, na ghat ka* (a washerman's dog who has no real use, neither at home nor at the washing places). Which is also how I feel that I fit culturally and ethnically in the U.S. However, I feel like I have found a little niche here in San Francisco that gives me certain things: I have a certain degree of personal freedom and, most importantly, I have a few friends who are progressive gay, bisexual, or heterosexual South Asians who accept me and share many of my feelings.

The hardest struggle for me has been, in general, to be a sexual being as a woman, and particularly so growing up in India, where women (at least those from the middle class) are not supposed to be sexual at all. In India, homosexuality is closeted for sure, but hell, even heterosexual sex before marriage is a big deal. For me to say that I have sexual relationships is an achievement. It is obviously easier here because of the anonymity, but there is a lot of pain and guilt associated with being away from your home place. Guilt at abandoning family, grandparents, pain for the time, the relationships, and the sharing that are lost with family and friends just by not being there. There's a feeling of missing a great deal.

There is also the demystification of the dream of America that some deal with and others don't. All of the propaganda about the easy life and democracy and equality in the U.S. is false. This place is racist, classist, and it is not easy to make it here. But there is room for personal freedom mainly because the society is so individualistic – let everyone do her own thing and so shall the invisible hand of the free market work. There is freedom here to pick your bubble of friends, choose what you want to do and with whom, whom you want to love and live with. Homophobia is still a harsh reality, but I do live in the gay capital of the U.S; if you don't feel safe holding your sweetheart's hand on a street corner, you can always run down a couple of blocks to the gay district, where you can kiss her in the middle of the street.

Living honestly

Feroze*

I was born twenty-four years ago in Mombasa, Kenya, the second son of a beautiful young Indian couple. Originally from the Indian state of Gujarat, my family had lived in eastern Africa for three generations. Despite the decades spent away from our homeland, my family, like most Indian families in Kenya, had retained its Indian culture. The language they spoke, the clothes they wore, the food they ate were all identifiably Indian.

I have sometimes wondered why the Indians in Africa retain their identity so strongly, unlike the Indians who came to the Caribbean, for instance. Perhaps it is because the Indians brought to the Caribbean were unskilled laborers, transported en masse to work the Britishers' plantations. Those who went to Africa were of a more middle-class status; they knew better the workings of the British system and were instrumental in helping to raise and maintain it.

My memories of growing up in Africa are vague. With regard to the deaths of my father and older brother, this is something of a blessing. I was an infant and had been left with my grandparents when the rest of my family went on a trip. There was an auto accident along the way; my father and my three-year-old brother were killed, my mother was badly injured but survived. This tragedy redirected the focus of my mother's life. She decided, consciously or unconsciously, to sacrifice her own needs to better meet mine. Eventually she would give up her own comfort, her parents, and most of her family just to give me the best opportunities.

When I was eight years old my mother moved us to England. Her brother was going there with his family, and she figured England would provide me with better educational options. We first lived with my uncle in Birmingham, a rather rough town in the central part of England. The move was a traumatic experience for me, and the first few days of school were especially hard. I was terrified, felt alone and alienated. My mother and my aunt would force me to play with the other kids in the street; they felt this would help me to fit into the mainstream of British boy culture. They brought me these footballs to play with. What a bloody nuisance! I hated football (soccer, for the American reader). I didn't know what to do with the ball, so I would give it to the neighborhood kids.

In South Asian society it is not considered proper for a woman to live alone, so widows like my mother often end up living in the house of a male relative, most often a father or brother. Living with an adult son is acceptable also, but living alone with a child is not. There is also, of course, the financial issues a woman raising a child alone must consider.

In my uncle's household my mother was, in some manner, the second woman. I hated the idea that she had no voice in household matters and was somehow a burden to my uncle's nice little nuclear family. As a kid, I managed better than she did. My mother is an English teacher and as such, she is a perfectionist. My uncle's main concern is money. Not surprisingly, they had a typical brother-sister love-hate relationship – they were constantly at each other's throats. This was exacerbated by their working together in the import business.

I could feel my mother suffering. I hated her condition and yet, ironically, I took it out on her. I would tell her not to argue, but to go along with what my uncle said just to keep peace in the house. My aunt did not escape my anger either. Once I got so angry that I slapped her for reprimanding me and told her never to talk in that manner to me again.

At the age of thirteen my family moved to London for business reasons. By this time I had turned into a real "coconut" (brown-skinned on the outside, white on the inside) – a good little English boy. I had gone to a good prep school in Birmingham; my mum paid good money so I could have a proper education. Later I got a scholarship to a good grammar school, also in Birmingham. At the time of the move, I asked to stay behind. Mum was in no position, psychologically or financially, to live on in Birmingham with just her and me – which was what I so desperately wanted to do.

I'm sure my mum wasn't too happy, but it was decided that she would go with them, while I would stay behind and take advantage of my scholarship. They put me up with friends of the family, a young couple who were Boré (a branch of Shia Islam, pronounced *boray),* like my own family. The arrangement seemed suitable at the time, but I would come to regret it.

Throughout this time I lived a fairly sheltered life, but I got an earful from my all-boys school. The favorite topic of conversation seemed to be sex, and I had no idea what on earth it could be. I don't recall at precisely what age it dawned on me what this "nasty" business was all about. It was a stage-by-stage process I'm sure; there was no cataclysmic episode that opened my eyes to everything. Watching the telly, observing the people around me were all a part of my learning experience.

I remember wanking (masturbating) with a cute neighborhood kid named Paul. We went into the woods once and explored a cave. I said something like "I can come these days." Of course he insisted on a demonstration, which I was only too happy to give. Paul and I got to talking about our willies. We ended up masturbating together.

I had a few of these "I'll show you mine if you show me yours" experiences, some with girls. Gender was not an issue, though I remember finding Paul particularly attractive. Though I can remember experiences like this, I did not have an intellectual concept of homosexuality at the time. Once, while still in Birmingham, I saw a picture of gay policemen in San Francisco kissing – I don't remember the specifics. My aunt said, "They're all gay there." It really struck a chord in me, yet I still didn't know why.

My first proper sexual experience, if I may call it that, happened just after my mum left for London. The family I stayed with was dreadful. The woman was a very nice Indian mother – long hair in a *jhoti* (braid) down to her bum (ass). A cute, bright little baby. And a nightmare of a husband. Why are Indian men so awful? He was a quite nasty piece of work – fat, ugly, and horrid. Over Christmas they were having repairs done to the house. The wife and baby were sleeping at her sister's house, leaving me alone in the house with the husband. One night when I came home it was very cold. The bastard had managed to shut off the storage heater in my room. My room was an icebox, and he said I could sleep in his room. I felt some trepidation but went with him.

I should have known better. I woke up in the middle of the night to find that he had taken off his clothes. He had positioned himself so that his penis was lying in my open hand. I was completely horrified and incredibly excited. It was like watching a frightening film through the cracks between your fingers, wanting to know but wanting to hide. He didn't rape me, thank God! But he did make me play with him. There was one point during the night when we talked a bit. I told him that I didn't know how to wank. He said he didn't either, but that he thought it went something like this, then proceeded to show me.

This sort of activity between us happened on a few other occasions. After the repairs were done and his wife came back, the horrid man became more creative. While she would be cooking breakfast below, I would go to his room. He would pull back the covers and show me his willie. On one occasion I had to sleep in his bed; they had a female guest and, because of the lack of space, the women slept together in my room and I was placed with him. The next morning his wife walked in while I was in bed with him. I wasn't wearing a stitch of clothing! He muttered some feeble excuse, and she left the room without a word. I was crushed. He tried to coax me into bed many a time after that, but I refused.

Was he a closeted homosexual? I don't think so, at least I don't want to. To me the term *closeted* suggests a rather beautiful person who is sitting in a shell just waiting to emerge into a beautiful thing – chrysalis and butterfly. I guess that is the distinction I make between homosexuality and being gay. I don't use the word *closeted* to refer to someone who engages in opportunistic sex with a kid of thirteen. Simply put, he used me and made it clear that I must tell no one else.

I soon discovered what an awful man he was in many other ways. He beat his wife terribly. He would pull her around by the hair and there would be blood everywhere. Fearful of violence, I literally hid, shaking, in the corner of my room.

154

I liked his wife very much, though I pitied her. We shared some pleasant times and some rather painful experiences. A lot of racism existed in our neighborhood. I remember one incident rather clearly. She was walking me home from school. People driving by, calling us bloody Pakis, and throwing eggs at us. One egg hit her in the head. The egg trickled down the length of her braid. She just knelt on the ground and cried. "Suppose it had hit my son," she said (her baby was two years old at the time). Some of our English neighbors walked past, but they did not stop, did not say a word. I felt disgusted by them, by so many things – white people, her husband, oppression. I suppose it was a great political moment for me, an awakening to the ugliness around me. Later I would find the experiences of homophobia to be quite similar to racism.

Despite the violence in the household, I stayed with this couple for two years. By that time the husband had begun to beat me occasionally. I told my mother about the beatings the wife received, but I did not tell her about my own beatings; she felt bad enough about my having to live in such a space.

Soon my mother arranged for me to stay with a family that lived in a very Punjabi Indian–Pakistani Moslem neighborhood. At this point I was quite conscious that I found blokes (men) attractive and that they seemed to go for me as well. I was regarded as being quite beautiful at school – small, hairless, a gorgeous face. I would often get sex mail: "I masturbate thinking about you at night," "Come meet me at such and such place," etc. Boys would flash themselves at me in the showers. With all of this going on, you would think that I would have I engaged in some overt sexual activity, but I took no part in it.

When I reached the age of eighteen, I was fortunate enough to get into Cambridge. I knew at that point that I wanted to be in medicine and did quite well academically. I still hated sports, however, and found novel ways to avoid them. I would pretend that I was fasting in commemoration of some religious day and, the teachers being quite unfamiliar with our customs, I would get out of participating in whatever sport. At times I actually went to the length of fasting and thus ensuring my escape.

As much as I detested sports, I loved school. Many of the teachers at school made overtures to me, some subtle, others annoyingly blatant. Sometimes one would suggest that I come and stay with him when his wife was out of town, but I would find some excuse to decline. I lived on campus during this time. It was a wonderful experience, really, like staying in some hotel paid for by the government.

At Cambridge, I had my first proper relationship with a man. David proclaimed that he was straight. He was a good friend of mine and had been a source of much support. When he stayed, we would make the most of the nights. One night he said, "This isn't right, it shouldn't be." But he managed to put up with it. For months.

I needed to be with someone who was comfortable with himself. Someone who could help me. David was constantly running away from himself, declaring that he was not gay. His attitude was demoralizing and depressing, so I eventually ended the relationship. Emotionally, it was not difficult. Sexually it was a bit harder; I had grown used to sleeping with him. But there had been so much pretending around our friends, lying still in the dark so as not to arouse suspicion. Such things made the end easier. David could not bear to see me in a new context, however, and our friendship also ended soon thereafter.

After breaking up with David, I went to India for a year. My major academic focus in India was the study of Persian. I traveled a great deal in India, much of it with Anita, a Cambridge friend who was from New Delhi. Anita came from an upper-middle-class family and seemed to know everyone in the city. We even came together sexually at one point, and it was nice to know that I could experience intimacy with a woman. But make no mistake, I'm not waffling; it was clear to me that I was much more attracted to blokes.

India was quite educational for me. I learned a great deal, and it very much felt like a second home to me by the time I left. I was now much more together as a gay person, though I had lost some of my academic desire.

Upon returning to England I began my study at Oxford. I also became involved in a series of relationships with men that helped me clarify what I was seeking in another man. In my first term I had a relationship with a very tall, very white man who was traditionally upper middle class and horrible. A few days into our relationship Mark said, "You know, Pakis were pretty high on my general dislike list, but you've changed that a bit." I knew then that it was doomed. I did not want to base a relationship on a strictly physical basis. It doesn't make sense if two people are not politically in tune. One's partner must appreciate other characteristics beyond the surface.

Mark was another coward who proclaimed that he was not gay at all. As a matter of fact, his conflict was so strong that he went to the trouble of engaging in a heterosexual relationship while he was seeing me. The woman he chose happened to be a good friend of mine who knew what was going on between Mark and me. I soon found the situation unbearable and, after four months, ended the relationship. I decided then that my next relationship would be with an openly gay, stable man.

Not long after, I was pursued by the sexiest man at our college, a Scotsman named Allen, and I succumbed to his abundant charm. This relationship didn't last long. I don't know what he wanted from me. Perhaps I was a conquest for him, and once he had me he lost interest. I really like him, however, and my confidence was shot when it was over.

After I stopped seeing Allen I began to wonder what was wrong with me. Was I bad in bed? (Even though we had had great sex.) What was it? Nothing, I know now. I don't think Allen tried to understand me. The lesson that I learned from him was that it is not enough to be like-minded politically. The other person must appreciate your multicultural factors and the inherent complexity. He must understand your inability to relate to some Western things. Allen was an open and politically active gay man, but he was not interested enough to make the effort to get to know me well.

I had other experiences during this time. None of these were long-term, nor did they possess much potential. But they were important in the consolidation of my gayness. Saying you are homosexual is an expression of your sexual preference, you see, and I had not expressed this. My time at Oxford has helped me to do this. It has helped me to define myself as a gay man.

The issue of my sexuality has come up with my mother several times over the past few years. I have told her many times that I am gay and that she should not entertain any notions of my settling down into heterosexual wedded bliss. I have made it clear that I still love her a great deal and hope that I can help her to understand my life. She knows that I don't want to cause her any pain. Once she told me that I had been keeping her in the dark. I said I did so only due to a foolish desire to protect her, but that I would do so no more. I need her support, I need to share my life with her more fully. I've tried to explain to her that my gayness is not the only thing important to me, but that it is a very central issue.

I would like to give my mum the joy she has hoped for — I think I have given it to her in all ways but one. But just as I want her to understand me, I cannot lose sight of her situation. She is a product of her society, her time, her family — she does not possess many of the coping mechanisms that are a part of my generation's character. She is a Muslim woman who looks to the Koran to define the world around her, and she is convinced that God expects me to be heterosexual.

At first, Mum used to cry during our discussions and made me promise to change my ways and to pray for help. Foolishly, I would agree. Who among us can stand to see his mother cry? Now I tell her that I can pray, but not to change, only to help her understand me. She has sacrificed a great deal for me and I love her very much; I want her to always be an important part of my life, but I want to live my life honestly as a gay man.

A happy life

Nimal Silva*

I am often told by people that I seem to be an unusually happy person, and I guess that really is true. From my childhood days in Sri Lanka to my life in Boston right now, I cannot remember ever being seriously depressed. Oh, I've been sad now and then, but not much more. I think that the world has been good to me, and my life has pretty much fallen into place. Even being gay has never been an issue; rather than going through some agonizing process of coming to accept it, I've felt fine about myself from the first day I realized I was different.

I was born in the capital city of Colombo on the island of Sri Lanka, or Ceylon, as it was called then. Sri Lanka was a beautiful island full of promise at that time, before economic woes and civil strife encroached upon its idyllic lifestyle. Unlike the majority of Sri Lankans, who are Buddhist, my family is Catholic. The part of Colombo we lived in was heavily Catholic, so I didn't really feel out of place. My father worked for the government, my mother took care of the household; every day she would go to the market for fresh fish and vegetables. My family was upper middle class and my three sisters and I grew up with a few privileges. Servants cooked and cleaned in the house and took us kids to school, and often they brought us hot lunches from home.

A lot of gay guys I talk to say that they did not have their first sexual experience until they became adults. My experience was quite the opposite; childhood was full of exploration. I started at the age of six with my best friend, who lived next door. We were inseparable to begin with, and then one day we played a game of "you show me yours, I'll show you mine." We soon progressed beyond this little game and continued to fool around with each other until the age of thirteen.

I don't think that either one of us felt any sort of a romantic attachment. There was an emotional bond, but that was just the continuation of our friendship. We would come home from school and, if my mom was away, we would "play." We didn't really know what to do then; we would touch each other, our little peepees would get hard. There was nothing in the way of pornography in Sri Lanka at the time, so there was not much for us to go by. We did graduate to oral sex eventually, but that was about it.

In Sri Lanka, there is no gay life to speak of. The only people I remember who could be gay are guys who are professional dressers – that is, they traditionally dress the bride for her wedding. There aren't that many of them, and many of them are married and have families. They are pretty feminine, though, and they dress different-ly, wear their sarong differently than other men. For Sri Lankans, that's pretty much the definition of a gay man.

At the age of twelve, my friend started to develop crushes on girls. One of our neighbors had a couple of daughters, and he would talk to me all the time about one of them. I would listen, but it was nothing I could relate to. I knew then that we were headed in different directions. Today he is married and is raising two kids, yet when I visited Sri Lanka a few years ago, we ended up fooling around again. I think most boys have sex with other boys at some point or other, regardless of whether they end up being gay or straight as adults.

When I was in the seventh grade, I had another experience, this time with an older boy at school. There was a bank at school, set up as a teaching tool for the students. The guy in charge of the bank was an eleventh grader, and one of us had a crush on the other – I can't remember who. After school, I would sneak into the bank, and we would fool around. I also fooled around with one of my cousins. He was older, but I was the one who made the first move. I remember that he could ejaculate at the time, while I couldn't, and I was fascinated. Today he is also married and has kids. I never really thought of what I did as being right or wrong in any of these

160

instances; I was a happy little kid, and what I was doing was rather innocent and felt right to me.

My sexual explorations came to a halt when my family moved to the United States. I was thirteen at the time. Sri Lanka was having an economic crisis and just about everything was being rationed. My family, like any emigrating family, was allowed to take a total of 100 British pounds in currency with us; the government wanted to make sure that an exodus of citizens' money did not further weaken the anemic economy.

I spoke a good deal of English in Sri Lanka and that, along with the fact that I was young, made the transition relatively simple. It was more difficult for my parents. They really had to start over. We lived with some relatives in New England for the first six months. My parents worked long hours at menial jobs in the beginning, but they were driven and eventually worked themselves into an economic position comparable to what we had in Sri Lanka. They really made a lot of sacrifices for my sisters and I, and for this I respect them a great deal.

In those early years in the U.S., I didn't think that there were any people like me in this country. I soon found out what the word *gay* meant, and I decided there might be hope for me yet. There were a couple of guys in high school who everyone thought were gay. I remember that this guy named Eric, who was gorgeous, took a fat, unattractive girl to the prom; I was sure I knew why. I dated girls myself, but they only served as cover. Without the option of being with another boy, I entered a period of sexual dormancy that would last years.

When I was nineteen and in college, I was flipping through an X-rated straight newspaper one day and came across an ad for a gay movie theater. I was so excited. I called the place, got directions, and went. A fortyish guy with a fantastic body approached me after the film was over. He was married and had a couple of kids. He asked me to go for a drink at a coffee shop, and I agreed. Later we went to another place, something like a bathhouse, and ended up having minimal sex. He gave me his phone number afterwards, and I gave him mine. I was living at home and could have gotten into so much trouble. I did see this guy once more but that was all; I felt guilty because he was married.

I continued to live with my parents after I finished college and got a job teaching here in Boston. My parents have always respected their kids' privacy and living in their house was almost like living in a hotel; I know all of my friends were envious of that when I was growing up. Each one of us in the family had a key to his or her bedroom, and no one else had a duplicate. Thus we could do as we chose in our own space, stay out as long as we wanted to.

For this reason, and many others, I have never thought of my family as something that I need to move away from. Sure, we all need to differentiate from our families to some degree, but mine was never oppressive toward me, so I never really felt a need to rebel against it. Even today, I have moved out on my own into a house only for investment purposes; I could still be quite happy living with my parents.

I have never discussed my being gay with anyone in the family. I worry about how my parents would react. I love and respect them so much, and I know that they will eventually find out about me. My sisters do not know either, though I have fewer apprehensions about them finding out; they've been raised here so I think it is less likely to be a problem with them.

I have been single throughout the years that I've been gay. I think my relationship with my family has made it easier, and preferable, to not have a lover. I don't feel the emptiness that a lot of guys seem to when they talk about wanting a lover. I feel like I get the love I need to survive from my family, so I am not driven to get it from another man. Also, I would only want to be with a guy who is discreet; I don't want to stand out at this point, in my family or in society at large, and I would not want to be with someone who would jeopardize this.

Only lately have I had any great desire to have a lover. In college I was very focused on my studies and felt that a lover would only interfere with things. It was easier to find someone for sex without having to make a great commitment, and I've never had trouble separating love and sex. I rarely go to bars, and the guys I've connected with I've met through ads or parties. Today I'm glad about this, what with AIDS and all. I've always used protection, even before it came to be seen as necessary; I considered it a part of good hygiene. So, in both instances, I feel rather lucky.

I must admit that at this point in my life I would like to be with someone romantically. I've got almost everything I want: a great family, lots of good friends, a job I love, a nice new home. The only thing missing is that one special person to share it all with. Not a lover in the stifling, together-every-minute sense, but more of a companion, someone with whom I could share my life but one who would give me the space I need.

My own space is still very important to me, perhaps because of the respect for privacy that my parents instilled in me. Living with someone involves so many compromises, and I have become a bit spoiled living by myself; everything in my space is as I want it and I have so much freedom. This would have to change if I were to live with a lover. I suppose I would be willing to make these compromises, but only for the right guy.

So what is a "right guy"? For me, that means someone who has his act together, is ambitious. It doesn't matter if he is working or is a student, as long as he is focused on some clear goals. Also, he should be understanding of cultural and ethnic differences. I think I blend into the American mainstream, but I am still bicultural and I need to be with someone who acknowledges that.

Most of the guys I've been with have been white, but I've also dated Latinos, East Asians, and a couple of black men. Sometimes I think it would be great to be with another Sri Lankan – someone who has had the same life experience as I have, someone who speaks Sinhalese and understands Sri Lankan culture. Overall, though, what is most important is whether I click with the person, not his color or ethnic background.

I hear a lot of my Asian friends complain about racism in the gay community, but I haven't encountered too much of it. Once a white guy I had been to bed with turned around to me and said, "How does it feel to sleep with a white dude?" I didn't know exactly what he meant. I got so angry. I told him that this brown-skinned guy could have any white guy he wanted. He started apologizing, saying that he was only kidding. This is the extent of the racism that I've faced.

I think so much of how the world responds toward you depends on how you feel about yourself. I get my share of attention if I go to a bar because I feel good about myself and it shows. I don't want to generalize, but I find that the Asian guys I know have low self-esteem, especially when it comes to sex. They seem to think of whites as being better — it really makes me feel sorry for them.

I don't know when I will find someone who fits the bill of what I'm looking for, but I'm in no hurry. I'm quite happy with the way my life is going. My family is great; unlike many Sri Lankan families, they put no pressure on me about marriage. I also have some great friends, some of whom don't know that I'm gay (mostly friends I've known since childhood). I tend to be more open with the friends I make now, and I have a lot of gay friends, some of whom are South Asian. I am a teaching professional, which is a very important part of my life. All in all, I think it's a pretty good life, and I'm happy with it, like I have always been.

Many journeys in one

Four women engaged in sexual play. (Temple carving from the city of Khajuraho, India)

Giti Thadani

Yaari

Raj Ayyar

Over the past few years I have come to realize that my meandering path through romance, sexual liaisons, and friendship has been, and still is, but a search for a singular relationship that can encompass all three of these elements. Such a bond as is embodied in the Indian concept of *yaari*. A *yaar* is an individual with whom one feels a deep, almost intangible connection. Definitions of this term have varied through time, sometimes denoting a lover, at other times a friend. For me a *yaar* embodies elements of both a friend and a lover, and I yearn for just such a connection with a man in my life.

As a youth in Madras, I fantasized a great deal about loving men. I was not really aware of the idea of homosexuality, at least not in any positive or even neutral sense. *Ghandoo,* an extremely pejorative term for a homosexual, was the only word I had heard in reference to sex between men. This term seemed quite alien to the wonderful images I created in my fantasies, so I did not apply it to myself. Still, I had a need for some sort of framework for my fantasies, so I became a voracious bookworm. The images of homosexuality that I found in literature helped me to become better acquainted with my own feelings. Jean Genet, William Burroughs, and Walt Whitman were among the authors whose works I devoured. Luckily, my parents, who were well educated, did not object to their only child reading any of these writers; they encouraged reading regardless of subject matter.

My sexual experiences during adolescence were strictly of the hole-in-the-wall variety — very closeted. My first childhood sexual experience was at the age of twelve. A friend of mine and I went up to his terrace and played with each other. We never talked about it; it was simply something we did. We called it wrestling to take the sting out of it. Don't misunderstand me, we were not ashamed of it. We just knew we should not let anyone catch us at this sort of play.

Around this time, I also had sex quite regularly with a friend of mine named Mohammed. He wanted to experiment with anal and oral sex, but I remember that I would not go beyond mutual masturbation; whatever guilt I carried would not allow me to do so in any of these adolescent experiences.

At the age of nineteen I left Madras for New Delhi, where I was to attend St. Stephen's School. This was an all-boys school, an extension of the Doon School that is patterned after the British private education system (actually called public school in England). These English institutions possess an inherent element of a ritualized sort of homosexuality, and this has been grafted onto their Indian counterparts. There is a certain acceptance of homosexuality within the circle of the school, though it is quite often done under some sort of pretense. Within this environment I first applied the homosexual label to myself. I could not think of myself as a *ghandoo,* however, so I embraced the idea of loving another man only in terms of romance and friendship; separating sexuality seemed to make my rationalization easier. I told a few students about my feelings for men and found some support.

While at St. Stephen's, I fell in love with Anil, a fellow student who was a bit younger than me. I did my bit of rationalization and thought of him as a friend for whom I a felt romantic, affectionate attraction. In a sense, I was living a fantasy of love. The object of my affections was a known homosexual at school. I suppose that today I would describe him as being queeny. Paradoxically, ours was more of a physical relationship; thinking of him as a *yaar* allowed me to continue compartmentalizing my feelings.

This split between the emotional and the sexual has been a pattern in my gay life. Consequently, real *yaari* seems to have eluded me. *Yaar*. There is really no English equivalent for this concept, no word that approaches its breadth and depth. *Friend* is not enough.

Buddy is superficial, reeks of Budweiser beers and backslapping in bars. The word that possibly comes closest is *camerado,* a word used by Whitman meaning "brother-in-arms." In India a world of romantic images revolves around *yaari.* There are tales of *yaars* dying for one another. Even a wife must many a time take a backseat to a man's *yaar.* (The women's equivalent of *yaar* is *saheli,* a concept that is equally rich in meaning.)

Even within a heterosexual context *yaar* has, and always has had, many homoerotic overtones, embodying values such as loyalty and strong commitment. A *yaar* is someone to whom one can reveal his darkest, deepest secrets. Thus one never has more than one or two *yaars* at one time. It is likely that during their early years a lot of *yaars* have some sort of sexual connection before settling down to a socially accepted heterosexual life. They most often continue to express their physical affection openly, however; many a Western gay man has been puzzled by this, not realizing that the affection, for the most part, carries no overtones of sexuality.

Perhaps it is my own insecurity, but each time I go back to India there seems to be less of this affection on display. I don't know if the memory of my own adolescent years is exaggerated or if westernization has brought to India a heightened sense of homophobia and taken the innocence out of physical touch. The urban Indian youths of today are fairly aware of the international gay scene; it comes to them through androgynous clothing styles, rock music, etc. Many college youths claim to have a chic attitude about homosexuality, but they carefully disclaim it for themselves.

During my time in Delhi, *yaari* was more important to me than sex. Really, I'm being quite honest. I could always wine and dine my own hand if necessary, but the emotional bond was precious. This bond never really formed with Anil. After three months of sex, we came to a parting of ways. It was he who rejected me. He began to put up walls, and I said nothing; I was not terribly assertive. He was quite promiscuous, and we never discussed our "fun" in any detail. I think he may have been afraid of a lover relationship, threatened by the fusion of friendship and sex that I so desperately wanted. Neither one of us had had any previous experience of such a relationship.

I was aware at this time of other gay relationships in the context of the school. I also knew about the blowjobs traded in the parks, but I was much too afraid to do that. I was not promiscuous, at least not until I experienced the United States years later. I do recall a near-experience with a *scooter-wallah* (a three-wheeled motorcycle-taxi driver) soon after Anil. He propositioned me, asked me to go to his room. I was scandalized. There was no emotional bond involved, no *yaari;* he just wanted to fuck. I could not do that.

There were other instances like this one. During one train ride from Delhi to Calcutta, where I was going to meet friends, I shared a private compartment with a friend of my father. The man tried to seduce me. He called me Mar Kandeya, a boy hero who was a favorite of the Indian god Shiva. I was disgusted and excited by him. I had a hard-on as he talked, but I couldn't follow through because he reminded me of my father. At some point I told him that I felt soiled. In retrospect, I think I was rather cruel to him. He was only acting on his desires, and, when one stops to think about it, it is actually quite life affirming. But there was no *yaari* and he was too old. I was then, and still am, attracted to younger men. Perhaps it is my own father issue; I would rather play daddy than have one.

In 1975 I received a fellowship to study in the United States and wound up in out-of-the-way Carbondale, Illinois. Because of my leftist leanings, I was initially hesitant to come to the U.S. After all, I was not diving into San Francisco, but into conservative Middle America. Still, Carbondale was a college town, and it even possessed a gay bar, called the Underground, and a small gay scene. In these surroundings I became increasingly comfortable with my gayness. I shared this truth about myself in my classes and became quite politicized. At this time I also started having a series of promiscuous encounters, adventures that continued when I later moved to Florida. Some part of me, however, was still searching for *yaari,* and I found the average gay American quite incapable of this bond.

During the halcyon days before AIDS, everybody was ready to fuck everyone. I had men of different sizes, races, and shapes. I went to bathhouses and found the courage to check out the parks. Today, during the age of AIDS, it is fashionable to disclaim promiscuity, but I'm not ashamed of that period. It made me aware of my own body, as well as increasing my comfort with being gay. I really enjoyed oral sex – giving it and receiving to the point of orgasm. I enjoyed the taste of cum. The safe-sex prohibition against swallowing cum has been the hardest for me – it makes me feel deprived in a way. I've had little in the way of anal sex.

I still feel a bit of anger regarding the end of my promiscuous period; I suppose that, at a base level, it is a control issue. I was moving out of promiscuity at this time, but I was not ready to stop altogether. When the specter of AIDS hit, change became an immediate necessity. I resent the decision having been made for me. I had to put the brakes on abruptly and, in a sense, never had the opportunity to say good-bye to that scene. I have a strong feeling of having been cheated.

My transition from the fear that possessed me in India to the promiscuity that I slipped into in the United States was done with little conflict. The sex in the bars and bathhouses was, in a sense, protected sex; the fear factor was totally missing. I felt like I had found a haven within which I could endlessly explore bodies. As an intellectual Brahmin kid I had been extremely horny, but I had expressed this desire only through masturbation or through ultimately unsatisfying experiences. There had been no full-fledged celebration of bodies – of nipples and armpits, crotches and asses. Now a whole dimension was opened to me. Yet this dimension was faceless, spiritless, and did not hold any promise of the *yaari* I longed for. It was ironic. In India I found sexless *yaari* in abundance, and here sex was available in abundance but *yaari* was an alien concept.

I had no contact with gay Indians during this time. I was something of an anomaly in both the gay and the Indian communities. Even in India I had known of only one overtly gay man, a journalist I knew during my college days and with whom I never had sex. Today he is married, though he acts and sounds as gay and campy as ever. Spending time with him now is rather unpleasant for me; he talks nonstop about his new baby, and about his wife's endless shopping trips. I must confess that I feel betrayed by him.

I knew and socialized with many heterosexual Indians in both Illinois and Florida. There was always the issue of why I was unmarried at my age, and I'm sure they must have done their share of speculating. They accepted me as a part of their circle in a very Indian way; as an unmarried Indian, they were quite protective of me. Coming out to them would have been too much of a risk for me, so I never opened up on that level.

171

When I first came to this country I was often mistaken for an Iranian and treated like Khomeini's nephew. It bothered me a great deal, but it is only one face of the tremendous amount of racism I have witnessed in the American mainstream. It is clear to me that, in many ways, it has been easier for Indians to assimilate in this country than it has been for blacks. Perhaps this is because of our colonial hangover; Indians seem not to express their hostility and rebellion issues, while blacks and other groups do. This can make us appear less threatening even to racist whites.

Many Indians in America have cashed in on the available opportunities and are seen as success stories by those in India. Nonsubmissive Indians, on the other hand, seem to threaten white Americans even more than blacks. Maybe this is due to the cultural difference, or perhaps it is due to the Indians' knowledge of and comfort with both the Eastern and the Western experience.

Racism is present in the gay subculture as well, though it is much less overt. There is a patronizing, sometimes indulgent attitude. Cliques of gay white men in the Castro area of San Francisco, for instance, think that they are the center of the universe. They often regard nonwhite gays as poor, wide-eyed Third Worlders who come to the Castro to sip coffee and pay homage.

On the other hand, because I am an Indian, I am considered exotic. During my promiscuous period this made it fairly easy for me to pick up guys. Yet when the possibility of a relationship arises, the American gays seem to feel threatened by the exotic. Thus the acceptance is but surface, and even then only in a particular context.

My lack of success in finding a happy coupling of *yaari* and sexuality in Carbondale eventually led me into a marriage with a woman. I don't think I was ever truly bisexual. I think my marriage happened because I found women more emotionally empathic, and my ex-wife, whom I met in a class, was no exception. Geraldine knew of and accepted my gayness. She even went to gay bars with me. We started as friends, but eventually had sex together at her suggestion. At some point I began to think of it as love. We ended up getting married, and stayed together for two and a half years. The relationship was a mixed bag, however. My stance toward her seemed to become more macho the longer I stayed in the marriage. I was turning into the traditional husband because I resented the marriage. I was faithful to her for quite a while, but after about two years the marriage began to fall apart and I started going to gay bars once more.

Toward the end my marriage, I had a relationship with Mark, a beautiful young white man who tried hard to please me. What a thrill to be with someone who did not see me as simply being exotic. He was even willing to learn South Indian cooking for me. Imagine! A man who would cook my native food and have sex with me! Could this be the *yaar* I was looking for? However, after three months my guilt about my wife reasserted itself, and I rejected him rather cruelly. My time spent with Mark is the closest that I have come to having a relationship with a man.

I eventually separated from Geraldine and moved to Florida, where I taught at Orlando Community College. My mother visited during this time and taught for a bit in Ft. Lauderdale. We had never discussed my lifestyle. I thought this might be an opening, but no! As soon as I mentioned my gayness, she held up her hand and said she did not want to hear about it. She said it was okay for me to be myself and that I should be careful. We haven't spoken about it since, though she no longer pushes marriage on me. I think she accepts me to some degree, but I do wish we could discuss the issue more deeply. It leaves me feeling a bit repressed and angry, yet I have to acknowledge that she has made a great deal of progress since my adolescence.

Talking to my father about my gayness is out of the question; we both would be made uncomfortable by it. But my father is very intuitive, and I'm sure he must know something. On my last visit with my parents in Bangalore, India, I became infatuated with a local waiter. My father gently kidded me about this, teasing that I seemed to be in love with the guy. I sensed no malice in his teasing.

The tug between the culture I share with my parents and the sexuality that is foreign to them has not abated within me. I feel loneliness and anger. I could try to reject my gay self and conform to the image of Indian normalcy, but this enrages me. I feel angry at the Indian culture for not fully accepting who I am. I also feel angry at the West. Despite its talk of freedom there is hypocrisy, and I feel that it has met my needs only sporadically; probably there is some vestigial colonial anger working here also.

Gay life has been affirming and painful for me. It has also been very lonely, except for a few short relationships and body explorations. I do acknowledge that only I can dispel this loneliness. I am still seeking the balance between sexuality and *yaari,* and I think I now have a better idea of what I want. The problem is, I don't know how or if I will find it. These days I am thrilled to be in touch with other gay Indians; through my association with them, I am seeking to unravel my identity. The idea of an Indian lover is seductive. Someone who could share my love for Indian food, Hindi music, and a thousand other Indian things. I also find myself more physically attracted to darker men; I think I had my share of vapid blonds in Florida.

Recently I have also discovered a newfound attraction to East Asian men, and being bicultural, I think they would understand me better than the average American. Do not misunderstand me; I am not ruling out a relationship with a white man. It is just that I have become aware of how difficult it can be for them, being monocultural, to appreciate a culture different from their own, and I have not met many who possess the exceptional openness needed to do so.

So many revelations, endless discoveries. Here I am today, a gay Indian man living and doing graduate work in San Francisco. When I look back, I see myriad experiences, so much pain, pleasure, awakening, and growth. Much has changed, about my perceptions of my world and about my sense of self. One thing has remained, however, one need that tugs at me – to find that special connection with another man. I continue my search for *yaari.*

An improbable pair

Kiron*

My first image of Jerry is still crystal clear in my mind. I had walked down from my second-floor office for a bite to eat in the cafeteria, something I did nearly every day. When I saw him, this blue-eyed, strawberry-blond-haired boy-next-door with freckles, I could not take my eyes off him. I had no idea who he was. I knew only that he worked on the first level of my building. It was late spring of 1983 and I was living in Philadelphia. I was a 27-year-old architect who had no idea that he was about to stumble into the sort of love we all dream of but so rarely find. After that first glimpse, my eyes would search for him each time I walked into the cafeteria. To say that I was attracted to him is to say that the Himalayas are large. It got to the point that I could feel him walk into the room without looking; I could sense the electricity in the air.

For eight months I watched, unable to think of a way to connect with him, unable to keep myself from obsessing on him. Finally, in January of 1984, I decided to take a risk. I sent him a telegram. I had discovered that his name was Jerry, but I had no idea whether he was gay or straight. My message was simple: "Jerry, I see you on the first floor and admire you from a distance. If you would like to be my friend, I would like to talk with you. " I signed myself as "Gandhi," included my telephone number, and sent the communiqué before I could change my mind. It was a good thing that I acted impetuously; as soon as I had a moment to think, I began to wish I hadn't sent it. I mulled over my action, tried to figure out how I could cancel or intercept the telegram, but a part of me refused to do so.

When my three roommates came home, I told them of what I had done. Victor, Doug, and Vladimir thought I was crazy and were convinced that I was headed for trouble. It was done, however, and a part of me was still willing to gamble. The next day I rushed home to my answering machine, my face tense with anticipation. Nothing. I was dejected, but not without hope. On the second day, nothing still. On the third day my eyes lit up as brightly as the light flashing on the answering machine.

"Yes, Gandhi, I would like to meet you. Please call me at this number so I can learn who you are," Jerry's voice drawled as I played the message.

I screamed! I ran to find my roommates, shouting incoherently. They still weren't convinced. They thought I was being silly and were yet afraid that I would get into trouble.

"How do you know it isn't a setup?" Victor demanded. "Maybe he's straight and is just setting you up. You could get fired. You are fucking crazy!"

As my closest gay friend, Victor was only looking out for me. I had known him even before I discovered that I was gay. As a matter of fact, it was through Victor that I had ended up, quite innocently, at the very gay Castro Street Fair in San Francisco in 1979. It was later that year, at a party, that I had my first adult sexual experience with another man.

Victor was a good friend, but his warnings could not make me change my mind now. I had liked Jerry too much from day one to give in to any doubters. So I picked up the phone and called him. We made small talk and all the while I was dying to know if he was gay.

"Did you go out of town for the holidays?" I asked, positioning myself for the all-important question.

"No, I stayed home," he replied. "What about you?"

"I went dancing to this place called Studio One. Have you heard of it?" My heart was racing as I waited for his answer.

"Oh yeah, I used to go there a long time ago," he replied matter-of-factly.

I took a deep breath.

"Are you gay?" I asked.

"Yeah, I'm gay."

The first bridge – a successful crossing.

"Oh, I didn't know," I said, quite truthfully. "I'd like to meet you sometime."

"But I don't know who you are!" he responded.

"Can't you guess?" I was certain he must have noticed me watching him.

"No."

"I'm the guy on the second floor. You must have seen me looking at you."

"I don't know anyone on that floor." His answers were honest, uncomplicated. I sensed no pretense.

The fact that he couldn't place me did not deter me. I asked if he would come by and join me for a drink. He said yes, so I gave him directions and quickly jumped into the shower. When the doorbell rang I was still in my bedroom, slipping into my clothes. I could hear my roommates telling him that I was crazy and that he would like me. I put on the finishing touches and headed out the door. I was crazy all right. I was crazy nervous as I joined them in the kitchen. Jerry looked at me as if he had been caught off guard.

"You? You?"

"I'm Kiron," I said, trying not to sound nervous.

"I've seen you!" he responded. "I didn't know you were gay. Oh my God! This is such a pleasant surprise. I was afraid it was this guy from the fifth floor."

That was music to my ears.

"I'm really happy to meet you," he continued.

I believed him. He seemed enchanted, his face full of light.

"Well, looks like a match," Doug piped in.

That broke the spell, but only momentarily. Jerry and I slipped past my friends and headed for the bar. We had not been in the club long when I found myself kissing him.

"I can't believe this," I told him. "The other day I was craving you and now here I am, kissing you!"

"I can't believe it either," he replied.

That was how it started. It was like a fantasy, one I might have written in my most optimistic mood. When we finally came back to my apartment that night, we ignored my roommates and went immediately upstairs. We lay on the bed and kissed. And kissed and kissed. He asked me if I wanted to have sex, and I told him no. It was special for me, I didn't want to do it on the first day. He agreed. In all the time we were together, he never stopped being so agreeable.

During the next few weeks Jerry and I learned a lot about one another. We were different in many ways, perhaps an improbable pair if you stopped to think about it. But love doesn't require you to pause and think. Jerry had grown up in Baton Rouge, Louisiana, the only boy in a house full of girls. His parents were prime specimens of the redneck phenomenon, though I eventually grew to like and bond with them. They had not been very understanding when Jerry came out to them. He had been seventeen years old at the time and soon found himself out on the street. Jerry and his family did eventually reconcile, although they never accepted his lifestyle. He did manage to finish high school, despite the lack of support, but that was the extent of his education. The jobs he had worked were clerical, menial, and that was the sort of work he was now doing in our building.

My life experience had been as far removed from Jerry's as one could expect. I was born in Madras to an upper-middle-class Indian family, the first of four sons. My father is South Indian, my mother is from Hyderabad. Though they spoke their native languages, English was the only language spoken in our home, perhaps because we were Anglican. The idea of an Indian Christian is not as strange as it sounds, not when you consider that Christianity reached India nearly two thousand years ago. The neighborhood I grew up in, called the Colony because someone from each household worked for some subsidiary of one giant Indian corporation, was quite diverse. There were Moslems, Hindus, Christians, and Jews, and in this melange I grew up for a secure, fun-filled ten years.

Jerry laughed and was amazed when I told him of my first sexual experiences at the age of six or seven, the vast majority of them with boys. Our sex basically consisted of touching, kissing, and sucking. There was one boy, Mohan, who was perhaps my most regular partner. Mohan loved to suck, and he was ready anytime I wanted him to do it.

In 1963 my family immigrated to Canada. After six years in Toronto, during which I shut myself off sexually and sublimated my sexual energy into schoolwork, we relocated to Boston. Again, I studied hard and kept my sexuality dormant. It was not until I entered college that I had my first post-pubescent sexual experience, and that with a woman. I continued to have relationships with women until that weekend with Victor in San Francisco. By the time I met Jerry, I had been actively gay for about four years.

Despite the differences in our backgrounds, both Jerry and I were convinced that we were meant to be together. My intuition certainly told me that this was the love of my life. I would watch him dress each morning as we got ready for work, and I would marvel at how beautiful he was. I would be thrilled that he was mine. Mine! I would feel such a surge of love for him. Jerry would constantly tell me how different I was from anyone he had met before. You're so nice, he would say, no one has treated me so well. I could not fathom how anybody could mistreat him, this handsome creature who was becoming my lover.

Jerry and I became inseparable. Soon we were best friends, and all of my other friendships, Victor included, fell by the wayside. We met in January. In November the lease for the apartment I shared with my friends was up for renewal, and Victor suggested that Jerry move in with us; Doug was leaving, so there would be plenty of space. I had to say no. I could not have other people living with my lover and me.

That was my main reason for wanting to move out, but there was another equally important consideration. Victor was sharp, the epitome of West Hollywood. He was trendy and wealthy, as were all of his friends, and they could all be quite vicious when the mood suited them. Jerry was their antithesis. He was innocent, simple, of the working class, and they could easily have torn him apart. There was no way I could allow that to happen. I loved his innocence, which was a reflection of some part of myself, and I would do all I could to protect it.

Things fell into place quite smoothly when we moved in together. I set about the business of looking at apartments, found three and showed them to Jerry. When I showed him my first choice, he loved it. He had a few things, I had a few, and what we didn't have we

179

bought. I earned a lot more money than Jerry, but it was never an issue for us. I would ask him what he wanted, and we would get it. I would never make a decision without consulting him, and I think that was important to him. It was a very happy time for us and, in all the time we were together, we rarely fought.

"This is forever. I know it is." I don't know how many times Jerry said that. I would get a shiver up my spine each time he said it. Somewhere inside of me I knew that nothing is forever. So I would say to him, "Yes, Jerry, but nothing lasts an eternity." "But I know it's forever," he would say again, and I would say, "I hope so, I really hope it is." It was so sweet, yet it gave me the strangest feeling.

The intuitive connection between us was incredible. I remember the time that I met a rather attractive guy at the gym. This fellow suggested that we have an affair, but I said no; I would not sleep with anyone but Jerry. He accepted that, and we became friends. Sometime later I was meeting him for dinner, and he came over to our apartment to pick me up. I introduced him to Jerry, then my friend and I left for the restaurant. When I got back, Jerry was not very happy with me.

"Don't ever bring him here again," he told me.

"Why?" I asked.

"It's the way he looks at you. I know what he's thinking, what he wants."

"How can you say that, Jerry?" I argued anemically, but he was right. It floored me. He had intuited what I had not told him! I sometimes wonder if I will ever have such a connection with anyone again.

One of Jerry's dreams was to go to Europe, so we went in 1985. I must admit that it was a little difficult for me. I am a free bird when I'm traveling; I like to get up early, wander all day, and see as much as I can. Jerry preferred to sleep in and couldn't keep up with my pace. I felt a bit burdened, but luckily it was not my first time. It was Jerry's and I loved showing him the sights.

Sometime after we got back from Europe our idyllic life began to unravel. In July of that year Jerry began to cough a lot. He was a smoker, so I didn't think too much of it. It persisted, however, and I began to worry. This was 1985 and Rock Hudson and AIDS were in all of the media around us.

"Jerry, you should go to the doctor," I told him one day. The cough had been with him for two months now. "I'll go with you if you want." I knew he hated doctors.

He told me no, then went to the doctor on his own.

"See, it's only bronchitis," he told me when he got back.

"Fine, but please take care of yourself." I still had an uneasy feeling.

We were lying on the sofa together a few days later, and I noticed that his body felt really warm. I told him this, but he shook his head.

"No, I'm not. You're just imagining things."

"It's not right, Jerry. You're coughing and you feel so warm. I think you should get tested." I couldn't shake the feeling of some shadow drawing near.

One night I woke up at two and found the sheets drenched. Jerry lay sound asleep beside me.

"Jerry! Jerry! Wake up, the bed is wet," I said, shaking him gently.

"What?" he asked groggily.

"Did you pee or something?"

"No," he replied. "What is this?"

"It looks like a night sweat," I told him. "Have you ever had this before?"

He said he hadn't, but it didn't look good. The cough, the warm body, the night sweat. I knew a good bit about AIDS and all three of these were symptoms. We changed the sheets and slept uneasily the rest of the night. The following morning we were supposed to go to San Francisco to see my close friend Carl. I didn't want to go now, but Jerry insisted. When Carl and I had a moment alone, I told him about everything and how it terrified me. I could barely function. Carl was supportive, telling me to take Jerry to the doctor and to monitor his health closely. Besides, Jerry looked fine and had not lost any weight; it might be nothing serious.

The moment we got back home, I made an appointment for Jerry. He was nervous and asked me to come along and do the talking for him. So I told the doctor what symptoms Jerry had been having.

"We're gay," I told him. "I think we should have him tested for AIDS."

"Okay, if that's what you want," the doctor replied. "But I don't think there is anything to worry about."

"But all these symptoms—"

"Sure," he continued, "people have night sweats with other conditions, like TB. The cough — well, he's a smoker. And the warm temperature — there's a lot that science simply can't explain. You guys are just being paranoid."

"I sure hope so," I replied.

The doctor performed the tests as we requested. When he came back into the room, his face told a story we did not want to hear.

"Well, Jerry, your T-cell count is kind of low — out of the normal range. I would suspect that you have some kind of an immune deficiency."

"I can't have it. It can't be AIDS!" Jerry's voice was trembling.

"You never know," the doctor replied. "It might not be; you might just bounce back."

I asked Jerry how he felt, if he was tired very often. He said he wasn't, and I believed him. After all, he biked to work every day while I drove. We went home, and he seemed to put it out of his mind. I couldn't. When I was alone I would weep, because on some level I knew everything wasn't all right. I remember pulling off to the side of the road and crying on my steering wheel. Now I knew why I couldn't tell Jerry that our relationship was forever. Something had held me back from agreeing with him, and now I knew what that something was.

He's going to suffer, I would think. I had seen pictures of people with AIDS, and I couldn't accept that my beautiful Jerry was going to die that way. Ironically, I never thought about myself. We had been monogamous, were equally top and bottom, and we had never used condoms, but I did not think about my own status.

I remember that I once asked him about his past, something I had never cared about. I loved him so much that his past didn't matter, but I needed to ask now. He said that he had been to bed with one guy who had later come down with AIDS, and that only once. I didn't push the subject. It was pointless. We simply had to deal with the reality at hand. Jerry was eventually diagnosed as have AIDS-related complex (ARC). He did not accept it from day one.

"I wish I were dying of leukemia instead of this shit," he would say. "What are people thinking of me now?"

"It doesn't matter what people think," I would respond.

In November Jerry was diagnosed as having TB, but he was in the hospital only three days. They gave him some medication; he recovered from it fine. He had lost all of four pounds, which he quickly gained back. By February he was back at work. He was fine throughout the spring. In June of that year, 1986, things began to slide again. One day I found Jerry holding his head.

"I've got this headache that just won't go away," he told me.

"Maybe you're under stress," I told him. "Maybe you should stop working."

"I don't know, but this is a weird headache. There is a weird sensation in my head."

Later that night I found him on the floor in the kitchen, holding his head again.

"I can't take this anymore," he cried. "My head feels like it's expanding, like it's going to explode."

It was two in the morning. He wasn't running a temperature, but I was taking no chances. I drove him to the hospital and told the doctor about his condition. Jerry could not even talk. A few tests were done, it turned out that Jerry had meningitis. The doctor suggested that I take him home that night, get his things ready, and have him admitted to the hospital in the morning.

Jerry was admitted the next day. I had to go to work, of course, and I hated the thought of leaving him alone. What would I do when he came home and needed someone to look after him while he recuperated? I called Jerry's sister and told her that he had ARC. I asked her advice in dealing with their mother. She suggested that I not tell their mother about the ARC, but say only that Jerry was not well. I followed her advice and asked Fay, their mother, if she could come out and help me take care of Jerry. She agreed, and I arranged for her to fly out to Philadelphia.

Fay was wonderful about staying with Jerry. I would drop her off at the hospital in the morning and she would keep him company all day. As soon as I finished work, usually about five in the evening, I would rush back to the hospital and stay there until ten. I would usually take some paperwork to finish while I sat at his bedside.

One day, as I sat beside him, I said to Jerry, "When you get well, we're gonna go to Puerto Vallarta and have a nice long holiday."

"Where's my purse, where's my wallet?" he responded frantically.

"What wallet, Jerry? You're in the hospital," I answered, baffled by his words.

"Oh yeah, Alaska would be nice," he muttered back.

"Who said anything about Alaska, Jerry?" I was getting an awful feeling in my stomach.

"You did."

"No, I didn't" was all I could say. Something was seriously wrong.

The next day, on another visit, I heard screaming and shouting coming from his room as I came through the hall. Inside they were restraining him. There was shit on the bed. His facial expression was weird, so weird. I put down my files and asked what was going on.

"He's having an episode," I was told.

"A what?"

"He has encephalitis and is in delirium."

I could see that he was losing consciousness and could not recognize anyone. I asked to see the doctor right away.

"The infection has gone to his brain," the doctor told me. "Sooner or later he will be unconscious."

"But he's in pain," I protested.

"No, he's not. When they're this far along, they don't know what's going on and don't feel any pain."

"But look at him! His hands are moving, his eyes are rolling."

This wasn't my Jerry. This was not the pretty boy I loved to look at. It was awful, but I didn't have too much time to think about crying or dying. I was just too busy, trying to make him feel better, holding his hand. He would come out of it for an hour or so, then go back into delirium. In a flash he would drift away. One time he came out of it and nearly broke my heart.

"I don't want to die, I don't want to die," he kept repeating.

He was crying, and I didn't know what to say. I couldn't tell him that he had to die, but I also couldn't lie and say everything would be all right. It wouldn't. So I just held him. Clinging to me, he kept repeating that he didn't want to die. What the fuck do you say to someone like that?

There was a chapel downstairs in the hospital and I went there regularly. Usually I was the only one in the chapel. There was a book – a prayer book, I guess – in which people had written prayers and thanks. "Please let this operation help my mother," "Thank you for saving my son." I was too angry to get down on my knees and beg for God's help. "Fuck you, asshole, for putting anyone through so much pain," I wrote. "Fuck you!" I shouted at the chapel. The next night I wrote the same bloody thing. "Fuck you for letting people have AIDS!" I hoped everyone would see it. It seemed so hypocritical. My Jerry was dying upstairs and this God, who is supposed to be loving, was letting it happen.

Going to the chapel was my release. I would vent my frustrations, then walk back upstairs feeling better. So often the doctors would tell me that Jerry had perhaps three days to live. I would make all the necessary arrangements. Thank God! I had a wonderful secretary. She covered for me, told me over the telephone if anything needed my attention. She even visited Jerry in the hospital during her lunch hour. I don't know how I would have gotten through it without her help.

Victor and my other friends were also quite supportive and visited Jerry often. Jerry's mother was especially impressed with my friend Mike. Mike had been the senior class president at our high school, and he and I had been best friends at the time, but neither one of us had known that the other was homosexual. I came out to him in 1982. He was married at the time and did not come out to me for another year.

"He's so wonderful," Fay would say of Mike. "Did you know that he's married and has two kids? Oh, if only Jerry could be like Mike, married and happy."

She did not know that Mike was divorced and gay, and he saw no need to tell her. Fay was convinced that someone was to blame for Jerry's condition. She wanted to know why he was sick and who had done this to him. I could not convince her that it was no one's fault; she had to find someone to blame. It used to make me a bit defensive, but Jerry needed her, so I managed to deal with her questions.

One day the doctor looked at me and said, "There's nothing more we can do for him. It's time for you to take him home."

"I can't take him home," I replied. "Look at him, he's a vegetable. Who will take care of him? The insurance won't pay for anything once he leaves the hospital."

"I'm sorry," he said quietly, "he's beyond our help now."

His mother looked at me. "What do we do now?"

I asked her to stay on a bit and she agreed. Fay asked if her husband could join her. They had little money, so I flew him to Philadelphia the following week. We were such opposites. When I would be watching "Good Morning, America" in the morning, they would be tuned into "The PTL (Praise the Lord) Club." We didn't have any fights, yet it was damned difficult sometimes. It was for Jerry's sake, however, so I was willing to put up with anything.

I had always had a paradoxical relationship with Jerry's parents. They were really redneck, such racists. I remember them saying, on a previous visit with us, "You sure do have a lot of niggers here in Philadelphia." I couldn't believe that they used that word, but it was a regular part of their vocabulary. I thought, what must I be to them but one more nigger? I remember once asking Jerry how he felt about my brown color.

"Oh, I don't think of you as being colored," he had replied. "You're white, aren't you? You know, I never thought of you that way. I don't think my parents think of you that way – they never say anything. Besides, I just think of you as being Italian or something."

"But you know I'm from India, Jerry."

"Yeah, I know," he answered quite innocently.

He was right. His parents never said anything about it. His mother stayed with him in the hospital, then both of them watched over him when he came home. A month later he lapsed into total unconsciousness, and the doctors took him back. It was the Labor Day weekend, and his mother stayed with him round the clock.

I really thought that Jerry was going to die that weekend, but he kept hanging on. I called a pastor from the local Metropolitan Community Church (a predominantly gay church), and she told me that people sometimes can't let go while their loved one is in the room.

"Maybe you should go," she suggested.

"I want to be here when he goes," I told her firmly.

"But some people hang on," she pressed me gently. "Why don't you tell him to let go, then go home yourself?"

"I can't. I've been here since day one, I can't go now and not come back."

I did leave at about one that night, while his parents stayed with him. At six in the morning I got a call from them. Jerry's dead. I felt so good. I had been released from a burden, and Jerry was no longer in pain. There was an incredible sense of relief. I had gone through so much grief in the previous few months that the end brought only this sense of relief.

Everything about Jerry's funeral had been planned in advance, and it all went well. I came to the hospital and saw Jerry, but the body, the face looked nothing like him. I couldn't cry. I could only ask, is that Jerry? I touched his face softly and closed his eyes.

"If you're in this room, I'm saying good-bye, " I said quietly as I looked up at the ceiling.

As soon as we got home, his parents started taking down pictures of Jerry.

"Fay, don't touch anything," I said wearily. "Those are my pictures."

"But they're Jerry's," she responded.

This was the worst part. They wanted everything that had been Jerry's, and so did I. Would they have done this if Jerry were straight, and I were his widow? No way! It could have built into a real fight, but I was too tired.

"Fine," I told them. "Take anything you want, just ask."

They took, but they didn't ask. I wanted to tell them not to touch one more fucking thing, but I was too emotionally exhausted and didn't feel like fighting. Then I thought, maybe it's better this way. If they take everything, I won't have anything to look at and cry.

Jerry's parents left the next day. Mike came over with a friend of his and they took me out to lunch. While we were eating, Mike showed me a poem called "The One Who Was with Us." I cried as I read it. My Jerry was gone, really gone, but at least he was not in pain anymore. As for me, the whole experience has made me appreciate life so much more. It's made it possible for me to accept anything in life, including my own death when it should come. Jerry gave me so much in life, even taught me a lesson in death, and some part of him lives on inside me.

The lion skin

Suniti Namjoshi

Previously published as a part of "The Lion Skin"
sequence of poems in the author's *The Blue Donkey Fables*

(iii)

Dispense with disguises. The lion's skin
is a skin after all. Spread it on the ground,
so that no twig or stone in this forest clearing
shall hurt or trouble us when we both lie down.
Or should the weather change and we grow cold,
let the fur cover us and warm our sleep
till we wake again and are brave and bold.
And if the stars choose to peep, let them peep.
What can stars or moon or sun discover?
That the lady is a woman, and I,
who lie so close beside her, am her lover?
The stars will not shriek, will make no outcry.
The stars are sensible, and would not sever
woman from woman or lover from lover.

A fragment of his eye

Singh*

My lover's vision rests upon another,
even though his heart rests upon mine.
He watches you, young man!

O young man of age and desire,
your youth is resplendent.
Your mouth still childlike and luring,
to which your teeth add a mischievous glitter.
Your cheek is pale,
and upon it your lashes drop shadows of innocence.
But your gait exudes manhood,
and those thighs wear brazen shades of lust.
I know he watches you, young man.
I see in your eye the color of his desire.

Will you become my child, young man?
I will cradle you as your mother wished she did.
Canopied under my gaze,
I will rock you to sleep.
I will blow gently upon your face
to break loose fragments of his desire
that rest upon your cheek.
I will command this listless breath of mine
to pursue one stray, floating fragment

190

to come rest upon my face.
A particle of his eye upon my face
is all that I have ever wanted.

My child,
how may I no longer grow fond of you?

The man with the one golden arm

Singh*

In the golden arm of a man
who has no face
I salivate in silence.
My mouth fills with the liquid of the moon.
I promise to let moonlight
turn into lead this time.

But he too must betray
the golden cavity
that has opened between our bodies.
He too must fall out of
this luscious embrace,
and steady himself
in the privacy of a shower –
check his datebook
to set priorities straight.

It is not I, who you fear,
O lover of mine with one golden arm.
It is not even my desire

that horrifies you,
but the harrowing silence
in which our bodies must untwine.

There is nothing gentle about parting
of faceless bodies that hold no promise.

Love?

Hyder Ali

I met you after a year—
no, a year and a half—
so changed
and yet the same.

Your thin chest
now big as mine,
your smooth chin
rich with stubble.

The soft petals
of your boyhood charm
all but lost
in the armor of the man.

Yet the same eyes,
the same twinkle,
the same depth.
And the same smile.

Still you look up to me,
and as always,
I get annoyed;
I don't wish to play God.

I do not wish to grow old,
I do not want a son—
or worse, a father—
all I want is a friend.

A comrade and equal,
the weakness of a man,
the glory
the greatness.

My friend

S.D.G.

We met on the cold busy floor
of the center,
your black G.M.H.C. t-shirt
tucked into pale blue denim.
We shook hands
and you guided me
around fellow counselors—
counseling the inconsolable,
they say.
Being negative was positive—
we weren't.
Our evening coffees
became invitations to dinner.
We talked into the dawn,
your straw blond hair flowing in the firelight,
your Southern accent foreign to my New York.
We laughed,
we shared friendly kisses,
but the knowledge of our work,
the tears and blotched skin,
hung in the background,
gray and heavy.
One night the ghost of the pain
threatened to push forward.

Panicking,
we turned to each other,
kissing urgently,
hands groping, legs entwining,
our clothes shed like skin.
We fucked urgently,
with a strange tenderness
behind the gasps.
That day changed our lives
as if the dark ghost
that had prodded us   love
withdrew without a trace,
leaving the flush of beauty vibrant
between us.
With almost nihilistic ardor
we fucked daily,
no safe sex and warnings of swallowed semen
touched us.
We were half gone anyway.
I wept
as your warm come spurted into me,
wanting, yet knowing
that the pleasure wouldn't last.
You are too weak now,
your hair flaxen and thinning.
I remain the same,
as if life is playing with us—
your beautiful body emaciates
as I remain.
The three stems of tuberose
on your coffin
disappear under the falling mud.
I turn away, my heart aches,
like it did at fifteen,
when I dreamt of holding a man like you.

Fires of our pasts

Lakshmi

Previously published in *Shamakami*

Kashmiri shawls and silk saris burn
patchouli and Indian oils gyrate,
California seduction in cold November.
You glitter like an uncut stone,
found by surprise,
lodged in the sand,
your body hard,
cinnamongoldbronze,
mixed over centuries with intensity.
Fires of our pasts burn in the wind,
consumed with passion.
Bursting with light coming together
you have marked me.
Your breasts like that of a bronze statue
Indian goddess
you leave me trembling
with a new page of my life open
I can never forget,
our palms will always merge.

APART

Rakesh Ratti

you spoke of mist
        i sang of monsoons
you dreamed in pastels
          i in mango hues
you were an island
           i a drop in a sea
you felt with the mind
             i thought with the heart
sometimes i wonder
how we managed to start
this love of ours
so   far   apart

     yet mind and heart
      meld as one
       within a mist
        of green and gold
          monsoons thunder down
         lavender rain
           upon an island
          within the sea

Ute

Zariamma Harat

Ute
when you walk
there is a dignity quiet as the charm
of a gentle mountain stream
bending and light in its appreciation
smiling and letting gentleness
radiate
when you walk there are days that turn to
supply
lack flees and I know there is a better
way
smiling and singing and letting your
eyes that turn to color the morning or the day
as it sets dance
I wish a better tomorrow
to know one another
freshly,
smiling,
beyond the what was – let it let go
I will
A day of the walk through Teuffelsee and a
new remembering
seeking in the others taken that their brownness
yellowness redness blackness otherness

meant yes it meant perhaps it is nice as well
but let me tell you Ute
that in knowing them I have come to see
that your walk is the song of a day that is beyond
no compare, only observe
time and space and I am shy. I like you very much.
Love
Ute
come walk with me
tell me some of your stories
I am tired of telling mine
I will listen
I am unloading the overload
and listening to your walk.

A redefinition

Ian Rashid

I lie here on this vast rumpled ocean, your bed,
completely naked but for my skin
which is also a sheath.
This sheath itself you can make a weapon, and a fine one:
It gleams nut brown or bronze or cocoa
or other such magazine words
polished by the sucking of maggot and pests,
waxed, with a veneer of spices and feces,
washed by urine which men have spurted against
makeshift dwellings by which I have lain.
I am a catastrophic beauty (this will make you smile)
—an insistence of immortality.
Through my pores are amplified the shouts
of street merchants and photogenic urchins,
(this makes your smile disappear, yes?),
the offensive cries of burning brides,
hopeless milk screaming inside their searing, succulent,
honey-colored breasts. Listen carefully: hear
the music, melting, bubbling beyond...
so sweet, so sweet...

I am not even a complication, not worthy
of being one. My words enter the clarity
of your gaze like a blade but what comes back

is cornflower blue, dazed, a trifle
embarrassed, no hurtful words, no afternoon
television dramatics ... you reach for me, large
white spider against my darkness and I am
yours, now and for the first time.
For you see, my big, blond, perfume-soaked Sahib,
you have, through your polite – your civilized – grace,
brought down my New World.

Coming home

Maria

Gentle amber rays stream out of a deep blue sky that is dotted with billowy, gray-white clouds forever on the move. It is a crystalline day, fresh, clean, the type that San Francisco is famous for. I stand with my lover and some friends on the corner of Market and something – it could be any street – as the parade crawls past. We are but specks in the sea of humanity, 300,000 strong, that lines the parade route to watch what is a yearly ritual of pride and affirmation: the Gay and Lesbian Pride Parade. I watch them file past, dancing, laughing, singing, shouting their joy and self-love. Lesbian mothers and gay fathers, doctors and lawyers, African-Americans, Latinos, East Asians, Jews and Catholics – every segment of the gay and lesbian community asserting its pride and power.

Immersed in a conversation with a friend, the vaguely familiar music of an approaching contingent barely reaches my consciousness. As it gets louder, however, it reaches into the crevices of my mind, brings to the surface a torrent of memories. I turn to find the source of the music and stare at the blue pickup truck, its sound system blaring from the flatbed as two figures, both quite androgynous, dance atop the float.

The man, his hair falling to his shoulders, is dressed in a *kurta* (long shirt) and pajama; saffron, gold, red, and olive hues dance across his ethnic clothes. The woman, her shiny black hair styled short, wears an equally bright *salvar* and *kameez* (baggy pants and long tunic). All around the truck are more dark-haired, dark-eyed men and women, adorned with every color of the rainbow, dancing, clapping, rousing the crowd. The sounds and colors of these marchers are those of my home, a home that I have drifted from for a long time.

❖

Home, my original home, is Bangalore, a city in the southern part of India. From Bangalore my father left to study in England after the Second World War. While walking in a garden in England he met and fell in love with my mother, a young Italian woman who worked in a factory. After completing his studies, my father went back to India and began to prepare his family for his sweetheart. My mother went to Italy to do the same. Eventually she took a boat to India and, soon after her arrival, married my father.

Not surprisingly, both families were appalled. He was a Brahmin, she a Roman Catholic. His family was orthodox vegetarian, she ate meat. My father's family took four years to finally come and visit him and his wife, but over time they did come to accept her as a part of the clan.

Ours was not a very typical Indian household. To begin with, the double standard for men and women that is so pervasive in Indian society had no place in our home. My younger brother and I were always encouraged to achieve from a very early age, a teaching that has greatly benefited us in our adult life. My environment was also rich culturally. My mother taught me Italian, which I still speak fluently. My father spoke English at home, and as it was also the required language in school, I became proficient at it. I also spoke various Indian languages at one time or another; my father's job called for us to move around a lot and I picked up bits and pieces of the local languages.

No matter where we lived, Indians did not look at me as one of them. There is a good bit of prejudice against Anglo-Indians in India, and, since there were not many Italians around, I was often lumped with them. What prejudice there was came not from the kids, but from the adults. They wondered why we didn't observe the various holidays and customs of Hindu India. The whole thing left me feeling different sometimes, but I did not feel depressed or deprived.

I just blew such prejudice off. I never felt that I did not fit. Later, when I became conscious of my sexuality, I came to feel that I didn't belong.

I can remember being attracted to women at a very early age. I've often wondered if the society in India fosters this attraction. There are so many restraints on men and women spending time together, so you naturally form bonds with those of the same gender. You can embrace these friends, hold hands with them in public, show affection in myriad ways that would be labeled romantic or sexual in the United States. All of my close friendships throughout childhood and into adolescence were with women. Of course they were seen only as friendships; as one grows up, labels like homosexual and lesbian are applied to certain types of behavior.

I had one very serious crush during my early teens. I was fourteen, Rani was four years older, and the two of us attended the same Roman Catholic school. My attraction to Rani was very strong; I had to be around her constantly and spent a great deal of time at her house. I remember that we were becoming especially close right before my family left India. I often wonder what would have happened if we had stayed. We did leave, however, and whatever feeling was growing between us could only fade.

I was fourteen years old when, in 1967, my parents emigrated to Canada. Their first choice was the U.S., but such an arrangement was more difficult, so we ended up in Quebec. Overtly this move was made to give the children better opportunities. I suspect, however, that a larger motivating factor was the possibility of my parents finding a better life. The West offered more independence, a value that was especially important to my father; he had rebelled constantly against the tight controls of India.

I experienced certain difficulties in adjusting to my new home, not the least of which was the need to learn French just to get by. Even the Canadian English was different than what I was used to and seemed like learning a new language. I also found myself in a coed school and mingled with boys for the first time.

During this time I experienced a lot of peer pressure to date. There were no boys I wanted to go out with, but when it came time for the prom, I found someone to accompany me just to feel a part of my group. My father, who was very protective, tried to make certain that I did not date too young, although he held no illusions of arranging my marriage. He went to my school and told the principal that I, being from India, was very naive about many things. He wanted the principal to monitor what places I frequented and I was to be kept out of the snack shop, which was reputed to be a hangout for drug addicts. The whole thing was very embarrassing for me socially, but it didn't stop him.

I did have one relationship in Canada; I was still trying to fit in and succumbed to the warmth and affection that this one fellow offered. I did not, however, experience any deep feeling of love for him. I was conscious that I was not straight, but I wanted very much to change my orientation. When I had a flicker of a crush on a senior boy, I was thankful that I was going to be "normal."

I had no concept of what it meant to be homosexual or lesbian before I moved to Canada. The first time that I saw a couple of lesbians was at a restaurant – I was there with the guy I was then living with – and I spent the whole evening looking at the two women. That was when it began to click in my mind that people could love in this manner, that it could be more than just thoughts and fantasy. Yet I was still frightened of the idea of lesbianism; I thought that all lesbians were mannish, wore sensible shoes, and were not very attractive. I was only seventeen and I could not really think of living my life as a lesbian.

After a few years in Canada, my family's entry papers for the U.S. came through and we moved to New York. I was having a hard time at home by now; I had lots of feelings for women but did not know how to handle them. I had started attending college and a guy in my biology class invited me to a party. The party turned out to be twenty gay men and me. I felt something open up inside of me that night, some feeling of kinship. Some of these guys told me about a gay bar in Albany, and I knew that I had to check it out.

I had no car, but that did not daunt me. I attended one class at school, then hopped on a bus for Albany. I was at the bar before it opened at noon. There were these huge dykes, old-fashioned, men's clothes and all. Before long I developed a massive crush on Marty, a bartender who was in her late twenties.

One night, after I drank a bit much, she offered to drive me home. My bedroom was above the garage and had a separate entrance, so we were able to make it inside unnoticed by my family. Drunk, we engaged in some rather noisy lovemaking.

Drawn by the racket, my parents entered my room just as a naked Marty was stepping out of my bed and into her clothes. My parents chased poor Marty, struggling to pull her clothes on, down the stairs. Mom and Dad talked to me all night. My mother insisted that I confess to a priest. She and my father alternated in taking me to church, where I confessed my "sins" to an old priest who had no idea what I was talking about. It was a very traumatic time for all of us.

My father decided that he would drop me off at school and would pick me up after my last class. I still managed to grab the bus and see Marty at the bar, however; I just skipped some classes. This eventually waned when I became attracted to another woman in the same bar. She was older and was raising four daughters. Things were getting pretty rough at my house, so I moved in with this woman. For seven months we played house. She went to work, I stayed home and took care of the house and the kids.

My routine as a "housewife" became boring very quickly; I had a need to be self-supporting and I wanted to be even farther away from my parents. My ultimate goal was to be an attorney. That was not feasible at this time, so I joined the army. Not only would it get me out of the house, it would also pay me and teach me something. My parents liked the idea, figuring that the discipline would make me a woman. Little did they know that the army was full of dykes, and there I really came out. In the military, the lesbians all knew one another, and we went out to bars after hours.

In many ways, the army was a bit of a playground. It was a period when I wanted, and had the chance, to be with women. I took ample advantage of the opportunity. Those three years, the company of these women, really helped me become more comfortable with myself. I was stationed in San Antonio when I left the military, and I decided to stay there for a while.

Throughout this time, my Indian self was basically dormant, trotted out when it suited me – usually when I figured that the exoticness of it would set me apart. The extent of my forays into my culture consisted of occasional Indian music and food. Interestingly, I have never identified myself as an Italian. I have always thought of myself as an Indian, perhaps because that is the culture I was born and raised in. Because of my longing for the Indian part of me, I would stop Indian-looking people on the streets of San Antonio and ask them what part of the country they were from. They would look at me as if I was crazy, since I don't look all that Indian, and would only believe me after I told them my last name and that I was from Bangalore.

I still had not really accepted myself. I knew I was a lesbian, that was real enough, but I wasn't comfortable with it. Texas is not the most nurturing place for gays and lesbians, and I did not want to spend all of my time battling the world. At times I actually tried to force myself to be straight, but I never felt a deep attraction to a man.

At one point, after ending a relationship that had made me very unhappy, I went to a bar and met a tall, slender woman with the kindest eyes and very pretty hands. Her name was Georgia, she was eleven years older, and she seemed fun, stable, and responsible. We felt an instant kinship. We began to date, bought a house, and generally settled down to "coupledom."

We lived in Texas for five and a half years before moving to northern California; I wanted to pursue my long-held goal of being an attorney, and Georgia had a sister who lived in Sacramento. We joined with her sister to open a catering business. During this time Georgia was very supportive and gave me the chance to work through many of my personal issues.

One problem I had with Georgia, however, was her inability or unwillingness to acknowledge my being Indian. I suppose that isn't too surprising since I did not acknowledge it either, and yet it bothered me. Even my close friends were never very interested in my heritage. I came to feel that by bringing up my Indian side, I was somehow imposing on them. I felt uncomfortable talking about this aspect of myself. I sensed little support, so I closed it off.

My studies consumed most of my time during my stay in Sacramento. We had no gay friends there, so Georgia and I would go to San Francisco to get some sense of community. There was a gay and lesbian group on my campus, but I was too afraid to join them; I was apprehensive that being visible might jeopardize my chances for a well-paying job with a big firm.

While in law school, my relationship with Georgia started to fall apart. The age difference between us was becoming more important. We were at different stages in our lives, both personally and professionally.

After graduation, I secured a position with a law firm in San Francisco. We should have been finished with one another at this point. The process of disintegration had been slow, and we had done much of the grieving during the last stages of the relationship, but a nine-year relationship was hard to relinquish. We stayed together, under one excuse or another, for nine more months.

My mother had passed away by the time I started law school. I think she had begun to realize that I was a lesbian during her last few years. On one of my visits with her, she mentioned an article she had read about gay people. She told me that people should do whatever made them happy. I wasn't sure then how I should take her statement, but I suspect that, in her own way, she was acknowledging her acceptance of my lifestyle.

I did come out to my father more directly, and he surprised me by telling me that he had had feelings for men at times. On some level I think I knew that he had a bisexual potential, perhaps because we were raised in the same culture. I remember that there was a cute male attendant at a gas station my father frequented. Dad told me that he had some sort of feeling for the attendant. I think this sharing really strengthened the bond between us.

I did not come out to my brother until 1989. He is very different from me, being ten years younger and having spent all but four years of his life in this country. In thought and attitude he is very American. Four years ago my brother was diagnosed with HIV, and he has begun to show symptoms. A while back he was involved with a woman who, unknown to him at the time, had been an intravenous drug user, and we suspect that he picked up the AIDS virus from her. Last year I decided to come out to him. His response to my sharing was very positive; my being lesbian seems no different to him than my having gray hair.

At that time, I knew no Indians in the gay community, and I was still out of touch with my native culture. I figured that there were probably gay Indian men, but it didn't seem likely to me that there might be Indian lesbians. The Indian women I knew in childhood were all strong, contrary to popular demure images. They exercised their strength overtly, not from behind the scenes. Yet, for some reason I cannot fathom, I could not visualize an Indian woman being a lesbian.

One evening I went to a party organized by and for business-women in the Bay Area. In the course of the evening I met an Israeli-American woman named Rena. She wanted to learn more about India, I was curious about Israel. I found her fascinating. I remember telling her that Rena is an Indian name and that I liked it very much.

Over time I found that Rena and I shared a lot of commonal-ities. Like my family, Rena's family first moved to Quebec and later to the northeastern U.S. She was not Indian, but she was multicultural, multilingual, and as such she respected my bicul-turality. We didn't even need to talk about such issues; there was an intuitive understanding.

❖

That was over a year ago. Rena stands beside me now, puzzled by the faraway look on my face. "Where are you going?" she asks as I step into the street and hurry toward the colorful, wonderfully noisy marchers. My walk turns into a run. The first member of the contingent I reach is a beautiful Indian woman in a blue *kameez* and *salvar*. I grab her arm; she turns to me with a startled look on her face.

"Is this an organization? Do you people have a phone number?" I ask excitedly.

She tells me that they have a booth in the festival at the end of the parade. I immediately drag Rena and my friends to the festival and locate the booth. Behind their table hangs a turquoise banner; the name of the organization, "Trikone," and the words "Gay and Lesbian South Asians" stand out in bold violet letters. I tell the people at the table who I am, and there is immediate, wordless acceptance when they realize that I am Indian. They invite me to a party that they are having tonight. I assure them that I will be there.

I am flying! I have been in the process of coming out as a lesbian, and now I feel like I am coming out as an Indian. Two parts of me that were alienated are beginning to come together. It is almost unreal, the bright clothes, the melodic music, and the Indian eyes of my childhood, here, in the midst of this mass of gay and lesbian humanity. It feels like I'm coming home.

Breaking silence

Sharmeen Islam*

Dupitara Chowdhury and Nandini Datta are two lesbians living and loving together in Bombay. The following interview is excerpted from a longer article published previously.

Sharmeen: How did you come to know you were gay and to accept yourself?

Nandini: Looking back at my childhood, I can make connections to my homosexual feelings. I grew up among girls; we used to get very physically close on picnics or day trips, but I didn't know about homosexuality. Not until I went to college and started reading about it. I read and supported progressive discussions of literature about gay rights, but I was scared to probe my personal feelings. However, when I got involved in the left political scene in India, I started developing strong feelings towards a woman "comrade." I was courting my future husband at the time, but the feelings couldn't even compare. My comrade and I worked together in the trade union and we spent a lot of time together. We were subjected to a lot of laughs about our constant intimacy. We ourselves cracked jokes!

Sharmeen: You mean you cracked jokes about being lesbians?

Nandini: Yes. But we thought it was safe, since [lesbianism] was a "distant, Western phenomenon." Later she married another activist. After her wedding, I was very disheartened. I went off to Sri Lanka and had several unsatisfactory affairs with men. When I came back to India, I knew I had to have a female companion. So, I started to

213

look for a mate who would share my children, my household, my life with me. And that's how Dupitara came into my life!

Dupitara: And here I am! My past is very similar as far as close bonds with women are concerned. I came from a conservative Muslim family in the village. The concept of an alternate sexuality or lifestyle is unheard of! I mean, people accept women being with other women – as long as it is not in a sexual context.

Sharmeen: When and how did you come to realize you were a lesbian?

Dupitara: From the very beginning I was extremely conscious about my relationship with men. I disliked them thoroughly. Being a lesbian is very much a political statement for me in that sense. I know what marriage is, at least in Muslim families. I also know what men are. I knew I didn't want to get into it. So, I came to Bombay looking for a household with women. And I found Nandini.

Nandini: When she came to my house, she was very vulnerable. She had never had sexual feelings, or known an orgasm. I was much more experienced and had to control the vigor with which I wanted to explore my sexual feelings for her. She felt very scared initially, along with her mental reservations about whether what we were doing was right or wrong. But, the key was that her mind and body responded.

Dupitara: All my life I've been close to women. But, I think it's only lesbians who are free to touch other women freely and in places they would like to touch. Every other woman is scared out of her mind.

Sharmeen: Dupitara, after you came out through your relationship with Nandini, how did you accept your sexuality?

Dupitara: I met an Indian lesbian who lives in the States. Then I met another who lives in New Delhi; she gave me a lot of strength. Our feminist friends were very hostile towards Nandini and me. They

Our feminist friends were very hostile towards Nandini and me. They didn't say much to Nandini, but I was young and vulnerable. They advised me to leave the relationship, to stay away from her. Despite their efforts, we survived and became closer!

Sharmeen: How did you meet this lesbian in Delhi? Are there more lesbians in Bombay?

Nandini: We met her through our friend in the States. Apart from our friend in New Delhi, we know one other woman in Bangalore. Her lover is Greek. A group of lesbians from the West came to India at one point. They stayed with our feminist friends, who told them there were no lesbians in India. Finally, one of the ex-editors of *Anamika* [a South Asian lesbian newsletter once published out of New York] came to visit her home state. She insisted that there must be other lesbians in Bombay. That's when one of the feminists called us up and asked if we wanted to meet another lesbian; since then, we have opened up our communications to the international lesbian world!

Sharmeen: So, the so-called feminists deliberately misdirected lesbians from abroad by telling them you don't exist?

Dupitara: Yes, but we know many many friends now from all over the world. Moreover, we are hearing of many lesbians who are not urban, middle class. Recently, two nurses hung themselves because they loved each other and would not be married off. In another village, two women registered their union as "marriage of friendship," called *Maitrikarar*.

Sharmeen: Tell me about *Maitrikarar*.

Nandini: For women, the whole thing started with the two police-women in Bhopal. It struck the minds of lesbians throughout the country. Two primary school teachers from Gujarat registered their union as *Maitrikarar*. *Maitrikarar* is an old, heterosexual concept used by businessmen to wed their mistresses in order to give them some commitment.

Sharmeen: Is sex between people of the same gender punishable by law?

Nandini: Homosexuality between men is defined in terms of penetration and it is punishable by ten years [incarceration]. But, when they wrote the laws, they didn't even think of homosexual acts between women. That's why the police tried and failed to indict the female police officers on a ten-year sentence for being homosexuals.

Sharmeen: It's amazing that lesbianism is not punishable! Moreover, it's okay for two women to marry each other under *Maitrikarar*.

Nandini: In Bhopal, the homophobic tank commander said that marriage is all about sex and those two women couldn't possibly have a "real" marriage. But the police commissioner said that marriage is a union between two souls – and soul has no gender! In the midst of this confusion, people of the same gender are fortunately being allowed to celebrate some sort of a union. However, the system is very conscious of refusing to legalize, institutionalize, and give social acceptance to lesbian and gay people.

Dupitara: Actually, there is extensive evidence of lesbian sexuality before the British Victorian culture came to India. When I told my aunt of the Bhopal marriage, she shrugged her shoulders and said it's quite normal. Recently, we got to know about a lesbian couple working as prostitutes. When one of them came down with AIDS and died, her lover spent her life savings on her funeral and grave site.

Sharmeen: How did your feminist friends react to the Bhopal wedding between the two police officers?

Nandini: First, there was tremendous hesitation. Nobody wanted to go to Bhopal. We collected many signatures, though. Finally, a few lesbians from here and a few Indian lesbians from the U.S. went to Bhopal to talk to the women.

Sharmeen: It's sad that feminists are discouraging you to be lesbians! What can be done to change that?

216

Nandini: I think lesbian liberation is closely interlinked with deconstructing patriarchy. It holds women behind, no matter who they are. The first thing Indian women need to do is to come up with an analysis of marriage and defy it through a movement. Indian feminists are still working on peripheral issues around patriarchy, such as wife battering and dowry deaths. The center of patriarchy is held up by marriage. In Kanpur recently, three sisters committed suicide simultaneously because they refused to get married! And then four sisters did the same in Kerala a week after. Marriage is like slavery to women.

Sometimes, the mainstream press does more of an anti-marriage analysis around these incidents than the feminists. A radical straight woman named Kamala told the press, "Damn marriage!" She also gave the press details of her sexually active life. In support, another senior male journalist wrote that he would rather spend his money educating his daughters than his sons and that no woman needs to get married!

You see, women in India need to be independent, allowed to earn their livelihood, set up their own households; only then can they explore their sexuality. Otherwise, they never have the strength to come out of the closet. How can they?

Sharmeen: Is the number of single, young working women increasing at all? If not, what can be done to encourage women to be independent and to come out of the closet?

Nandini: Only in urban areas are women living independently. A lot of these women have high education and well-paying jobs. They are only a handful. I think if women can develop themselves, if they can take charge of their lives, other things would fall in place.

Sharmeen: What is the hardest part of being gay at this time in your lives?

Dupitara: I think the fact that I'm not married. You see, Nandini was married and has two kids. Nobody bothers her about remarriage. But, most people question why a young woman like me is living with another woman with children. And why am I unmarried? I think the hardest part is that I can't tell anyone I'm a lesbian. Everywhere I go, people ask why I am not married, who is my boyfriend. It is humiliating and disempowering. I cannot share any of my happiness or problems with them. It's like I am two different people. Another complication is that I am Muslim. Nobody understands why I'm living with a Hindu woman, away from my family.

Nandini: I feel I'm in a slightly different position than Dupitara. I have come out to people at work. I really don't have many problems being a lesbian here. People are more willing to accept me because I have been married and have two children. I never give a het [heterosexual] image to my family and friends. They come to my household as it is. In a way, I don't care too much for acceptance. I think a little distance from family is good. Sometimes, though, I'm scared that when I die, my house, children, and everything will go to my ex-husband.

Dupitara: I also think I miss having a community. Sometimes, I feel we are not growing because we have nobody except each other in our relationship. No one to go and talk to safely.

Nandini: The Trikone chapter [in Patna, Bihar] and the lesbian marriage both took place in economically depressed regions of India. I think that, ultimately, the revolution will spread from rural India. I think one day we will be free.

Chai wallah (Tea seller)

Susil

A semi-autobiographical story

I was born on the day of the full moon after *Divali,* the Indian festival of lights, and, according to my now-tattered school certificate, I turned thirty-five last week. My life in the tea shop started the day after the funeral of my late father, who died in a rather gory mill accident. I was in the third grade at the time. The mill owner gave my mother one thousand rupees, more to shut her up than out of compassion. She immediately purchased gold and deposited it against a loan through the bank, available to her because she was a widow. She had to provide for the family now (three sisters, a brother, and me), so two days later she purchased a rather elderly but very pregnant water buffalo.

I rarely heard my mother get up in the predawn light to milk and feed our much-loved buffalo and her calf. After finishing, she would shake me awake. I would tumble out of bed and swish a bit of water over my face. Then I would walk whatever milk there was six paces to the tea shop next door. This shop was built with palm leaves, had its own well, and stood in line with all the other houses against the mill wall. Often I arrived at the shop before the owner had started to kindle the charcoal briquettes for the first pot of tea. Usually a *rickshaw wallah* (driver) going home after a night of gathering odd fares, perhaps men sneaking home from the red-light district, would be the first customer.

Who can list the number of jobs that a boy in a tea shop does at the age of nine? If you have been one, you don't want to list them anyway. My routine was to slip a *neem* twig (often used by rural Indians to brush their teeth) into my mouth and work it around while I filled one tub of water after another for chai. I developed the art of twisting it around so well that my teeth would be clean by the time the last tub was full. Then I scraped the twig across my tongue to clean that as well. Funny, but I've noticed that foreigners don't bother with cleaning their tongues. Oh well, they are an odd lot anyway.

If my timing was good, I finished in time to get the third *idli* rice cake off the tray as the owner's wife peeled back the steam cloth. The first two went to her son, who was a year older than me. I didn't mind that; he was my first love, and I couldn't be jealous of him. In later years, when he went off to college, I would rearrange my whole life just to have an hour with him.

The tea shop used to open just as the street lights went off and the sun poked its face over the wall. It closed by eleven in the morning, then reopened at four. It closed for the night by ten. During the winter it would close much earlier; the cold coming off the mountains drove most sane Indians indoors where they could sit before a cow dung–fueled fire to ward off the chill and the mosquitoes.

On one of these cold winter nights my eyes were opened by Prasad, the owner's son. He had started to wear a cloth that was tucked beneath his waist-string in the front, went under his crotch, and was tucked under his waist-string once more in the back. I was puzzled; we had always gone to the canal at lunchtime and bathed naked, so I asked him why he was wearing this cloth. He told me that he had started to get hard when he bathed. It was not news to me; I had looked at him more than once, out of the corners of my eyes, as we dried ourselves in the sun, but I never said anything. I had also noticed that he didn't have any pubic hair, whereas I was already sprouting a few.

By this time I had started to stay in the shop at night so that I could light the stove in the mornings and give his father an extra hour of sleep. Now my mother brought over the milk each morning, and she would stay on to scrub the pots with ash from the stove and a burred end-piece of a coconut shell. Soon I was allowed to actually make the tea, a new step in my career. As I lay in the shop at night, half-asleep, I would think of various men who had come to the shop that day, pick one, and wonder what his body looked like. My penis would be hard, and I would hold it tight but I ventured no further. I had no idea what more there could be.

One night, when his parents had gone to the cinema and we were curled up under a blanket on the countertop, Prasad asked me if he could feel my pubic hair. I was so delighted by the thought that I nearly fell off the counter. Ten minutes later I thought I was falling off the face of the earth. This incredible something crept up from inside my crotch and splattered all over Prasad. I just lay there in a daze for what seemed like forever. I have never experienced that time warp again, but it is close to the feeling of being stoned on *ganja* (marijuana). I suppose in reality it was not much more than a minute later that he asked me a question.

"Do you know what that was?"

"No," I gasped weakly.

I don't know if he described it to me in the same terms that our beloved Rabindranath Tagore (a Nobel laureate Bengali poet) would have used, but I understood him all the same. At that moment I realized that I still had my hand on his penis, and he was holding my wrist and moving it up and down. I learned a lot that night. Three years and many joint adventures later, Prasad went off to the nearest big town to attend upper high school. I felt absolutely lost.

Prasad came home at the end of his first term. We eyed each other all day and passed smiles and brushed together. His father gave him one rupee and I went to the cinema for the first time in my life. At intermission we decided not to go back inside the theater, but instead went to the canal and took a bath. When we got home, he told me that he had talked his father into allowing him to rent a small room near his college.

My two smaller sisters were now entering puberty, and my older sister was nearly a young woman. Our house was at one end of the mill wall, and at the other end lived an old man who had no family. When he was feeling well, he would pull one of the oldest bicycle rickshaws (a rickshaw that is pedaled, not pulled) I had ever seen. It made him cough a lot. At times I wondered if he was moving the rickshaw or if it was moving him. Every morning, even if the cough nearly drove his balls into his throat, he would wander out at some early hour of the morning and rasp out a "chai." Sometimes he reminded me of a parrot stepping out of its cage. It was my job to

221

stop what I was doing and bring him a glass of tea with an extra spoon of sugar in it.

On the same day that Prasad came home from college, the solitary old rickshaw driver died. He had really been dying for months, and people along the wall had been bringing him meals, taking him to the doctor, and generally looking after him – something not uncommon amid the squalor and poverty we lived in. Up to his last moment he had been quite appreciative of anyone who called on him. Three days later, I heard loud voices shouting. The mill owner, who had threatened to pull down the old house and reclaim the spot for one of his workers, was having to retreat from the angry neighborhood. It seemed that I had inherited the house and the rickshaw, and my neighbors did not want him to claim what had been willed to me. All because I had often helped the old man wash his vehicle during the summer and had given him the least amount of grief among the kids on our street. The women divided up his other belongings, while his clay pots were broken, in keeping with tradition, and his cot was cremated with him.

What was I to do with a rusty old rickshaw and a room full of holes? Prasad's father gave me all the answers I needed. He lent me enough money, against my future wages, to repair the rickshaw and pushed me into having it painted. I sat for many a night after the tea shop closed and scraped off the rust. Prasad's father arranged to have the rickshaw rented out during the day, and he collected the rent until my debt to him was repaid. I pushed the bloody thing from closing time at the tea shop until after the end of the late movie. The cinema often let out as late as two a.m. and a long fare sometimes took me an hour. It was hard work. It was good, though, to see the cash mounting on the slip of paper that Prasad's father and I kept together. Over the course of a year I saved enough money to buy a new rickshaw.

After a hard day of work I would fall into bed exhausted. I even had difficulty staying awake long enough to get myself off thinking about Prasad. The summer before he went off to college I did not push the rickshaw except to take him somewhere. He had many friends now and often three of them would pile into the rickshaw. I would take them to one another's houses or perhaps to the cinema, where I waited outside for them until the film was over.

"And now I will pay you for the rickshaw ride," he would say when we got home and curled up on the cot.

Except for a patch in the pubic area, Prasad was hairless. He turned me on more and more. He told me that summer that he had watched the hair grow up from my navel and slowly spread across my chest. He said that when he came home after each term he was anxious to see if it had spread to my nipples. He must have run his fingers across my face a thousand times during that summer. Everything that he did turned me on. My favorite of all his tricks, however, was when he would catch me on a night when I had just shaved and run his tongue all over my face.

That was a hot summer in many ways. Working in the tea shop and keeping up with Prasad left me exhausted. The old man's house, now mine, had finally met its end; the last tenant had left because the structure was so decayed. Prasad's father kept saying I must do something about it. I agreed, but finding the time was harder than finding the money. Prasad decided to pull the house down for me. The four main roof beams were still good, so we saved those along with a handful of bamboo. The palms were only fit for burning. The local experts said the mud was still good, so Prasad piled it up on one side with all the stone pieces that made up the floor.

For the next few months I would stop beside the road, when I had no fare, and pick up any stray bricks I could find. I borrowed money from my mother's gold loan to get new poles and palm fronds. Prasad's father came down the path one day with a spade and showed his son how to dig the foundation out. One morning, in the middle of his digging, he dropped the spade and rushed to find me in the tea shop. I assumed that he just wanted tea or water, both of which I had ready.

"I need Susil for a few minutes please," he said to his father.

His father, who now sat most of the time and just collected money from the customers, simply nodded. As we walked back to the digging site, I figured that Prasad merely wanted my help in moving some rock. He said nothing.

"Keep quiet and look under that cornerstone," he said softly when we finally stood in the trench.

I found a small stainless steel tin that he had already wiped clean. When I look inside I spotted a *manglastotram* — the gold wedding piece that a man ties around a woman's neck during their marriage ceremony. I had just turned it over when Prasad plucked it from my hand and put it in his pocket. I looked up in surprise.

"Well, get back to the tea shop. Do you think my father pays you to hang around building sites?" he said. The tone of his voice made me shiver, but with excitement, for this particular tone meant that he had some mischief in mind.

He came in covered with mud and dust at five o'clock and said that we should go and bathe. He also thought that we should take a coconut to the temple and seek a blessing for the start of the real work on the house, which would begin the next day. At the temple, in one dark corner, Prasad put the gold piece on a string, which he then wound around my waist.

"Now you belong to me forever," he whispered.

The next morning a mason came to work on the house. He was about the same age as the two of us and lived in the compound around the corner. Prasad went and labored with him. He came back at lunchtime and told me that he had spent most of the morning watching the mason.

"The gold must be very thin," I said, feeling a bit jealous.

This evoked no more than his usual "Uh-huh" grunt. I knew from experience that it was pointless to argue.

"I have been watching the boy too," I finally confessed. "You're right, he does have a beautiful body."

I must have been terribly naive in those days. I would look at everyone yet never think it possible that they might possess the same desire that Prasad and I had for one another. I rarely thought about what he and I were. We did what we did, and we did not need to know more.

The walls of my new house crept up slowly with the mud, brick, and stone. On the fourth night Prasad told me that he intended to ask the mason to come to the cinema with him the next day. He asked me to bring a bottle of toddy; he figured that on the way home we would stop by the canal, drink the toddy, and play it by ear. I was in an absolute dither the following day. I nearly spilled the milk. I made a whole pot of tea with no sugar in it and got shouted at by a poor rickshaw driver who had just pulled a load of potatoes to the market down the road.

That evening I lounged on the cement apron of the canal with Prasad and the mason. We sipped quietly from the bottle I had brought. When the bottle was empty, we sat there in silence. I could think of nothing, and Prasad seemed to have lost all of the ideas he had told me about the night before.

"Do the two of you have it off with one another?"

It came from Ramana, the mason. We said nothing, and I imagine that he must have been in a total panic, not knowing how we would react. Slowly Prasad turned onto his side.

"Why, do you want to join us?"

It was the last week of the school holidays, and Prasad was kicking himself for not making his move earlier. We took more night baths and went to more cinemas that week than we ever had before. Prasad's mother kept grumbling about the late hours we kept, but his father, as always, said nothing. I tried to act real cool the morning Prasad got dressed and, with his father and mother, went off to board a bus to Azidur. He was on his way to a college, where he had secured a position with his good marks at the upper school.

Ramana was still around. He turned up almost every other night, just in time to get the last cup of tea before I turned the stove out. He would wait until I closed up, then we walked along the rice mill wall to the house that was now nearly completed. There was not much light near the sidewall, so we would climb over it and into the rice mill compound. One night Ramana told me that he had been coming to the tea shop every morning for three years just to see if he could spy an erection left over from the night before. I realized that Prasad and I were virgins compared to him.

The house was eventually completed and rented out. I also owned two rickshaws, which gave me a good income, so I decided to stop pulling the rickshaws at night unless one was not rented out. I never thought of a job other than the tea shop, however; the tea shop was me. The house rent and the income from the two rickshaws were extras that allowed my mother to stop working. Prasad's father now left the whole show at the tea shop to me much of the time. Often he would collect the cash, and infrequently he made a special pot of chai for some of his longtime cronies.

One day Prasad sent a note to his father asking me to visit him for two days. His mother packed a whole bag of goodies for me to take for him, while his father sent him a bit of extra cash. I caught the early-morning bus, and he met me at the station. The first time I visited him we had walked to his room. This time we took a rickshaw. I had never actually sat next to him in a rickshaw in all those years; it had always been me pulling while he sat.

"See the way his ass moves from side to side, that's the way yours looks, only more beautiful," he said to me as the *rickshaw wallah* stood up on the pedals and pushed harder on a slight incline. "So many times I was tempted to reach out and squeeze your cheeks, but I was afraid that you would tip the rickshaw or maybe cum on the spot."

"Probably both," I responded.

Prasad had one room in a house opposite his college. He got the room with the understanding that he would also tutor the owner's three small children. It was a good deal, but nothing like the deal he laid on me. Here was this college, at the end of town, on a main highway, and no one had built a tea shop, maybe because a barbed wire fence, instead of a wall, separated the college from the road. Whatever the reason, I could not believe that no one had claimed this spot.

"Why don't you sell the two rickshaws, use the rent from the house, borrow against your mother's gold, and build a tea shop here?" he suggested. "You could even get a loan from my father – provided he isn't too angry at you for leaving his shop."

I went home on the last bus the next night with aching balls, drained but with my mind in a spin. My promise to Prasad was that I would say nothing to anyone for a few days. The following weekend he would come home and discuss it with his father.

That same week my mother asked me if I was thinking about marriage. She went on and on, as all Indian mothers do about their children's marriages, moaning about how if my marriage was left too late, my younger sisters would have no chance for marriage at all. I hemmed and hawed and said that the girls should be married first because we could not afford to go into too much debt. She agreed; I think that on some level she was actually pleased with the idea.

The next weekend Prasad came home and spoke with his father. His father asked me a few questions, nodded and, although he was a bit angry that he would now be left alone with the tea shop, he agreed. He would give me the cash in advance and arrange to sell

226

the rickshaws at a good price during the summer. We then spoke with my mother. She had a fit. Eventually Prasad's father calmed her by telling her that he would be responsible for it all.

❖

Everything happened as we had planned, and the memory sits near the top of my thoughts. Near the top, however, for at the very top is the tragedy of Prasad's death a year later. Killed by terrorists on a bus. He and six others, all of them headed for a picnic that they would never reach. He was twenty-five years old. His mother wept and his father retreated into a liquor bottle. I simply fell apart. I visited his parents only three or four times; it tore me to pieces to even see their place.

After a year passed, Prasad's mother began to make it through some days without crying. His father stood up one day, threw away the half-empty bottle of liquor, and began to remodel his tea shop. I just remained fractured. Over time I let my hair and beard grow. My new tea shop was a gold mine, and it helped me keep up a good front. I got through the day with a smile for everyone and wept almost every night. If I got an erection I put my hand on it and thought of Prasad. It would collapse immediately.

Not long after I opened the shop, I hired two boys to help me. By the end of the first year, I had trained them to manage the place while I took a week off. The man in the house opposite the shop, who had rented a room to Prasad once, took a week off and came to collect the cash for me. We had become quite good friends by this time, and I was in the habit of taking a pot of tea to his house every morning as soon as his front door opened.

With time on my hands, I decided to go to Benares, the holy city, so I could do a prayer for Prasad. I cut my beard off and wrapped my hair into a bun atop my head. I put on a new white *lunghee* (a cotton cloth wrapped around the lower body) and draped a towel around my upper chest. The old swamis on the river steps looked on, chanted, and seemed to give me an inner smile. I had taken a step away from the world of males and females into the androgynous world of what in my part of India is whispered to be an "evening person." I had seen many men dressed like this. I had never asked anyone, but I just assumed that they preferred to look more feminine than masculine. Some of them went too far, I think, wearing makeup. Don't ask me why I decided to do it. It's just the way I felt. I felt that I would never marry, and at this stage I only wanted to try to heal myself of the loss of Prasad.

My change certainly attracted attention and business upon my return. No one had any idea that I was gay until this time – well, no one except Ramana and, of all the people, the owner of the house across the road, who said to me one day, "If your outward change makes you feel good or happy, then that's good. I realized on the first day that you came to stay with Prasad that the two of you were in love with each other. I thought it was just a thing that young people do at the time. But no matter what, you are welcome in my house."

By the end of the first month, I had a dozen well-honed replies for the smart-assed students who tried to get a laugh from their peers by teasing me. They all took it pretty well though, because I always smiled, winked, and added an extra dash of sugar to their tea.

Prasad's brother, Chitti, turned up at the shop one day. When he saw the change in me, he went outside and stood by the roadside. I sent one of the boys after him with a glass of tea. Eventually he came back in and smoked a cigarette while he sipped another chai. The tea shop was quite busy but he sat there patiently, just taking it all in.

About eleven o'clock I told the boys to clean up so that I could go into town for lunch. I turned to Chitti and said, "Well, are you game enough to come with me?"

He nodded, walked over, held my hand, and said, "I suppose I'll have to, if I am to marry your sister next month."

So that was why he had come. We had lunch in a *pukka* (orthodox) Brahmin restaurant, and he told me more news about the upcoming marriage. He went home saying that somehow he would explain my "change of dress" to everyone. I sent him off with a set of new clothes for him and his whole family. I told him that I could not come to the marriage, not because of my "change of dress," but because it would tear me up to be there and think about Prasad. He looked at me for a long time, then nodded knowingly.

The following week I was surprised to see Prasad's father, my mother, and my two sisters all getting down from a rickshaw and coming toward my tea shop. I wanted to just vanish, but I stood rooted to the spot. Again the shop was crowded, and they all just sat down and ordered chai and *idli*. When the last of the students had gone, I closed the door and sent the two boys off to the matinee. Now I was alone with my visitors. They didn't seem bothered by the change in my appearance. My two sisters teased me a bit. My mother seemed to adapt to the situation, as mothers do so well, while Prasad's father criticized the color of my countertop. In the end I agreed to attend the marriage ceremony.

The ceremony went on for three days, as is our custom, but I stayed for only one. I used the tea shop as an excuse to leave. The next afternoon, as I sat in the shop, I was jolted when one of the boys whispered to me that some guy wanted "a rice mill special tea." He asked me what kind of chai that would be. Ignoring him, I slowly put the teapot down and scanned the room. Ramana had returned and found his way to my new location.

It was still the early part of summer and the crops in the surrounding countryside had failed. Consequently, there was little being built anywhere in this part of the state. Ramana turned up looking like a mason, though, with a gunny bag containing his trowel and other tools. I was in the middle of making cardamom tea for a government officer from the municipality, who came once a month to collect my roadside rent, so I didn't see Ramana walk in and sit down. Nice guy, that officer; he always paid for his tea.

Ramana had no work, so he decided that we should get some bricks and fix up my place a bit. I had thought about this for months, but, being overly careful with money, I had put it off. Ramana masoned and I labored. I hired a rickshaw and carted bricks, mud, sand, and cement. The few college boys who lived near the tea shop were amazed to see me doing these things. A gang of them actually came over every afternoon and fixed tea while I shouted instructions. They thought it was fun, and their tea wasn't half-bad. Often Ramana would entertain them with bawdy stories.

It was a great summer, the two of us repairing the shop and Ramana healing me. He was what I needed right now, and he knew it. He got me to talk about Prasad while we were having it off together. He teased me about Prasad until I opened all the doors I had sealed the year before. In the end, I was feeling a bit more whole and my tea shop had an extension, a separate room on the side; the college girls could sip their chai in semiprivacy now. When the work was finished and the college reopened, Ramana went off to find work in the south. He said that he might be gone a year, or perhaps a week, but that he would return.

When the college girls realized what I had done, they were delighted beyond words. There wasn't a tea shop in town that had a separate room just for girls. It blew their minds that they could sip their tea a safe distance from the boys, with my counter forming a divide, and yet still flirt with them. It wasn't long before I was put in charge of passing notes back and forth. Then one day one of the girls called me *Akka* – elder sister. It floored me! The boys working in the shop giggled so hard that I thought they would wet their pants. The next day I heard, "Akka, give me a *samosa* (a spicy, triangular vegetable roll) with my tea" a few more times. On the third day the whole tea shop nearly collapsed when one of the gang of boys who had fixed tea over the summer for me said, "I don't know about Akka – I saw him taking a bath once, and I'm blind if I didn't see a cobra clinging to him." Laughter swelled across the shop, causing people on the street to wonder what was going on.

My shop continued to do well, and during the next year I had a larger, more solid house built for myself. I also asked my mother to come and live with me. She happily packed her belongings, sold her land to Prasad's father, and moved into my new home. I was a relatively wealthy man now; things were going well, but I was also lonely.

There were times, not too often, when I would see two "evening people" go past my shop on a flat-top rickshaw that would be loaded up with vegetables. Soon they took to stopping the rickshaw and coming in for chai and sweetcakes. I have found that it is usual for "evening people" to be very extroverted and make talk constantly among themselves; perhaps it is their way of dealing with people. But in the tea shop these two said nothing, though I could feel them staring at me constantly. When I would turn quickly and catch them looking, they would just keep staring as if I was a mirror.

Winter came early that year. The sudden cold meant that the streets were almost deserted by seven o'clock. I would keep the fire going until eight, sometimes just for the occasional lorry driver who stopped by. Every Wednesday my boys went to the cinema, and on these nights I would clean up the place. One Wednesday night the cane door groaned and in walked my "evening people." Over the previous ten days they must have stopped by at least three times. They always had a young guy to help them load and unload the baskets of vegetables. For the last two weeks, however, I had noticed that they had a new helper.

Who would not have noticed this new helper? He was a piece out of the sky. His whole body was different, somehow confusing to me. He was tall for whatever his age might be, and had the Oriental shape to his eyes. He might have been Nepali but for his height. His skin was the lightest shade of bronze, and lips — those lips really caught my attention.

The pair stood at the door and asked, in unison, if they could come in. I asked them to sit down and have a cup of chai with me. I remember that they tried their best to pry the secret of my sweetcakes out of me, but to no avail. After they had finished their tea, they hesitated for a moment.

"Would you like to come for supper tomorrow night at our place?" one asked.

"If you don't know where we live we will send a rickshaw for you," the other added.

I tried to maintain a level head; I wanted to be fair, but I did not want to get into a tangle I might regret later. It was difficult to think at all, however, and I ended up saying, "Yes, send the rickshaw. What time will it come?"

I didn't sleep much that night, wondering endlessly what one should do when one receives such an invitation. If Ramana had been there, he would have known an appropriate answer. What should I do? I couldn't go to their place empty-handed. I went to the bazaar in the next town, which was larger than ours, and bought matching *lunghees* for them and a polished white cotton shirt with a rose embroidered on the pocket for their helper.

I hopped onto a bus and was back in my tea shop by the afternoon's opening time. As soon as the crowd in the shop thinned out, I got myself a bucket of warm water and bathed. I got dressed, which is not an involved affair when you wear something as simple as I do. White cloth on the top, white cloth on the bottom, no footwear. I tried sandals once and thought they were murderous. My hair was about the only thing that I could spend time on, and for once I did. I even added a rosebud behind my ear, which elicited comments from my boys. They tried to pry out of me what big affair I was going to, but clammed up when I told them that I was going to the cinema, a line I used when I wanted them to mind their own business.

The rickshaw arrived and took me across town. My hosts lived in a small mud house with four verandahs all around and a neatly kept garden. I found Ganga and Tipu, as they now introduced themselves, sitting on mats on the front verandah with the young man. They all stood up and greeted me warmly. It suddenly occurred to me what an asocial creature I was, hardly ever venturing out of the shadow of my tea shop.

When I handed them my gifts, they seemed stunned. We soon settled down to a rather mixed yet wonderful meal; I had not eaten so well since my sister's marriage. After dinner, we chewed on *paan* (betel leaves), and they brought out a water hookah with six pipes, along with some very good *ganja*. While all of this went on, the young man just hovered around us, pouring water and moving plates. I still did not know his name. He smiled a lot, and when he seemed to purposely brush me, my body shuddered.

"I think you are curious about our friend here, eh?" Tipu said, pointing at the young man as we lounged in a circle.

I nodded as I sucked on the hookah.

"His name is Pratap. He is a mute, born that way. He met a couple of 'evening people' in a town a little ways from here. They took him in but passed him onto another couple after a year." He took a long drag from the hookah. "The second couple, whom we know, were not very kind to him, so he fled from them. We didn't know what to do except to take him in. I want you to know that we haven't slept with him – not to say that we wouldn't have liked to."

As Tipu was telling the story, Ganga was doing some incredible sign language translation for Pratap. He nodded and soon came and settled down near me.

"We started to take him around with us," Tipu continued. "When he first saw you, he wanted to know who you were. He has told us that he would like to go and work with you in the tea shop."

By this point Pratap was leaning against me, and I was as close to joy as I had been since my first love. The feeling filled me, stunned me. I dared not take another puff from the hookah, and yet I did. It laid me out for a full hour. When I finally recovered, I told them that I was in agreement with them except for one detail: I did not want Pratap to work in the shop. I wanted him to stay at home with my mother and keep my part of the house spotless. And perhaps to learn to cook for me. I did not want him to come home with me that night; I had to go to the temple first. I also had to pick up a few things, not to mention giving my mother some explanation.

The next day I again went to their house for dinner, as we had agreed. I was so happy that I showed up bearing more gifts. It was a wonderful evening, one I will never forget. I brought Pratap home with me, and we embraced and loved one another until dawn. Thus began the last of my healing. Now, four years later, I still think about my first love, but with Pratap by my side I am happily reminded that it was not my last.

Finding community

Meera*

I fell in love with Bijli when I was thirteen and she seventeen. How do I describe the Bijli I fell in love with? She was – is – very headstrong, a quality that could at once be endearing and frustrating. She also had a very kind heart. Bijli was good-looking, with a firm jaw that showed her resolve; I found that irresistible. She had a beautiful voice and sang well. Since I played an instrument, we would often play together at my house. We went to movies together, took walks with my dog. We even took a few trips together, though these were always done in the company of other friends.

Bijli and I didn't just discover one day that we were in the throes of a full-fledged love; it happened gradually. It was a part of play, at first. We liked each other a great deal, and one afternoon, when we were alone, it seemed natural to kiss each other. Being older, she had a better sense of what one does in this situation, and I enjoyed every moment of it. At home, I had the luxury of having my own room, which allowed us a good deal of privacy. It is natural for friends to spend nights together, and we took advantage of this. I had two beds in my room. Every morning we would mess up the second bed to give it a slept-in look.

Bijli and I lived in Poona, a small city southeast of Bombay. My parents were upper middle class and my siblings and I grew up speaking both English and our native Sindhi. Like many of my peers, I attended a Catholic school even though I was raised Hindu. I may have thought my feelings perfectly natural, but my world, especially my school, had other ideas. Sex education was a part of the moral science curriculum at this school. I soon learned through these classes that the kind of feelings I was having were wrong, immoral.

This new information made me feel guilty and upset me terribly because I could not change my feelings. I tried to force myself to be interested in boys, and at times I actually thought that I was becoming "normal." But I was fooling myself. At some point I heard the words *lesbian* and *homosexual* and was able to connect them to Bijli and me; I really thought that we were the only two such people in all of India.

The fact that Bijli and I were very close and spent as much time together as possible caused problems with our families, though not quite as you might expect. Customs being as they are in India, it is not unusual to have a same-sex friend, a *yaar* or a *saheli*, who becomes your soul mate, at least platonically. So our families did not at all suspect that we had any sort of romantic involvement. We were out of the house so much, however, that rumors started circulating about us. Because of our budding adolescence and the usual context for adolescence being a heterosexual one, it was passed about that we must be whoring around with boys. Our families were not pleased.

The malicious gossip did much damage and the impact was a lasting one; to this day I will not be party to any conversations or interactions which pass about rumors. At the time, I reacted to the gossip by turning inward. I became more introverted and did not want to have anything to do with people. Having Bijli with me was the saving grace; we gave each other the support needed to get through this horrendous time.

My family was concerned about these rumors about boys, but they were also not crazy about my being with Bijli so much. She came from a middle-class family, and this made a big difference to my family. It is pervasive in India, this disapproval of the mixing of classes, and it made life harder for us. Had they known how we loved one another, they would have come down on us much more harshly.

Context is so important to one's understanding of any situation. It shapes your reality, and it defines your visions of the future. The hopes that you have, the fears that you carry with you, are all based on the knowledge you have of the world around you. We were being raised with the idea that the only possible life for a woman included the presence of a husband. Thus both Bijli and I explored our feelings for boys. I used to tell Bijli that we should find a pair of brothers to marry so that we could live in the same house and continue our relationship. It seemed the closest thing to what we viewed as normal.

When I started college, a lot of the boys I met expressed interest in me. There was one fellow, an Iranian, who was very nice, and I tried to establish some sort of emotional link with him. In the end, with no semblance of this thing called love in sight, I had to tell him that I wasn't attracted to him. He almost slit his wrists. When he told me this, I knew I had to break from him right away. We had spent a lot of time together but had not been involved in a sexual way; we had not even kissed.

Bijli was quite upset about my seeing him. She couldn't understand it and saw it as betrayal. This reaction seemed unreasonable as she was dating a man as well, although she went to great lengths to tell me that I was the one she loved. I saw no reason why I should not have the same option. I knew that I was a lesbian, but the pressure to move toward heterosexuality was too great and I suppose I needed to show myself that it really was not an option for me. I was also jealous of the guy she was dating, although he was the sweetest man. This situation caused much friction between us.

I told no one in my family about our relationship. I did, however, tell one of my schoolteachers; Bijli and I felt that we had to share it with some adult. I was good friends with this teacher, although she was the one who had told me that homosexuality was wrong. Surprisingly, she was rather accepting when I told her. I had spoken to her naively, for there was no guarantee that she would not tell other teachers, or perhaps my parents. She told me that heterosexuality was normal and better for me, but she did it very gently; she did not make me feel at all bad about myself.

I knew no other lesbians throughout this time; I had no idea of what to look for. When I was seventeen, Roy, my older brother, who was then living in England, came out to me. He wrote in one of his letters that he was "a kind of" bisexual. How is one a kind of

236

bisexual? I wasn't sure, but nevertheless, I was happy that he had confided in me. Later, when I went to visit him, I heard him comment on the men we saw in the street. It was fascinating; he appreciated men in a way that was quite unknown to me.

Even though he had opened up to me, I did not feel comfortable telling him about myself. I suppose I was a bit afraid of him. He is eight years older and had bullied me horribly as a child. It's taken me a long time to forgive him for that. Perhaps Roy told me and no one else because he knew that I was pretty open-minded and a feminist. He was also very supportive of my feminist views unless I challenged him.

As I searched for a bit of acceptance from the world around me, I was also struggling to accept myself. In this process I was inspired by the history of the nationalist movement in India. People fighting for their rights – I took that to heart. I figured that there was no reason to let anyone push me around. This caused friction with my parents, since there was the traditional double standard in the house. My brother had wanted to study overseas, and there he was, in England. I wanted to do the same, but they said no; I guess it wasn't enough of an investment for my father to support a daughter in this goal. The traditional Indian view has been that a daughter is destined to leave your household upon marriage, so what time and money you possess is better invested in the son.

I pushed hard against this double standard. My father was firm in his denial. My mother did not exactly stand up for my view either; she was afraid that with higher education I would have difficulty finding a suitable marriage match. What Indian man would want to marry a woman who is better educated? Angry with my parents, I decided that I would take it upon myself to make my dream come true.

When I was eighteen, I went on holiday to England and stayed with Roy. On this trip I got my first view of what it meant to live as a gay person. I would walk up a street and see all of these signs of a healthy, visible gay life. There were gay bars everywhere. It blew my mind! My God! I thought, people actually live together, even openly, and it's okay! I was excited, and I wrote a passionate letter to Bijli. Forget the whole marriage idea, I told her. We can move to England and live together.

Bijli was very happy to hear the news. When I went back home, we began to plan our escape. It became an obsession for us because we wanted so badly to live together. Coming back from England made me even more dissatisfied with what was available to us in India. I had a real hope now, not some vague dream. Several times in the past we had talked about killing ourselves, not because we were unhappy with our love for one another, but because the world around us was so potentially hostile that at times death seemed like the only way out. My trip to England made me realize that life offered a better escape than death ever could.

Since Poona is located close to Bombay, and because there is an ashram for the followers of the self-styled guru Rajneesh in the area, Bijli and I came in contact with a great many foreigners, including many from California. We made the acquaintance of many of these people, realizing that knowing them could make our escape that much easier.

I was twenty-one now, and my family was beginning to exert a lot of pressure on me regarding marriage. I was a bright student and had much ambition, however, and my family could envision me going to college. My sisters were very supportive of my education, though they had no idea of my sexuality. My brother lined up behind me as well. Marriage, of course, could only interfere with this education. So, until the age of twenty-four, college saved me from any more marital pressure.

By the time I turned twenty-five Bijli and I were finally ready to leave India and pursue our dreams. France was our first choice, and I lived there for one year in anticipation of having Bijli join me later. The United States was pretty much the last place I ever wanted to move to; I had always seen it as an imperialistic power. But when things did not gel in Europe, I looked farther west. A lot of the foreign contacts Bijli and I had made in India were with Californians, but it had taken us three years to get our papers in order and to be sponsored; would they remember us?

I came to the U.S. first, and Bijli followed a few days later. We landed in San Francisco, and because of our precarious financial situation, we ended up in the Tenderloin, the roughest part of town. It was fascinating to find that so many of the motels in this area were owned by Gujarati Indians, but of little consolation. Each night we would hear fights and screams. In the middle of the night ambulance sirens would pierce the air and our sleep. It was too much for us. We had some contacts in Santa Rosa, a smaller city in the wine country north of San Francisco, so we decided to head for a bit of peace and quiet.

Our acquaintances in Santa Rosa, some of whom were gay, were very welcoming, though it irritated me a bit that they looked at us as something exotic and expected us to be more spiritually evolved because we were from India. At that time, I wanted to hear very little about India or of my religion. But these people were kind, and we stayed with them as we tried to establish our footing. The rural aspect of Santa Rosa was quite strange, so different from the India we had known. There were no people in the streets of the city. There was little in the way of public transportation. Having Bijli by my side really helped to minimize the strangeness.

I was astounded to find so many women living a gay life in this country. All of my post-childhood life I had been trying to find an identity, a group to be a part of, and now all of this was in front of me. I yearned for a sense of community; I suppose one cannot get away from one's roots, and India is a very community-oriented place.

Now that we had made the journey, Bijli and I faced the challenge of finding work and settling in. Initially, I was willing to do any work to get us started. My first job was in a woodworking shop while Bijli found a position doing office work. I liked my job at first; it was something I would have never done in India. Later I worked at a hospital for mentally retarded people, then I taught English for a while. Eventually I decided to return to school and learn acupuncture, my current profession.

Being in a small city made it easier for Bijli and me to establish our household, but the provincial attitudes did not allow us to talk freely with our neighbors. We had to pretend to be roommates. Being foreign nationals from the same country made things easier; people could understand why we would want to live with one another.

Unfortunately, Bijli and I reacted very differently to our new home. I wanted to explore and see everything, she wanted a home with me. Before long this difference in our perspectives began to cause problems. Bijli had a hard time communicating with and understanding this new culture. I was willing to explore, she was becoming more introverted. We loved each other deeply, however, and we tried to deal with our differences.

Bijli and I received much support from the lesbian community, and for that we were grateful. Yet we both missed the Indian presence, regardless of how much we had wanted to leave my native country. We knew no Indian lesbians in the Bay Area; I did not even think that there could be such a thing here. Still, I discovered the existence of publications like *Manushi* (a feminist magazine in India) and *Connections* (an international magazine for women). They had articles about lesbians in India; this opened my eyes to another world.

In the midst of all of this, the need for an extended family still throbbed inside of me. Each time I thought I was learning something, there would be a new part to the puzzle. There were many things that I had in common with Indian women but not with Americans. Bonding was perhaps the most important of these. I didn't understand this about Americans – I still don't. There is such a big cultural difference. Not a difference between white and brown individuals, but more between those raised in an ultracapitalist system and those born in a relatively less capitalistic and technological culture.

For us Indians, bonds are the most precious things. In the United States, the individual is most important. People are seen as being dispensable. I was to see how this was also a part of the lesbian community in which I sought closeness. I couldn't understand how bonds could be disposed of so easily. I supposed that this was just a part of the bigger capitalist, patriarchal culture around me. I still don't accept this, for I think it deliberately alienates people. I have to be conscious of not taking on this transient approach to bonding. I talk to my white friends about this, and they listen, but I don't think they completely understand; they certainly don't seem to share my view.

After we had been in Santa Rosa for a while, a woman named Kate heard about us and drove into the wine country to see us. Kate had spent some time in India, and she was the first person in this country who seemed to know where I was coming from. I did not have to explain myself to her in detail as I had to with others. I soon found myself feeling an intellectual, comforting attraction for her. She taught me a lot about the feminist movement in India and I developed an immense fondness for her.

I had known Kate for a year when I realized the strength of my attraction to her. I figured that, if anything, it would be an affair, my way of making a family tie, so we became romantically involved. I told Bijli from day one; there was no question of deception. Understandably, it was difficult for her, but she also saw it as an affair and so it was a little easier at first. When things became difficult for her, I told her that there was nothing wrong with loving two people.

On an abstract level, I had always thought of myself as a nonmonogamous person. Monogamy seemed a limiting part of the old, oppressive system, though I never was nonmonogamous. Bijli was very definitely monogamous, in thought and action, and she thought that my view was just bullshit. I've changed my own view since then; I don't think a nonmonogamous relationship really works. I still think that there is nothing wrong with loving two people, but I don't think it is very practical; invariably someone ends up getting hurt.

I tried to time my visits with Kate around Bijli's schedule. Bijli was my primary connection, I was quite clear about that. I did my best not to let her miss me, but how could she not miss me when I was involved with someone else sexually and emotionally? It was disruptive and distracting, yet I felt that I had found a soul mate in Kate, just as I had found one in Bijli years earlier. I don't think one could have compared the two; they meant entirely different things to me.

I was twenty-eight years old when I met Kate; Bijli and I had been together for thirteen years. Eventually I told Bijli that I would not see Kate anymore − Kate and I had also decided that it wasn't working out. I told her that Kate and I would eventually be friends, but I don't think she wanted to hear that. I offered to never see Kate again. Bijli said that I still had not forgotten Kate, which, of course, I had not. I could not just banish Kate from my heart simply by not seeing her.

Bijli was pretty direct about how difficult it was for her, and it was quite hard for me as well. I always thought that we would be together forever – I still think in those terms. I think that all of these breakups we go through can be very destructive for us. Our separation process was long, and the emotional aspect of it took place over several years.

There finally came a time when the tension and pain became too much for Bijli, and she left Santa Rosa for New York, where she had some family. She did come back to Santa Rosa for a bit, but by that time Kate and I were in a relationship. It was rather neurotic; I kept telling Kate that Bijli was my primary relationship still. After Kate and I were together for five years (including the two years while I was still with Bijli), she asked me to make a commitment to her. I declined. To resolve the conflict, we agreed to seek joint counselling.

Through this therapy I realized my role in the turmoil. I realized I must tell Bijli that the separation was going to be permanent. She felt betrayed once again and I felt responsible. I needed to see her settled in her own life, especially since we were in a new country. Although painful for all of us, there was no other way.

Though my joint therapy sessions with Kate gave me some insight, they also left a pretty bad taste in my mouth. Our therapist was a white, middle-class lesbian, and she misrepresented herself when she claimed to be culturally sensitive. She placed no emphasis on my cultural background; how could she understand me without it? Rather, she conveniently put us under the model of codependency. In principle, I understand this concept; it is inherent to both Hinduism and Buddhism. The self has to be taken care of first. But ultimately, you surrender that self. There is a fine line between codependency and nurturing and other cultural variables have to be examined before either label is placed.

This therapist did not realize that Indians, for the most part, get their sense of self through their bonds with others; we have an extended sense of self. She didn't appreciate how inappropriate and destructive her approach was when it ignored cultural differences. Taking care of the self is fine, but getting stuck in that mode leads to selfishness. You know, "How do I love me, let me count the ways."

While Kate and I were undergoing these therapy sessions, Bijli settled in Spain, where her family was now living. Eventually, she began a relationship with a married man, an Indian who lives in New York. She is planning to come to New York next year. He is supposed to divorce his wife so that he and Bijli can live together. But divorce is not an easy matter, especially for an Indian, so who knows what will happen. Our relationship has changed; we are the best of buddies, and she often calls me for advice regarding her relationship.

When Bijli first told me about this man, I thought she had no idea what she was doing. My friends were surprised at how I could be so calm about her being attracted to a man, but that was not really of great concern to me. I knew that she was not changing her sexual orientation or any such thing; that is not under one's control. She had always been honest with me about the fact that she could be attracted to both women and men. Now she had simply met a man who attracted her.

It would have hurt me if Bijli had left me for someone, be that person a woman or a man. But I had already made my choice, and what mattered now was that Bijli had someone new in her life; the gender of that someone was not the issue. I know that Bijli and I will always be like family. Love changes its form but it doesn't go away. If it does, then it was not love to begin with.

My relationship with Kate lasted for six years. She eventually ended the relationship because she felt that I was trying to transform her into Bijli. She found some of the things I expected from her unreasonable. I guess the shadow of Bijli was tough for her, but I didn't see it that way. Before we met, Kate had not been in a relationship for about seven years, and some aspects were hard for her. Three months after I finally made the commitment she had wanted, she decided to leave. That was nearly two years ago, and she has not been able to see me since. It was difficult for me; I loved her very much and did not want to break up with her. When I make a commitment to someone, I can't close the door so quickly.

I guess that this clear break on Kate's part is a part of the American bonding experience that I still do not understand. She had become Aunt Kate to my nieces and nephews and was integrated into my family. She had even stayed with some of my family on occasion. Yet since we broke up, she has totally cut herself off from any of them. No phone calls, no correspondence. Even now that one of my sisters is seriously ill, she has not made any inquiries. That really hurts. How can she make such a clean break? I think it is inappropriate, and I don't pretend to understand her behavior.

Perhaps the difference is cultural, but I find it irresponsible. Feelings and ties should not just vanish like that. It is possible also that we, as gay and lesbian people, don't take our relationships seriously. This internalized homophobia may then make it easier to break away from connections we make through our relationships. After all, if we can break up with our lovers as easily as many seem to, then breaking of other ties is likely to follow suit. The anger and pain that I felt when Kate left have faded. Some sadness remains because Kate is a very fine person in many ways. The things she taught me about life and living were invaluable.

In the last few years I have come across many lesbians in the acupuncture field. I connect with them, but they still cannot relate to some part of me. I have come to realize that there are many different groups that I need and have something to give to, not just lesbians or Indians. There are also men, Indian and non-Indian, whom I consider my friends. In the lesbian community itself, there are many perspectives, which I find to be very healthy. If I had to label myself, I suppose I would say that I am a feminist.

I was very excited when I finally met other Indian lesbians. The first one I met, through Kate, was a woman in India. I don't delude myself into thinking that ethnicity has to be the litmus test for a friendship; what is more important is the way that two given personalities click together. But it is important for me to have the Indian presence in my lesbian community. I am building an extended family for myself now and Indian and non-Indian friends are equally important.

A part of me is still wary of becoming absorbed into any small community – small communities tend to indulge in a lot of gossip. It was long ago that gossip did such damage to me, and yet its memory is clear. Even today there are a few rumors lingering from my life in India. Recently I heard from my family of one such rumor. It's said that as a teenager, I fell in love with a boy from a different caste. When my parents refused to let me be with him, I swore that I would not be with anyone else for as long as I lived. I guess that's their easy way of explaining why I'm not married; people always want such convenient answers. Having seen the pain gossip can cause, I want no part of it.

Despite any difference I might have had with them, my family is as important to me as ever. My brother still lives in London and has been with his current lover for five years; he feels that this one will be lifelong. Our family has had a harder time accepting Roy's gayness than they have mine, perhaps because he is the only male child.

My sisters know about me, and they are my best friends. Since I am the youngest, they have always had a protective feeling for me. My oldest sister experienced the biggest problem with my being a lesbian. She had always been like a second mother to me, and she saw my gayness as just a phase. She took two years to come around, but when she did, it strengthened my faith in the ability of human beings to change. Both of my parents are deceased now, but I did come out to my mother before she died. She surprised me by telling me that she had had a relationship with another girl when she was thirteen.

Today I am thirty-five, and I find that I have gained a new appreciation for my homeland; I think India became more appealing to me when filtered through the distance of another culture. I'm now drawn to some of its philosophy and spiritual teaching. From here, I can choose certain ideals from it rather than buying its reality wholesale, and I am far enough away to not be touched immediately by the exploitation of its people. I feel happy that I have succeeded in finding a place where I can be myself and that I have found community in this new place, without losing sight of my culture and the community it offers.

What what doesn't
happen nowadays!

Kartikeya*

Pragati Maidan, New Delhi. The Indian government's showcase to the world. Site of countless industrial and trade expos, film festivals, and *melas* (fairs). Its architecture and vision of New Delhi itself – rough, uncouth, the twenty-first century without any infrastructure to sustain its facile technology and empty dreams.

Here, amidst the vast glittering magic of merry-go-rounds, puppet shows, and game stalls, I was swept off my feet (quite literally – into a Ferris wheel) by a streetside hero, stocked, barreled, who was now locking me madly in a deep midair kiss as we spun along the axis of the earth.

I had grown up in urban India but left it at seventeen for the seductive attractions of an Ivy League university in America. And though I vividly recalled boyhood sexual exploits with classmates and servants, I returned to India in 1987 assuming that Indian homosexuality belonged to an invisible geography, its existence at best a subterranean reality hidden deep beneath the visible surface of upper-class boarding schools and feudal work environments.

But a summer's night like this seemed to say otherwise. So many slender boys about, hair carefully coiffured, *kajal* (black powder used to line eyes) heavy on the eyes, wandering in dusky twosomes of delight. And my companion on the Ferris wheel drawing the love deep from my mouth, my head snuggled on his bare shoulder, his arm clasped around my yielding waist.

As Shankar and I dissolved in each other's arms that night, we discovered that we were both relative newcomers to the city, still looking for a way to survive and a community to survive with, he as an artist, I as an activist.

Shankar came from a lower-middle-class family which had ostracized him for being openly gay when he was fourteen. "When I was twelve, my father used to give me a weekly bribe to prevent me from showing up at his shop with a made-up face and nails," he recalled with a giggle. "Then a cousin who had just returned from the navy created a hullabaloo because I tried (successfully) to fuck him in the middle of the night. When my pious aunt found out, she shaved my head and conducted a humiliating public exorcism on me.

"I was totally shunned by the family, but this only made me bolder and more thick-skinned. I more or less dropped out of school in class nine, learned to walk the streets, and supported myself by painting shop-boardings and the backs of trucks. You know, 'O.K. TATA' (Tata is a huge Indian corporation), 'HORN PLEASE,' and all that.

"Then a rich designer who had noticed me working in shops near his house picked me up (not just for my artistic talents!) and promoted me for many years through his textile business (or, you could say, promoted his business through me). I got tired of it, and, one day, I just packed a small bag and left for Delhi! O.K. TATA! I was fed up."

Ironically, Shankar continued to send money to his large family every month. "What to do?" he would say. "Despite being perverted and a *harami* (bastard), I'm now the only earning member of the family!"

Within a month of meeting each other, Shankar and I had moved into a modest, sunny *barsati* (top-story terrace apartment) in Jangpura, a very middle-class colony, and we were excitedly setting up our home.

I had been very nervous when Shankar and I had first set out, newspapers in hand, to look for a place to live. We appeared to be such an odd couple, so obviously from different backgrounds, that

I was convinced that we would make all landlords suspicious. I just couldn't bring myself to ask Shankar to tone down his outfit, to not wear makeup for these weekend flat-hunting expeditions. But I prayed, nevertheless, that he would have the good sense to think of it himself.

But come Sunday morning as I waited tensely in the auto-rickshaw, Shankar would emerge from the room, dressed more flamboyantly and stylishly than ever, in yellows and purples and greens and oranges, all designed to make any landlord bolt. Jelly-legged though I was with fear, I admired his confidence and defiance and was exhilarated when we passed the test.

My sister and her husband had just been setting up house in Holland, and I madly wished that I could write long, detailed letters like hers to my mother about house hunting and setting up our new flat. But there was too much to do for the moment to feel sad. There had to be lots of plants for the small terrace, and pots and pans and cups and plates, a good stack of grains and groceries, and a desk and two beds (the extra one for visitors).

The first night together in the *barsati* was magical. Here he was, Shankar, soft and strong, stunningly beautiful, minus the gel, eye pencil, and mascara, kitten and acrobat all rolled into one. Our slender brown limbs heaved and entwined and scissored under the cool moonlight, hot and throbbing with the life force, rushing with flowing sap. Such delicate, subtle layers of desire, thrill unlocked from every bud, every pore on the body, breath drenched and delighted.

As we wrestled and rolled, locked in the most impossible positions, Shankar glimpsed four men standing on the terrace overlooking our bedroom, watching and silently stroking their crotches. He leaped out of bed to draw the curtains, but soon a half-eaten apple came hurling through the window, the pleading of frustrated desire.

Our neighbors were Afghani men who spent their lives packed together in two crowded terrace rooms similar to ours, starved for friends and freedom, temporarily marooned in a city that was hostile or indifferent to them. For several nights following our free performance, many of them would ring our doorbell, in desperate search for release and solace. Shankar and I were too scared of a rough gang bang to let them in. I mean, six of them would show up at a time, high out of their minds. Three would have been another matter! But so many. No, baba!

The half-eaten apples, part longing, part invitation, part threat, became a regular feature, both angering us with their intrusion and exciting us with their raw passion and potential. On some nights, noticing only one or two of the Afghani studs out wandering the terrace, lonely figures in the moonlight, we would discreetly leave the curtains to our dark, seething bedroom undrawn.

One evening, soon after we had moved in, I was accosted with rude gestures and loud, abusive jeers by a group of teenage boys playing cricket in the neighborhood park. I walked on, pretending to ignore them, but red in the face from shame and confusion, until I heard one of them shout, "Hey, homo, want to suck my cock?"

Desperately trying to maintain a calm, elegant front, but trembling inside with anger and fear, I stopped and turned around.

"Okay, who wants his cock sucked?" I asked, amazed at my own boldness.

There was utter, unbearable silence, except for someone's mother calling out from a nearby balcony to not make trouble and come right home. This was followed by the group of snickering, uncertain, macho boys nudging one of their own forward. His name was Rajiv, and he seemed to have made the remark.

"What happened?" I continued, flushed and sweating by now. "One of you is man enough to ask for a blowjob but too scared to actually get one! You can't get it up or what?"

At this, Rajiv lunged out, cricket bat in hand, his mouth pouring forth filth, his every pore playing to the cheering gallery. Seizing me by the collar, he hissed, "I'll ram your ass, homo!"

I immediately and firmly pushed him off. "You can't get it up for me to suck you off, how will you get it up to fuck me?" I scoffed and started to walk away. "Next time any of you wants a blowjob, come to Y-12!" And then, lest they get the mistaken impression that homos provide services for free, added, "And have the decency to bring some money with you!"

Before long, everyone in the locality and nearby market recognized Shankar and myself as the couple from Y-12, and, much to our surprise, left us alone, even when they saw us walking arm-in-arm and passionately kissing under trees and in auto-rickshaws.

Shankar was my introduction to the vast gay culture in Delhi, from the gullies of Chandni Chowk and cruising spots in Connaught Place, to the closets of journalists and bureaucrats, to the living rooms of glamorous designers. All of his friends were women or gay men. Some were dancers and hairdressers, some drove rickshaws, many were struggling artists, a few were prostitutes, and others were domestic servants.

The color and theatricality of their lives was overwhelming to me at first, as was the very fact of their existence. There were queens from Chandni Chowk, originally from northeastern India, who would work in dreary government offices during the day and do *mujras* (traditional dances of courtesans) on our terrace at night. There was Barry and his mother, Norma, both cabaret dancers from Bangalore, who were forever ready to organize mock weddings, whose vast network of Anglo-Asian friends always cheered us up when we were depressed, and who drank with us in celebration when we put together enough money to pay the rent each month.

Barry's sister, Lata (born of a Hindu father, Norma was quick to explain), mentally retarded since childhood, practically lived with us, and methodically circulated lurid details of the goings-on in our *barsati* to all the domestic servants in the neighborhood. "I know you are all homos," she would scream. "I saw you putting it into his mouth last night. Don't you try to fool me. My name is Lata, Lata, Lata!"

Our little *barsati* soon became a meeting point for all kinds of drifters and wanderers and, as my landlord once complained, "antisocials." This last label would puzzle me, as social interaction, eroticism, and homosexuality flourished all over those tiny rooms on the terrace.

In the beginning, all the flamboyance and wildness threatened my "straight" and "good-boy" self-image. "Why do you have to make such a point of being different, of standing out?" I would complain to Shankar, as I put on my starched white shirt while he deftly *kohl*-penciled (a black cosmetic powder) his eyes before going to work in the morning.

And he would respond angrily. "You straight-appearing men are too much! You wear a shirt and tie during the day and fling your legs up for another man at night. And then you say that something is wrong with me for 'standing out'! Let me tell you, I might paint myself and appear whorish, but at least I am not spending all my life trying to fit in to someone else's idea of what makes a real man."

He would say that this same masculine norm that I was trying to fit into was being used to define unmarried women and homosexuals as deviant and abnormal, even sick. It was that norm which was fucked up and worth attacking, not his "standing out" against it.

Each of our friends was wilder than the other, but the style and eccentricity seemed to me very different from the phony gender-bender fashions and posturing so trendy in liberal universities in the West and in upper-class cultures the world over.

We would drink and dance and gossip together, cook a meal, then go walk the streets and alleys and main thoroughfares, stopping trucks and taking wild, sex-filled rides to neighboring Haryana state, cruising around taxi stands and construction sites, propositioning policemen.

Sixteen-year-old Pakeezah would kick one ballet leg up toward the sky to taunt everyone who passed by. Twenty-year-old Bali would remove his turban and let his dyed hair down to shock the wits out of the ritzy crowd in Nirula's. Forty-year-old Mahesh, built like a mountain, would wear shimmering black dresses and a mad parrot on his hairy shoulder to crowded Connaught Place, not caring what people said to him because he could not hear, literally. He was deaf! (His parrot would pick up people's rude remarks and hurl them back at them.) As an aunt, on meeting some of my friends, remarked with characteristic frankness, "What what doesn't happen nowadays!"

And, in our colorfully constructed *"rundi* (whore) talk," we would share our hurts and cynicism about love and commit ourselves to acting like whores to straight men and respectable society. The language and the style were a way of making fun of a puritanical, perverted world that insisted on labeling homosexuals as perverted – us healthy, generous, kind, and sex-loving people.

An insane god

Hyder Ali*

A semi-autobiographical story

"Bloody hell! How can she say such things?" Shahab fumes, one hand clutching the letter he has written in response. He is not exactly fluent when it comes to English expletives, but he prefers not to curse his mother in their native Urdu, a language he has always used to sing her praises.

From the distance comes the ringing of the clock tower bells, signaling the townspeople to awaken to a new day full of work. This morning the bells mean nothing to him. He has spent the whole night in the courtyard, sitting or standing, more often pacing, sometimes lying down and futilely reaching for sleep. His restlessness is not unwarranted, for he is at the brink of a momentous decision.

Shahab scrutinizes his dilemma from every angle possible, yet each time his mother's eyes bore into him. From some angles her face shines with a smug smile; from others it fixes him with a characteristic severity. It is a face that has sheltered him from the world, a face that has deprived him from the company of other living things. He fingers the letter in his hand, feeling the tightness of the bond that she refuses to relinquish.

All through childhood she took great care of him, loved him as much as any mother could. Beneath that love was a desperate grasp that would not allow anyone else close to him. Nobody was good enough for him except she herself. She clung to him so tightly that she seemed to lose all sense of boundaries. He belonged to her, not as her child, but as her property. She thought of him as being shapeless, just waiting for her life-giving hands to mold him into something extraordinary.

Shahab's mother comes from a conservative, aristocratic family. The principality this family calls home was tiny, but it boasted, until recently, its own *Nawab* (ruler). Now that power is gone and the prestige waning, but the old ways and thoughts hold on tenaciously. As a youth, Shahab's mother had not been able to stomach this relic. She became a radical who thought she would take the world by storm, but the world turned out to be more sturdy than she had envisioned. Rather than admit defeat, she turned all of her energy and passion upon her son, guiding him toward her failed goals.

So often Shahab had fallen short, but who can blame him when the motivation always came from her? Too often his goals were to simply get through each day, to pass each hurdle that she set for him. He did all he could to keep her at bay, for if he did not, her retribution was swift and harsh: she would simply stop talking to him, and he knew no greater terror. The dependence he had built upon her, though of her design, would fill him with uncertainty and guilt. He had no one else to trust, no one to turn to, for she had long been his sole emotional link with life.

Even as Shahab grew older, she continued to monitor his every move. She would decide whom he should associate with, when, and where. She needed proof of his love for her constantly, and nothing he did was enough to satisfy her appetite. Consequently, he came to mirror all of her own insecurities. When he appealed to her sentiment, she would hold it up as proof that she was more genuine, more giving, than others. As a tool of sheer survival, he developed an uncanny ability to gauge her moods. He would submit to these moods, aware that only in this manner could he avoid her silence. Seizing upon his submissiveness, she would rail at him for not being manly enough.

A year ago, when he had finished his education and taken a job with a businessman in a nearby city, Shahab's mother decided her son should get married. All of his relatives and friends joined in, exhorting him to fulfill his destiny as a man. The marriage would bring comfort to his aging mother, they told him, and it would help him achieve *Sunna* in the Islamic tradition of the prophet.

If he had joined any of his friends who were "bad" enough to go womanizing, if he could have visualized women as something other than mothers, aunts, and sisters-in-law, he might have known what it meant to get excited, to fall in love, to get married. But he was the good boy that his mother and the rest of his relatives expected him to be. He did not know that double standards came as naturally to these people as they later claimed attraction for women should come to him.

As with many issues, he gave in to marriage. The ceremony was adequate, if not memorable. The girl chosen for his bride was named Ghazala, and he did not see her face before their wedding night. She was simple, nice in her own way, as "good" as any good girl. On the wedding night, and every subsequent night, their bedroom door (in his mother's house) closed behind them, opening only in the morning.

On the eighth day after the wedding, Shahab told his mother and Ghazala that he must now go back to his work in the city of Rampur. In keeping with tradition, his new bride would stay with her mother-in-law. As he left his mother's house and headed for the bus stand, he promised that he would be back on Sunday. Fortunately for him, the bus had arrived. He dropped his bag on one seat, then hurried to purchase a pass. As Shahab returned to the bus, he spied Abbas, the teenaged son of the village's lone postman, fidgeting by a broken gate.

"What are you doing here, Abbas?" Shahab asked warmly.

"Nothing, sir, nothing really," the boy replied.

At that moment the bus driver sounded his horn.

"Khuda hafiz." Shahab murmured the traditional Islamic good-bye.

"Khuda hafiz," Abbas answered in farewell.

The bus trip was uneventful, as was Shahab's work week. The following Sunday he went back to his village, as promised, staying but one night. Over the next few weeks he followed this same routine, inventing excuses that allowed him to stay away even when he had extra free time. Ghazala was a stranger to him in many ways. His mother and other relatives seemed to have no complaints about her, however, and for that he was thankful.

On a particularly bright Sunday in June, the postman came to see Shahab. He informed Shahab that his son, Abbas, had graduated from high school and had gained admission into Rampur College. Would Shahab be so kind as to take Abbas to the city with him and help him find accommodations? This was the postman's subtle way of requesting that Shahab allow Abbas to stay with him.

Shahab's residence was a small, dilapidated portion of a once-grandiose mansion, the legacy of a granduncle. It was somewhat isolated, as the nearest neighbor was a good half mile away. The one room had once been used for storage. It had never had a proper floor, and the roof leaked abundantly. The walls were still intact, and the porous ceiling was a good fifteen feet high. There was a nice verandah in the front, and an open courtyard that had once boasted the highest walls in this part of town, but was now over-grown with weeds and overrun by reptiles and rodents. During the monsoon season, staying inside the room was hazardous. Shahab had little choice, for accommodations in the city were beyond his means.

The postman, knowing all of this, still hoped that Shahab would take in his son, since he earned even less money than Shahab. Shahab made the offer, as was proper. The postman played his part in this curious game of etiquette, saying no, he could not possibly inconvenience his benefactor. Shahab repeated the offer a few more times and finally Abbas's father accepted.

Abbas and Shahab left on the bus the following day. Their arrival into Rampur was auspicious. The bus had barely pulled into the city when monsoon clouds broke open loudly. Shahab and his young charge were chilled to the bone by the time they reached the small room. The courtyard was flooded and the roof was leaking every-where but over one corner of the room, where Shahab had placed his one cot. He found a few dry crevices for the handful of items they had brought with them. Then he and Abbas changed into some dry clothes and slipped into bed.

Two grown men getting into bed together might seem odd, an invitation for something to happen. But in this part of the world, cots and beds are in short supply. It is natural for two men or two women to share a bed under these circumstances.

The rain lasted all night and throughout the next day, the water falling with a fierceness neither man had witnessed before. Lesser rains had brought cities like Rampur to a near standstill; this herd of thunderheads immobilized the entire town, trapping the towns-people in their houses. Shahab's isolated home was cut off. Had it not been for some homemade biscuits that Abbas's mother had packed for him, Shahab and the boy would have gone hungry.

With the rain unabating, Abbas felt truly miserable. If his admission card was not deposited at the principal's office today, his admission to the college would be revoked. Shahab could not bear to look at the youth's misery, and he decided to walk the admission card to the principal's office himself. He packed the paper in four plastic bags, one inside another, clutched his withered umbrella, and set out for the school.

Shahab was gone for seven hours. For Abbas it seemed like an eternity, and he was half-dead with fright by the time his benefactor returned. Shahab explained to the youth that the principal's office had not been open, so he had found the man's residence and handed over the card personally. Now he was tired, every stitch of clothing soaked. Wearily he slipped into his pajamas and crawled onto the cot.

Shahab had not been in bed long before he began shivering, feeling the chill as he had not outside. Abbas covered him with every dry piece of cloth he could find. Still Shahab lay shivering. After a few more minutes he began to slip out of consciousness. Abbas was truly frightened now. What more could he do? His mind struggled to think of how he could help Shahab.

As Abbas's mind raced frantically, he remembered a scene from a Hindi film he had seen recently. A young man and his woman friend were snowed in on a hillside, trapped in a small cottage. The woman was very ill, wracked with chills. Her lover had taken off every stitch of clothing, laid it on top of the woman, then crawled in beside her to keep her warm. In a matter of seconds he lay nude beside Shahab, all of his clothing draped across the sick man.

By evening of that second day Shahab had recovered from his chill. The rain did not let up, falling with varying intensity for another week. Shahab and Abbas, however, did not care if the clouds never dispersed. They had found more than comfort in the small bed. In the bodies and eyes of one another, they had discovered a whole new world. They were not ready to leave this world and the storm offered a perfect excuse to continue exploring one another.

After the arrival of Abbas, Shahab's visits to his home village became less frequent. They were quite happy together and the months passed without notice. Shahab's mother, on the other hand, was extremely unhappy. Her son had begun to ignore the commands he had never questioned before, and worse yet, he was beginning to talk back to her. Ghazala had followed suit, and the older woman now found her hard to manage.

On one of Shahab's rare visits, his mother asked him to take Ghazala back to her parents' house; she could no longer bear the young woman's presence. Shahab had mixed feelings about the request. It would be an affront to Ghazala and her family, and yet it would be tantamount to divorce and thus would free him from one obligation. So he complied. Poor Ghazala had no choice in the matter. She had never understood why her husband stayed away so much, but it was not her place to demand an explanation. In a way, she too was now being released from an uncomfortable situation she was powerless to change.

As the months passed, Shahab's mother began to grow restless. She thought that, at his age, her son should be married once more. She began a campaign to convince him, pestering him more each time he visited her. He reacted by returning home even less. About this time Abbas was finishing his first year of studies at the college. When the term ended, he returned to the village for the summer. In his absence Shahab found Rampur drab and unsatisfying. Three days later he gave up and followed his lover to their village.

When Shahab arrived at his mother's house, she seized the opportunity to wear him down. The poor fellow had no relief, for she had recruited many of their relatives to reinforce everything she had to say. Everywhere Shahab went in the village he was reminded of his need for another wife. Throughout the day he would be told to think about his aging mother and her happiness. If Abbas had not been there, Shahab might well have buckled under the pressure. Every day they would go to the mosque for sunrise prayers. After prayer they would go on long walks into the countryside and not return until well into the afternoon.

This routine quickly became comfortable for Shahab, and he lost sight of other annoyances. He was surprised then, when a group of the village elders confronted him one afternoon. They grilled him for hours about various details of his life. One of them had spied

Shahab and Abbas in a field this morning. They were not accus-
tomed to speaking about such matters openly, and made references
to the situation in rather oblique ways. Shahab was closemouthed,
which did not please the elders. Fortunately for him, a local politician
picked that afternoon to visit the village. As soon as the elders
received word of his visit, they dispersed and Shahab was left to his
own devices.

When the young man arrived home, his mother had already
heard the whole story.

"Why weren't you more convincing with your replies?" she
questioned. "Why did you not say anything?"

"What account of my life could I give anyone?" he replied
nebulously. "How can I give them any answers when they ask all
the wrong questions?"

Her reply was neither as opaque nor as gentle as his. She let him
know what she thought of him and his activities, and she was no
kinder toward Abbas. He was anathema to her, and she raked his
name through the mud until it made Shahab want to scream. Who
can bear to witness his lover torn apart by another? She railed at him
until she tired herself and withdrew for the night.

That was last night. Now he paces the courtyard, wonders if he
has the strength to make a difficult choice. What will happen if he
takes Abbas away from here, with no thought of coming back? Will
Abbas agree to leave everyone behind just to be with him? If he is
willing, what will they find out there? Won't the problems be the
same wherever they go? Will it be possible for them to really find
happiness with one another? The thoughts bombard Shahab, and all
are answered harshly by some corner of his being that is yet ruled
by his mother.

Shahab thinks back to the words his mother uttered last night,
words that left him feeling hollow. Now they only fill him with anger
and resolve. He sits down, closes his eyes. He is startled by the
morning call to prayers from the mosque. The same call he has
heard all his life is a signal for him, a call to action. He reaches for a
bucket of water, performs his ablutions. He reads once again the
note he wrote late last night. Yes, this is the only decision that he can
make. All others would lead him back to the oppressive yoke of his
unrelenting mother.

Shahab tiptoes into his mother's room, places the note soundlessly beside her bed. Gathering a few necessities, he moves through the courtyard quietly and is soon past the front gate. He pauses for a moment then, stares straight ahead at the mosque where Abbas will soon meet him. He looks beyond the mosque, to the bus stand. In a few minutes a bus will be ready to go. He is ready. Regardless of how his mother reacts, he now knows that he has made the only decision possible. Even if Abbas should disagree and turn away from him, the rightness of his decision would remain. He smiles to himself, confident of the first decision that is really his own. He takes one last look at the house, then takes his first step toward the sun that will soon rise to welcome him.

Outside her experience

Ashok Jethanandani

She emerged from the plane, the pink flowers on her sari fluttering in the wind. Except for the silver hair and a few more inches on the waist, she looked exactly like my mother – the small, round face, light skin, dark glasses, and flawless teeth that she flashed at me when she spotted me waving from the crowd. Soon we had our arms wrapped around each other.

"Did you have any trouble changing planes in Atlanta?" I asked. This was Putli Auntie's first trip out of India, and only her second flight. The first flight had been from New Delhi to Philadelphia to visit my brother Vijay. The domestic flight to San Jose was almost as long as the hop across the Atlantic, but she looked excited and energetic.

"No, Vijay explained everything to me," she replied. "Here, take these. I saved them for you." She rummaged through her purse and handed me a packet of honey-roasted peanuts.

"Tan musan Sindhi mein galhayo," I managed to say in my broken Sindhi, asking her to speak to me in our native language. *"Mukhe Sindhi galhayan ji practice khape"* ("I need to practice my Sindhi").

We were driving down the 101 freeway, just approaching the hills of eastern San Jose. It was an unusually cold December, and the hills were capped with snow.

"This looks just like Shimla," she exclaimed, comparing it to a hilly resort in the Indian state of Himachal Pradesh. I pointed out Lake Cunningham to our left and promised that we would go there for a walk soon.

As we parked the car and entered our house, Arvind came skipping down the stairs.

"Arvind!" Auntie exclaimed, not waiting for any introductions. She gathered him into a warm embrace. I beamed at them, amused to see Arvind's respectful Bihari *pranam* (greeting) muffled by the warmer, more physical Sindhi greeting. The sight warmed me, and I thought of how only a year before I had shown Arvind's photograph to Auntie and told her how much I wanted the two of them to meet.

That had also been during the month of December. We were all gathered in our home in the outskirts of New Delhi for my brother's wedding; Mahesh is my youngest brother and his wedding would be the last in my family. By that time my parents had reached an impasse in their attempts to change my mind about marriage. "We don't want to discuss it anymore," Daddy had remonstrated the last time the word *gay* had entered our conversation.

I did not bring it up anymore. Not with Daddy. But I continued to share my life with Mummy, my brothers and their wives, my cousin-sister, my favorite aunts and uncles, and my classmates from high school and college. In short, I shared it with everyone I felt close to, especially those who expressed an interest in my personal life.

"If you don't tell other people, what difference will it make to you?" Mummy asked me genially, her voice betraying the anxiety she felt.

"I can't pretend anymore, Mummy. I can't pretend to be single. Arvind is an important part of my life. I can't talk about myself without talking about him also. I will not hide my relationship with Arvind from the people I feel close to."

A dark cloud passed over her face then, turned her expression quite serious. "But do you think they will understand? This is so far removed from their experience. What good does it do to tell them?"

Every day more relatives arrived for the wedding. Space was limited, but no one minded sleeping on the floor. My younger cousins were having the greatest time chasing each other up and down the stairs. Their elders passed the time catching up on one another's lives. Mummy's relatives were given a separate room upstairs, but when I went up to that room, only Putli Auntie was inside.

261

"Oh, Ashok *lala* (son)!" she shouted in greeting, obviously in her usual joyous mood. "Come, sit down." As we sank into the cot it creaked. "I have seen just the right girl for you. You only have to say when."

"I am not getting married, Auntie," I replied. "I already have a partner."

"That is different. I am talking about a girl, a life partner, not a friend."

"Yes, Auntie, I know. That's what he is to me – a life partner."

"Are you telling me that you do with him what you would do with a girl?" She was catching on faster than I had expected.

"Yes, although not exactly. We have sex, we love each other. We live together and have a very complete–"

"But that's impossible. How can it be?"

"His name is Arvind, and he is really–"

"That is impossible." She was genuinely perplexed and wasn't listening anymore.

"Wait. I will show you a picture of him." I fetched our portrait photo from my suitcase downstairs. When I returned, she still had the same quizzical look on her face. She looked at the picture. Both Arvind and I looked rather stiff, me sitting on a chair, Arvind standing close by with his arm on my shoulder. We had worked up the courage to go to the studio and the photographer had immediately put one and one together, and pegged us as a couple. He did his best to get a good photograph, but all of his cajoling failed to make us loosen up. We did not hold each other tighter and his jokes failed to make us smile. We stared solemnly at the camera.

"He looks like a nice boy," Putli Auntie commented.

"He is," I replied. "I want you to meet him sometime."

❖

"Come, let me show you the house," I said as she now looked about the house I shared with Arvind.

Auntie marveled at everything she saw – the harmonium and the *tanpura* ("Oh, I can play these when I sing my *bhajans* [hymns]"), the batik paintings that I had bought in Calcutta and mounted in the frames myself ("This looks just like India"), and the spotless kitchen counters with the spice rack ("You even have *kukam* spice").

262

After she had her fill of the kitchen, I took her upstairs to the bedrooms. "This is Arvind's and my room," I told her.

Auntie peered in. Arvind and I stared back at her from our framed portrait that sat on the bedside table. It looked like any other bedroom, although neater than usual. The carpet was vacuumed, the sheets changed, the comforter folded below the pillows, the windowsills dusted, and the lube and condoms tucked into the drawer. She didn't say anything. Finally, I took her to the guest bedroom and helped her settle down.

During her stay, Auntie did not discuss our gay relationship. Arvind and I continued to sleep and shower together, and we cuddled each other in her presence. Putli Auntie, meanwhile, had established a daily routine of her own. Deeply religious and perpetually in a joyful state of mind, Putli Auntie was an easy guest to please. Every morning she would read aloud a *paath* (prayer) from the *Guru Granth Sahib* (holy book). Then she would follow me to the garage and watch me practice my *bharatanatyam* dance. She never tired of watching the same dances every morning. When I finished, I would find her lost in the stories about Lord Krishna or Shiva that I had enacted in my dance.

We could not keep Auntie out of the kitchen. At first, we insisted on cooking for her. Eventually, however, she had her own way. She would cook different vegetables with a variety of spices while Arvind looked on, jotting down the recipes on his writing pad. Always respectful of older people, Arvind gave her a lot of attention. When she offered to sing *bhajans* for us, he recorded the entire session.

During her stay, I realized that I had never really known Putli Auntie before. While growing up I had always thought of her only as Mummy's sister who always brought sweets for the kids when she visited. We would greet her respectfully, then go away to play. Her visits were always brief, and we would not see much of her until it was time to say good-bye.

Whatever I knew about Putli Auntie came from the bits and pieces of her life that Mummy had shared with me. The prettiest of the girls in her family, she had been married at the age of eighteen. They did not hear much about her except when she gave birth to a son. Later, a neighbor of hers had reported to the family that her husband was intercepting her letters and that her life was in danger.

263

Upon hearing this, her father and brothers had helped her escape from her husband.

My grandfather had been deeply shocked by this experience. He sent her to college and helped her get a job with Indian Railways. With time she divorced her husband, but she did not get custody of her son, who died a few years later.

"I was happy as a child," she confided to me one day, "and unhappy in my youth. But I am happiest now." She took great pleasure in describing her daily routine in detail. Getting up at five. Tea. Brushing her teeth, bathing. A visit to the neighborhood temple. Cooking breakfast and lunch. Taking the rickshaw to work. Then reading the *Guru Granth Sahib* for an hour ("My supervisor makes sure that no one disturbs me for an hour") before making entries to the accounts ledger.

Arvind and I took Auntie to many tourist spots in San Francisco – Golden Gate Park, Fisherman's Wharf, Chinatown, Twin Peaks – but she was happiest at home, chatting with us. All too soon, it was time for her to leave. We asked her to extend her stay, but she had already used up all her vacation. When Arvind said *pranam* to her, she hugged him and said, "Take care of my Ashok."

I drove her back to San Jose International Airport. When it was time to board the flight, she hugged me. "Next time you come to India, you must visit me in Ajmer. And bring Arvind with you. I have a small house with few modern amenities, but do come and stay with me."

It was windy out that day. I watched Putli Auntie's sari flutter as she climbed laboriously up the steps. She reached the top, turned around and waved at me, then disappeared into the plane.

Extended family

Lakshmi* & Arka*

Arka and Lakshmi both come from the Indian state of Bengal.
They are both bisexual, are happily married, and have been
together for many years. In this frank dialogue, excerpted from an
interview, they chart their experiences, individually and together.

Arka: From my earliest memories I know that I have been attracted
to both men and women. My first sexual experience occurred in
Calcutta, India, when I was seven or eight years old. I was visiting
a friend whose sister and younger brother were also in the house. At
some point in our play we began to explore one another's bodies. I
remember being especially intrigued by the girl's body and how it
differed from mine. Our exploration consisted of looking and touching, not much more.

My first sexual experience with a guy happened when I was
eleven. A neighborhood boy who was thirteen years old at the time
taught me how to masturbate. I don't think I labeled our interaction
in any way, and I had no clue about homosexuality as a concept. I
heard the word *homo* for the first time when I was twelve years old.
It sounded like a Bengali word to me. I certainly didn't connect it to
myself.

During adolescence I had some extremely close relationships
with boys, though I suppose these guys could not be called lovers if
sex is a prerequisite for the definition. The first happened at the age
of fifteen. I had a close friend in school who was, and still is,
extremely committed to me. We never had sex, but we were very
physically affectionate with each other. Today he is in India, and I
rarely correspond with him. But the moment I arrive for a visit, he
is there. I spend most of my time in India with him.

265

Lakshmi: He is very possessive, in a protective way. I think that his protectiveness is very much like a relationship.

Arka: In some ways I would call it a relationship. But I think he has no expectations of me, nor I of him. I rarely think of him except when I am visiting Calcutta. He knows that I am bisexual and has no problems with it.

Getting back to my adolescence, I recall that I was always equally comfortable with the company of boys and girls as friends. This embarrassed a few of the girls, for I would joke around them just as I would around the boys. Their sex role dictated, of course, that they be outraged by such behavior. Around the age of twelve I had my first crush on a girl. It remained that, just a crush. Then again, near the end of high school, I became involved seriously with a girl. This affair remained quite platonic; we were totally in love, but we never talked about it and nothing happened between us sexually.

Then I went to college. There was a guy in my class who was very different from me. His name was Arindam, and he was extremely outgoing, whereas I was shy. He was everyone's friend, and initially I hated him. But within two or three months we were the best of friends.

Lakshmi: Arindam is very closed off, focused, and seems to know just what he wants. He is quite uncomfortable if we talk about homosexuality, yet he is very devoted to Arka. When Arka and I met, Arindam tried to help our romance along. We all became quite close.

Arka: With this guy the physical aspect was much more pronounced. Maybe because it was at an older age (eighteen), and we were suitably hard and horny all the time. Nothing explicitly sexual happened with us, but a few times we came close. We would sleep embracing each other. He would throw his arms around me as we sat in public. Of course that sort of affection between men is accepted in India and is not considered sexual.

Lakshmi: Arindam interpreted it as affection only, but there was something else there also.

266

Arka: Just before I came to the U.S., our last year of school, things became pretty bad between us. I think we both had many unmet expectations. When we started to drift, he tried to revive our former closeness. He was quite hurt in the end. After I left, he got out of the relationship completely. Now when I go back, I feel affection for Arindam but nothing sexual. He got married a while back, but I think he has a strong latent bisexuality. I'm sure he's aware of it, and he came closest to expressing it with me.

The only real sexual experience I had during my time in India was with a girl. It was no emotional attachment, just physical stuff...

Lakshmi: [*Laughing*] Just fumblings.

Arka: Kissing and stuff. I did kiss a couple of my friends in a sexual manner, but nothing more. There was one guy in the college who wanted to have sex with me, but he was very homophobic. I turned him down. I was not politically aware or anything like that, but I didn't understand why he would want to do something that he thought was wrong. He is in the U.S. now and claims that he is straight. We are not close, but I am tempted to pounce upon him one of these days and make him face his feelings. It would do him some good. During the last year of college, Arindam introduced me to Lakshmi. That was seven years ago.

Lakshmi: It was five months before he held my hand. I was really out of it too.

Arka: I was very shy and cautious. It was my first time at a real relationship.

Lakshmi: It was a first for me also. I guess my first childhood sexual experiences happened without my being aware of them. I was the younger of two sisters and we were brought up in an insulated family. Romanticized ideas of marriage were our full expression of sex. As a child I am sure I was very sexual. I masturbated a lot without ever calling it that. You know, one has a sense of pleasure about one's own body, and I did. At home (in India), however, it is not really given representation. Still, my older sister and a girl cousin discussed sex a lot, so I grew up quickly in some ways.

My earliest identifiably sexual feelings were toward men. Starting at the age of eleven I was attracted to many. At the age of sixteen I had a major crush a guy who worked on behalf of slum dwellers, but I never did anything about it.

I had a few relationships during my years in a convent school. As is Arka's case, none of these were overtly sexual. This was an all-girls school, and these experiences were with my friends, one of whom I had known since I was four years old. She was my first best friend and was extremely possessive of me well into college. That was my most committed relationship, though it was not sexual. I think she is a lesbian. She went into a graduate program in India when I came to the States. She visited me last summer in Calcutta, when Arka and I were getting married. She mentioned that she was very close to a woman and had a lot to tell me. I waited for her to tell me more and wanted to tell her about myself, but in the end we both let fear get the best of us and said nothing about it.

I had a similar relationship with another friend who now is in this country also. She, one other friend, and I would huddle together under the covers on long, warm afternoons and talk about sex, including homosexuality. A lot was said about homosexuality in school, yet we never applied the label to ourselves.

I came closest to an actual sexual contact with another girl, one my mother did not care for and constantly warned me about. I always wondered why. There was nothing different in her appearance, though she was extremely sexual. Once we went on a holiday with our mothers and my mother was annoyed to find us sitting or sleeping together. I think that girls, in general, become aware of their bodies later than boys, but I knew at this time that I liked to hold my friend.

Then I went off to college. During my first year there I met Arka. People sometimes tell me that he is gorgeous, but that didn't occur to me when we first met. We were interested in the same things and just hit it off. Three months later we decided to have some kind of commitment. At the end of that school year he left for the United States.

That year at home I came to terms with myself in some ways. I had always thought of myself as being monogamous; it was an ideal.

I was coming to question that ideal. Arindam and I were still close friends after Arka left, and there were some sexual feelings. At one point we went to a festival, got drunk, and were physical with each other. I became aware that there were other people I could be sexually attracted to; it was not a function of Arka being around. Then came the question of whether I could allow myself to act on the feelings. I think this was the time when my feminist leanings first started.

I was not yet aware of my bisexuality. I was romantically committed to many of my women friends, but there was no overt sexual component, and I did not interpret it as evidence of bisexuality. Throughout that year Arka would write to me and discuss bisexuality on an intellectual level. I would say that, yes, I can appreciate the beauty of another woman's body, but is that bisexuality? Through our letters we would argue back and forth. Although my grasp of the subject was intellectual, the reality of it did not repulse, I did not feel homophobic.

Arka: In my college on the East Coast there were many foreign students. I was twenty-one years old, having come as a junior, while most of the others were eighteen. One of them, Stefan, was from Germany. We met through mutual friends. For the next four days we talked nonstop, withdrawing only to sleep in our respective rooms. Classes had not started yet. Within a month we were the best of friends. It was really nice. At home I had had so many close friends, and he was like them. He was only eighteen, but awesome. Bright, dazzling. Two months later, on a walk one night, he asked me what I thought about us. He had a girlfriend in Europe at the time, but things were not going well. I evaded the question.

Two weeks later I was visiting in his room. There was a storm that night, so I stayed over. The next night the same thing happened, but this time we became physically involved. At some point I tried to stop it. I told him he was getting too serious and reminded him that my girlfriend would be coming the following year. He didn't care. He was having a good time, he said, and wouldn't give up the present while thinking about the future. I thought that was an astonishingly good argument. So we went on, and none of the people around us figured out our relationship.

269

There was another Indian at the college who was the campus heartthrob. I knew he was gay, though he was closeted. Except for one short bit, we were not sexually involved. Both the foreign student population and the campus gay group were quite large. We came together and called ourselves "the Marginalists." It was a wonderful time, as the two groups mingled marvelously. People who were not gay seemed to take on a bisexual persona. This environment made me sure of myself and encouraged me to express my ideas. I became the catalyst in the coming-out process of others.

Lakshmi: He had also written to Arindam about his bisexuality.

Arka: Yes, I wrote to him. In realizing where I was at the time, I tried to look back into my past, and he was a large part of it. I actually asked him how he felt about us sexually. He never replied.

The summer after my first year Stefan went home to Germany, and I went to New York. The only person I knew in the city was the other Indian from my college. He worked during the week and would hook up with me on weekends to explore the city. During the weekdays I went out on my own, roaming the streets and going into gay bars. I am sorry now that I did not check out the bathhouses at that time. When friends (gay or straight) would visit us in the city, we would take them to Christopher Street and other gay areas. It was great.

One night in Studio 54 I met a short, beautiful man. He was a dancer, originally from Venezuela. He asked me to go home with him, which I had not yet done with anyone. I was worried. What if he mugged me? But I went with him. I remember that I tried to talk to him when we got to his place. I asked if he wasn't afraid of going to bed with a stranger. He said no, at this point he really didn't care. That upset me so much that I left immediately. Though I was not fully aware of AIDS at the time, I was somewhat conscious of the situation. The guy gave me his phone number, but I never called him back. To this day I still have a problem going home with a stranger.

At the end of that summer Lakshmi came to the U.S. to attend a college that was about fifteen miles away from mine. Stefan was also back from Germany.

Lakshmi: That summer Arka had written a lot to me about this friend of his who was homosexual. He also wrote of bisexuality in reference to himself, but only on an intellectual level. I began to realize what it meant on a real, social level, and the problems one could have as a result of others' reactions. The idea of bisexuality itself did not bother me; back home both of us had openly talked about the attractiveness of this man or that woman.

Arka: In my second year at that college I became active with the campus gay group. Stefan had already been assimilated into my life, and we had agreed upon an open relationship. Now I began to realize that I could sleep with other people who attracted me. I was especially attracted to one man, but our love affair was of the eyes-and-smiles variety. We never really came together, which made me rather sad. After the term was over, we corresponded and discovered that the desire had been mutual. Needless to say, we kicked ourselves for our inaction. At the end of that year I finished my undergraduate work and headed for the West Coast.

Lakshmi: That year, my first in the U.S, was probably my toughest year. On my first evening at the college Arka picked me up and took me to his campus. That night we slept together and made love for the first time. It was all a bit confusing for me. All evening he had talked about bisexuality and I could not understand why it was such an obsession for him. Before it had only been an intellectual concept. Now he was obsessing, and I had very little idea of what homosexuals were like. He also told me of his various experiences on campus, though he said nothing of his relationship with Stefan. It took me a while to assimilate everything.

During that term at my own college I developed a circle of friends. By December I came to realize that all of them but one were lesbians. Our socializing included slumber parties, and there was a bit of fondling involved. It dawned on me that I also had these sexual feelings, but I did not think of it in relationship terms. I began to think of myself as being bisexual. Thus coming out to myself and to others happened simultaneously. I am sure the accepting environment I was in made all of this possible.

Arka: That is true for both of us.

Lakshmi: I did fall in love with one woman at this time, but she was involved with someone else. That first year was lived mostly on an intellectual level and I was moving toward my feminist interests. I realize that this was a necessary process for me: I have to experience something in my mind before I can live it. During my second year at this college, which was my senior year, I went to the lesbian dances and lived what I had been thinking about. In the winter I visited Arka in California. Stefan was also there. I knew him as Arka's friend, and I grew quite fond of him. He was still attending Arka's old college. After Stefan and I went back to the East Coast, he visited me often at my college.

Arka: I found graduate school on the West Coast to be totally different from my New England liberal arts environment. I was now surrounded by people who would not talk about homosexuality. Most of the graduate students in my economics department were also Indian, and very conservative. Eventually I had to really unleash myself amongst them. I wasn't closeted with them, but a lot of my straight friends thought that my gay feelings were just a fad. My gay friends, on the other hand, assumed that my heterosexual aspect was simply a cover.

I was not happy with these friends. This whole time was quite difficult for me. I went to the campus gay group's meetings, but I didn't want a relationship with anyone. Then Anand came to our college. Anand was an Indian who transferred to my school from a college in Chicago. He was just coming out at this time and wanted to go out on the town a lot. Neither one of us had a car, so together we would take a bus to the gay district. Soon I found myself going out on my own when Anand did not feel like going. I did not need anyone along, I felt very comfortable.

During this time, Lakshmi and Stefan visited me a number of times. That first winter I suggested to Lakshmi, in a theoretical context, that I could not deal with monogamy. Up to that point it had been a tacit agreement. Now she had something to think about. The following winter I wanted to tell her about Stefan, but I couldn't.

Lakshmi: By that time I had thought over the issue for a year and realized that I could handle the situation, that it didn't bother me. When I first came to the U.S., I had found Arka a changed person, so I had felt quite insecure. But over time we both matured. Our relationship evolved, it did not fall apart. That was reassuring.

Arka: Finally, in 1987, I told her. She was upset, but only with the fact that I had not shared the truth sooner. She was mad for maybe two or three days. Honesty is important for both of us, and she felt cheated. But she now had her own friendship with Stefan, he was not just my boyfriend.

Lakshmi: I told him that I felt our trust had been betrayed, though I realize now that it could not have happened any other way. I really value my relationship with Stefan, apart form Arka. Stefan had resented me when I first came to the U.S., and if I had resented him also it would have made life very difficult for Arka.

Arka: I wouldn't have made a choice in that instance, however, because I had come to realize that monogamy was not for me. Right up to our marriage we talked about whether we could live with more than one person at one time. It would be difficult to do so, and, in any event, one must stop at some point. Thus it made sense to stop at the first one.

Lakshmi: You feel whole with that first person, but that doesn't mean that you cannot feel whole with any other. It is only a chronological choice.

Arka: I can't imagine Stefan not being a part of our life.

Lakshmi: During graduate school, in 1986, I lived with a guy who was gay, and I became very active. I also met this Indian guy, and we slept together. It was nothing more than that, but it was an important step for me. I told Arka about that when he came to see me. It was on that same visit that he told me about Stefan. Arka and I lived together that summer and our parents knew about it. They were also aware that we planned to be married the following summer.

The winter of 1987 was eventful for me. I met a woman named Olivia over lunch and knew that she was someone I could talk to. She jokingly said, "You're someone I'd like to sleep with." I laughed. By the end of the month I had fallen in love with her. It was very romantic. We both threw ourselves into it so easily because we weren't thinking long-term. She had a girlfriend in Canada, and I had Arka in California. We were both thrilled to find someone else who believed in polygamy.

The following summer, 1988, I went home to get married. Olivia spent the whole summer not being able to sleep with anyone else. She had broken up with her girlfriend earlier. She told me when I came back that the relationship wasn't going to work for her; she was feeling monogamous. I had built it on a different premise. We had a lot of problems that quarter. During the next quarter we went to Montreal and had a very nice time. At the quarter's end she slept with another woman and decided that she wanted to see more of her. The other woman insisted on monogamy, so we broke up.

Arka: But they are still roommates.

Lakshmi: We still sleep in the same bed, but we don't have sex anymore. For me sex is not a deciding factor in a relationship anyway. Our dependence hasn't really changed much. But she and her friend are trying to build a relationship, and Olivia is very sensitive to anything I have to say.

Arka: Olivia knew, as did Stefan, that we planned to settle down in India sometime after the completion of our studies. It would be ideal for us to live back home and go abroad every few years.

Lakshmi: We both want a family, and we both want to teach in our respective fields.

Arka: I believe in a pluralistic lifestyle. Everything in my life has to be as such. Wanting only one of anything is playing it safe.

Lakshmi: Of course there are some responsibilities that we have to meet, especially with family. We do feel very responsible to them.

Arka: They are not really pressuring us, though. We impose it on ourselves. We want to spend time with them. As years go by our parents become more dependent on our communication, and demanding in some sense, but that is only natural. We will, of course, face the question of our lifestyle in India. We will be open with anyone who wants to listen, however. Most of our friends already know.

Lakshmi: A lot of them don't really accept it. One friend thinks that I am needlessly complicating my life. Sexuality is not given that much value as a lifestyle. They think that now that I am married, I should have a child and feel fulfilled. They look at Arka in a different manner. There is a double standard.

Arka: In some ways I am the bad one in their eyes. Lakshmi is a nice girl that I have drawn into all this. They want to see her as being pure. I imagine there are many people we will not tell simply because we would tell them very little about any other part of our life.

Lakshmi: They never ask about my work or studies. They don't talk about large chunks of my life. Sexuality is one of these chunks. I could tell my sister, and I would like to tell my mother, but not yet.

Arka: My parents do know, though we have not talked about it. When Stefan came to visit, during my marriage, I was very open in my affection for him. My father even seemed to enjoy my bond with Stefan. My sister, who is studying in this country, knows everything. She has been to gay bars with us.

Lakshmi: She stayed with me at one point and began to ask me about Arka's bisexuality. Intellectually she found it easy to accept, but she did not understand the reality of it. I know I will eventually tell my sister and her husband. I also think it will show in my work, since I would like to edit lesbian anthologies.

Arka and I both want to have kids. I would like for them to be exposed to as much diversity as possible. I would like them to see Stefan as a part of our extended family as well; I don't want them to have just the mother and father framework.

People around us do seem to have a problem accepting us sometimes. Bisexuals are more of a problem to them than homosexuals, I think. They see bisexuals enjoying advantages on both sides.

The problem comes up with both heterosexuals and homosexuals. For the people back home Arka is the most important thing in my life. All else is a passing thing, a fad. For lesbians here it is the converse. They see our marriage as a facade, a matter of convenience. It peeves me that they must try to put me in a separatist category. The gay community has adopted the mainstream's concept of monogamy to some degree, whereas bisexuality entails polygamy of some sort, or at least serial monogamy. I'm not selling bisexuality, but I think that it should be accepted for those who are bisexual, instead of being categorized as "sitting on the fence."

Arka: Monogamy is too often seen as the only way, and if gay men don't achieve it, it is seen as some sort of failure. It need not be so. I find it quite frustrating when I just can't get this point across to people, especially close friends.

Last year, I got involved with someone named Gerardo. Right from the beginning, I was up-front about my existing relationships, but I also made it clear that he was very important to me. For a few months, everything was fine, but then Gerardo decided that he couldn't "share" me with other people. He also met someone else, who insisted on monogamy. When they started going out, Gerardo wanted us to be "just friends," meaning that our physical relationship had to end. We spent a torturous month fighting, then decided to leave each other alone.

After four months, he called, wanting to see me. I understood how he had missed me; I had been feeling the same way. He said that he wanted to keep in touch, to do things together. I get along very well with his lover now, but every now and then, tension resurfaces between Gerardo and me. There is so much affection, a lot of tenderness, and yet there is also a great deal of bitterness. I don't think we trust each other – there is a constant fear of getting hurt. He tells me that he has started to understand how it is possible to lead a constructive life with commitment but without being monogamous; I am not sure if he really does understand.

Lakshmi: There is a difference between polygamy and promiscuity. Promiscuity labels sexual relationships as random or obsessive, while polygamy entails working out a "relationship." When I was upset with Olivia, for instance, I could not have sex with her. Sex was not random or obsessive.

Arka: I really cannot be promiscuous. I've tried. I have been in three full-fledged relationships, and I am twenty-seven years old. Most monogamous people I know, who are my age, have had at least six or seven. The only difference is that I've tried to keep mine going simultaneously. That's not bad. Limiting yourself monogamously, saying that you can share everything with other people except the physical, is to give the sexual too much importance. Yes, it is intimate, but many intellectual interactions are just as intimate.

Lakshmi: Of course, as soon as I, a woman, say that I can see myself having relationships outside of my marriage, many people just assume that I am available for casual sex. Sex is used as a defining factor for a relationship, yet simply sleeping together becomes in many ways the most important act of all. If all you want is sex, you can simply do it with yourself. After all, who knows your body and its desires better? I think the importance given to sex in a relationship has to do with the way in which sexuality itself is conceptualized in cultures. Sexuality, especially women's, needs to be represented more positively. The same is true of bisexuality. If it is represented positively, I don't think people will have such a problem accepting bisexuality.

Arka: It seems that people repress the most obvious way of thinking about sexuality: as a continuum, with homosexuality and heterosexuality as the two extremes. Most of us fall somewhere in between, possibly closer to one end or the other, but because of social and cultural pressures, we veer toward one extreme as a pragmatic choice.

Arka & Lakshmi: The repression of homosexuality has forced some people to suppress their homosexual urges. Alternately, it has also caused others to affirm their gay and lesbian identities. The upsurge over the last two decades has brought homosexuality into the mainstream discourse, rather than allowing it to remain a deviance. In spite of AIDS, its backlash on gay lifestyles, and the resulting emphasis on monogamy, there is a greater awareness and acceptance of alternative sexualities.

Polygamy need not be a problem, but people seem to confuse it with mindless (and potentially fatal) promiscuity. To make such distinctions, people need to think and talk more of these repressed issues. With the availability of, and open discussion about, alternative lifestyles and sexualities, the imperative to make pragmatic choices is declining. There is much more of a chance to find oneself and to get what one wants.

The toughest journey

Sharmeen Islam*

I was so excited during my flight from Boston to San Francisco. More than a year of planning, of time and energy spent, would culminate this weekend in Santa Cruz, California. I did not entirely know what to expect, but I was certain that it would be an unforgettable experience. How could it not be? I would be spending the weekend with hundreds of other Asian lesbians. We would be coming from countless states and many countries. We would speak numerous languages and bring with us a collage of cultural histories. We would be so diverse, and yet we would all have two things in common: we would be lesbian and we would be Asian.

The occasion I was so looking forward to was the first ever national retreat of Asian lesbians. The desire for this event had been in the hearts and minds of many Asian lesbians for quite a long time, but it was the hugely successful (500,000 people) lesbian and gay march on Washington, D.C., in 1987 that helped to crystallize the idea. After the march, there was a good deal of money left over, money that the organizers of the protest allocated to a variety of lesbian and gay organizations. One of these grants was made to June Chen and some of her associates, specially earmarked toward a congregation of Asian lesbians.

I was excited by the possibilities this grant presented and had quickly joined the core group that would eventually make this event a reality. The money we started with was hardly enough for the retreat we had visualized, but it did get us started. At that time I was meeting many South Asian women, and I got some of them involved in the planning of the gathering. I also became one of the tri-chairs for the organizing committee and attended meetings in numerous cities all across the United States.

The retreat was planned for Labor Day weekend in 1989. For a number of reasons, we decided to gather in Santa Cruz. The headquarters for organizing the gathering was in the Bay Area. Santa Cruz has lesbian and feminist communities that are large and active. Also, the facilities at the University of California, Santa Cruz (UCSC), were much more affordable than those in San Francisco and its neighboring cities.

The first night, a Friday, the hallways were filled with screams and shouts of joyous women, some renewing connections, others meeting for the first time. The variety of women just boggled my mind. There were poets, writers, artists, and videomakers, as well as women from many other professions. Five South Asian lesbians made the trip from Boston with me, and we expected to meet more South Asian sisters; we were not disappointed. We had our own South Asian lesbian caucus – it was amazing!

UCSC is built on Native American burial grounds and, out of respect for those buried there, we decided to have a small ritual in which we asked permission of Native American women to hold our gathering on their land. Four of us addressed the crowd. Each one of us spoke in her native language; not a word of English was uttered during the ceremony.

The rest of that evening and the next three days were filled with workshops on topics such as South Asian Eros, racial hostility, interracial relationships, and safe sex. We played games, took a trip to the beach, made so many new friends. The feeling of connection, of shared feelings and thoughts was so like a fantasy that my politically active mind might have spun. Few fantasies manifest themselves without some discordant note, however, and as marvelous as this retreat was, even it could not be an exception.

That first evening included a slide show of Asian lesbians. As one image after another filled the screen, I found myself looking for South Asian faces, South Asian culture. We were almost completely excluded. I felt awful. Here, in the midst of a group of women who have often found themselves excluded from the mainstream lesbian movement, in an environment in which I had expected to feel safe and validated, I was feeling invisible. Some of my South Asian sisters, feeling the same sense of exclusion, walked out of the auditorium at various points. I sat and waited. And hoped. I hoped that the images I longed to see were still to come. I hoped that the betrayal I was feeling would prove to be unfounded.

When the show was over, I left the building in tears. It was nine p.m. I didn't stop crying until six the following morning. How could this happen? Two of us had been on the overall committee; how could this exclusion have happened? I didn't understand. So many thoughts filled my mind that night. I kept thinking of the faces, voices, and experiences that had joined together over my lifetime to form who I was as a person, a person whose existence felt invalidated once more. Coming to grips with myself as a South Asian lesbian had been a tough journey, perhaps the toughest journey of all, and images from that experience filled me that night.

❖

I was born in Dacca, the capitol of Bangladesh, and I became aware of my attraction for women at a very early age. The youngest of three children, I was a precocious child and had crushes on different women throughout my childhood. When I was three years old, I used to tell my father, "I'm going to marry your sister when I grow up."

My father, whose sister was quite beautiful, would say, "What am I going to do with you? You can't do that."

"Sure I can," I would reply. "You watch. I will grow up and marry a woman."

I received most of my education at an all-girls boarding school, which I did not mind at all. There was much intimacy between girls at this school, but this intimacy was mostly emotional; few felt safe enough to take it to a sexual level. I certainly knew that I couldn't afford to express my desires. One of my friends was found out; she was given electric shock treatment and told repeatedly that she was crazy. Today she is severely mentally disturbed.

In light of events like this, I'm glad that I didn't act sexually on my desires. I made a distinct choice that was safer at the time. This was one of the reasons that I began to plan on moving to the United States; I figured that I could live freely there as a woman and as a lesbian. This could not happen in Bangladesh. Surprisingly, the homophobia in Bangladesh comes mostly from the educated people who know words like lesbian and homosexual. The underprivileged women in rural areas are much more friendly, loving, and open in their attitudes.

After high school, many of the girls left their relationships with their classmates and enrolled in coed colleges. They seemed to slip into heterosexual relationships quite easily. It was more difficult for me, however, and it really hurt at times. I was very sure of my lesbianism. I told people that I knew I would never marry a man; if I stayed in Bangladesh, I would become a marriage resister. Back home, a marriage resister is a woman who refuses to marry on the grounds that the institution is exploitive of women. It is much safer to be a marriage resister than a lesbian.

My image of lesbians was pretty awful at the time. I had read a novel by Harold Robbins in which he portrayed a woman who was sexually unsatisfied with her husband and this somehow turned her into a lesbian. I hated this idea; the word *lesbian* took on a negative connotation for me. I was surprised, though, at how well informed my mother was about lesbianism. Both she and my sister were educated in the U.S., and they introduced me to the word. I was sixteen at the time, and I was getting ready to come to the U.S. My mother sat me down one day; I thought it would be the "birds and the bees" lecture, but I was wrong.

Mother looked at me and said, "Whatever you do, don't become a lesbian."

I was dying! I thought, oh my gosh! I hope it isn't showing. I knew that she would not say anything of this sort to my sister, so I panicked at the thought that she might know. I didn't want anything to jeopardize my leaving.

Education was my main reason for coming to the United States in the summer of 1981. I lived in the dorms at Wellesley College in Massachusetts, and I had no idea that my building was unofficially known as the lesbian dorm. As I walked through the common room of my new home, I saw women making out. I couldn't believe my luck! My heart beat so fast. This was something I had never seen

282

before. They stopped their kissing and looked at me. They smiled. I smiled back, then walked out.

Initially, I was very scared in college. I felt a bit insecure, being a new foreign student, and in class I was very shy. I was trying hard to assimilate into my new environment, yet I was also trying to hide my lesbianism.

Ann, my roommate, was overtly straight at the time, and I like her a lot. She always went to these straight parties – you know, incredible amounts of beer drinking. I would go with her, then come back and say that these were not the kind of parties I wanted to go to. I would tell her that I was a lesbian. She would say no, you're dreaming. I guess at some point we started liking one another more deeply. It all developed so naturally. One day I told her that I was sure I was a lesbian, and that I wouldn't play the straight game anymore. She told me that she was attracted to me.

When we finally fell in love, Ann and I did not go out for a week. People began to wonder and talk about us. The foreign students at Wellesley were very homophobic. Some claimed that homosexuality was a Western phenomenon and didn't exist in South Asia. My lover and I would often hold hands, and the more we expressed ourselves openly like this, the more my foreign student friends abandoned me. Consequently, I began to seal off my South Asian self; I did not think that it could coexist with my lesbian identity.

One example of the homophobia of the other foreign students is still clear in my mind. I had one professor who really liked me, but one day his attitude changed completely. I found out that a student from Spain, who was not talking to me because I was a lesbian, was very close to him. It became obvious that she must have talked to him. I tried to hide my lesbianism during the first two years, and experiences like this made it all the more difficult to stop doing this and come to terms with myself. Ironically, this same woman came out as a lesbian after we graduated!

Over the course of our four years at the college, my lover and I began to come out more and more. We went through a lot of struggles. Ann's parents became hostile toward her when they found out that she was a lesbian. I had come out to my brother and sister, who were in Bangladesh, in 1981, not long after I came to the U.S.

My siblings were initially disappointed, but both said that they weren't surprised; they had always figured that there was something different about me. Both at first assumed that my lesbianism was a Western thing, but in the last few years they have come a long way. Now they think it would be wonderful if I had a child and raised it with my lover, even though they know I have no desire to have one. My sister even insists that I must make certain to have the child myself; she and my brother seem to have a need to see me in some familiar context. What would be more familiar than a South Asian woman in the role of a mother? All in all, however, they've made tremendous progress.

I was with Ann through four years of college and two years after we graduated. Right after we broke up, I was going through a newsletter in Boston one day when I ran across an ad for a potluck party sponsored by a gay Asian group. I had been aware of Anamika, an organization of lesbian South Asians, but it had been out of existence for some time. I had tried out a number of other groups that ultimately left me wanting more. Somehow this ad struck a chord in me that these others had not.

Through the ad I met a whole network of Asians. One of the people I met was a gay Chinese man. In 1988, Jack and I formed an organization called AMALGM, Alliance of Massachusetts Asian Lesbians and Gay Men. That's when my activism really started. Initially I was the only South Asian, but later two other South Asian lesbians joined the group. AMALGM really got me in touch with the national Asian gay and lesbian structure, which got me in touch with my South Asian lesbian sisters in the U.S. This organization was a wonderful example of men and women, East Asians and South Asians working together.

AMALGM was a great experience, but I still felt a need to work more within the South Asian lesbian context. People had tried periodically to restart the Anamika organization but it never came about. Personally, I never liked the name; Anamika means "nameless," and I don't think we are or should be nameless. While I was traveling in India and Bangladesh to connect with other lesbians, I did a number of interviews. During this process I came across the Bengali word *shamakami* – the love of an equal. I thought it was a marvelous image, and it became the new name of a reincarnated Anamika group.

Throughout these years my brother and sister remained quite supportive of me, but I still did not talk openly about my lesbianism with my mother (my father was long deceased, having been killed in Bangladesh's war of independence). Until a telephone call just a few months ago. She was asking me to come to Bangladesh with Mary, my lover.

"Well, you know that Mary and I are partners," I replied, wanting no miscommunication.

"What do you mean?" she asked.

How could she not know? She had lived for a time with my lover and me on the East Coast. We had gone to visit her in Bangladesh, and she had seen us kissing. She had been disapproving of my girlfriends but had never addressed the issue directly.

I took a deep breath and said, "Well, you know that we are lesbians."

"No, no, you can't be!" she replied, quite distressed.

She said that she didn't know how to react. She said that she wished that she could be more supportive, but that she was devastated. A few days later she called back and said some incredibly harsh things to me. We exchanged letters. My mother is a dominating woman, and I resorted to playing the little kid for a while. There was so much guilt, and it took a lot to counteract that.

Three months ago I decided that since I had done so much political work, how dare I let anyone say these things to me. I would not have taken such words from someone during an AIDS march or a gay and lesbian rally, but here I was, back at square one with my mother. So I finally told her that if she continued to say these things to me she would lose me. I think that's when she crumbled. We're still going through some difficult times, but I now realize just how important it is to talk about these things. It is not enough for my family and friends to just know without the issue having been discussed openly.

A couple of months ago I found out that one of my mother's friends is a lesbian. Mother told me herself. This friend has lived with a lover for fifteen years in Dacca. Everybody knows, it seems. There seems to be some such tolerance for upper-class women.

"I do not want you to be lesbian because of the way she treats her lover," Mother told me one time. "Her lover never goes out of the house, has no identity. It is worse than a heterosexual wife's situation."

Apparently this woman, whom I've always referred to as an aunt, is a butch woman, and there is a lot of role-playing in the relationship. Mother asked me if my relationships are like that. I told her no, but I'm not sure if she believed me. I guess a lot of role-playing goes on in South Asia, because there is no identifiable lesbian culture; the only relationship role models are heterosexual. Thus, nearly all lesbians and gays are married or plan to get married to escape persecution; being single brings about the suspicion that one might be lesbian or gay.

All of my friends from school, with the exception of one, are married today. They don't consider themselves lesbians; they consider adolescent experiences with other girls to be a childhood thing. The exception is a woman who lives a rather isolated life. No life really, for she is so very depressed all the time. When my gay friends and I go back to Bangladesh, we try to revive her. It is such a lonely life for her, as I'm sure it is for millions of lesbians and gay men in South Asia.

❖

For every tear that I cried after seeing the slide show in Santa Cruz, I knew that there were countless South Asian women out there, on the Indian subcontinent and across the globe, who lived fearful, sometimes false lives simply because they were lesbian. Thoughts of these women, images of my lonely friend, the faces of my mother's friend and her lover filled my mind. I cried not only because I felt invalidated; millions of my South Asian sisters were having their existence invalidated by their exclusion from the slide show as well.

I was not the only one crying that night. All around me Asian women were in tears – not just the twenty-five South Asian women, but women of all Asian nationalities. A friend of mine started calling up other women, and they started calling me. They said they felt awful, that they could not understand how one could set up a conference condemning racism, homophobia, and sexism and yet so badly underrepresent South Asian lesbians. Most women kept saying that we must do something, but a few South Asian sisters did not want to do anything. They did not want to ruin the spirit of the retreat.

What could we do? The organizers were my peers, and I felt that I would be going against them. We could make a formal complaint. We could also talk to the woman who had put together the slide show. I told them that we had two choices: we could either leave the retreat with this feeling inside of us, or we could say what was in our hearts.

We made a collective decision. The next day, when everyone was gathered in the auditorium and before they broke for lunch, my South Asian sisters and I climbed onto the stage. One Canadian sister, who was in a wheelchair, had herself wheeled as close to the stage as possible. Even those who had talked about stage fright the night before bravely lined up before the audience.

"I could come up here and tell you that our sisters screwed us," I said to the roomful of Asian lesbians. "I could tell you that it is nothing, but it is something." I knew that I was going to cry, and I hated myself for doing it, but I couldn't control my tears. "What we want to do is to have each one of us on this stage say the name of her country, and we want all of you to repeat it."

India. Bangladesh. Sri Lanka. Two hundred women stood up and repeated the name of each country. We were so united, there was such solidarity and energy. Everyone was hugging and holding hands. I felt wonderful, and I couldn't stop crying. I heard later that everyone in the audience was crying as we were speaking. I think that it touched the hurt of marginalization in each one of us. South Asian women had shown courage in speaking out, but the conference was a safe space for this sort of action. Eventually, all types of women came on stage and cried. Mixed-heritage women. Bisexual women. Women from other countries who had felt excluded. Who among us has not been marginalized?

After our stand on the stage, an East Asian woman came to me and told me that when she saw the slide show the previous evening, she kept thinking of my face and could not make the connection. When I walked onto the stage, she immediately knew why I was up there. She too had realized that something was missing from the slide presentation. That day and the next, so many women came to us and showed their support. The whole spirit of the retreat had changed, expanded to include us all.

I learned a very valuable lesson from the events at this conference. I learned that any group, no matter how much it has been marginalized itself, is capable of excluding, consciously or unconsciously, another group. Any group, no matter how much hurt and betrayal it has experienced, is capable of subjecting other groups to this pain. This is something we can avoid only by being alert to it and by speaking out when it happens.

Visit from an old friend

Rakesh Ratti

He sits on the sofa, an arm's reach away from me. His appearance, though unexpected, is no shocking surprise; he has never strayed far from me. He is the personification of innocence, from the long brown hair sweeping across his forehead to the bony, slight body that trembles ever so lightly. He is full of questions, I am full of answers, and yet he does not speak. As always, it is my duty to draw the questions out of him. The fingertips pressed together in a steeple, he crosses his legs, uncrosses them, then stretches them full and crosses them at the ankles. This long-remembered mannerism brings a smile to my face.

"I've barely seen you lately," I say to him. "What brings you here now?"

"You've changed so much," he whispers, "I hardly know you anymore."

"It's a function of time; everyone changes," I reply. "I like to think that most of the change has been for the best."

"Does that mean shutting me out? That's what you've done. You've tried to banish me into some crevice so you don't have to deal with me. But you can't get rid of me, you know that. I see everything you do, hear everything you say."

I can't argue with the truth of his words, yet I would not change anything about my effort to leave him behind. Who would want to have his confidence at the mercy of an adolescent's fears?

"What have you seen and heard lately?" I ask.

"Too much," he answers, "and it scares me." He pauses a moment, then his voice rises, his words almost trip over one another as they roll off his tongue. "What the hell are you trying to do? Telling people that you're gay, those political organizations – that was bad enough. But a book? With your real name on it? Why?"

"Why?" I ask incredulously. "You of all people should know why. You know how much of a need there is for it. You and I, and so many other South Asians, have gone through so much pain, so many struggles, simply because we love differently. Our voices need to be heard. Others who are going through the same struggle need to know that they aren't alone!"

I watch him through narrowed eyes, and he is quiet for a moment. My eyes soften, I hold out my hand. "Don't be afraid; you can't live life in fear. Besides, our minds magnify whatever awful things may actually exist," I say gently.

"The hell they do!" he shouts, pulling away.

The tone is familiar, anger trying desperately to mask his fear. My skin feels warms, tingles in response to his words. If I don't watch myself, his fear will come to envelope me as well.

"I don't think you will ever change," I say very softly, trying to shrug off the fear. "But I can't listen to you anymore. You want to hold me back, make me hate myself. When you're like this, I don't want to look at you, I don't want to hear your words."

He looks hurt and it tugs at me, but I know I must steel myself. I cannot take care of him, I cannot give in to him without losing who I am, who I've become.

"Why do you have to do it?" he yells. "Why can't you let someone else do it, let them use their name?"

"If we all thought that way, it would never get done. We have to take some risks."

"But why do you have to live life this way?" he asks accusingly.

"In what way? Loving other men? How can you ask the question? It's not something I can change, nor would I want to."

He shakes his head. "Who said anything about changing? Of course you can't change! But do you have to scream it from the rooftop?"

"I don't have to do anything," I respond, trying to keep my cool. "I suppose some part of me does want to shout from the rooftop that I'm gay. It's the truth and I don't want to hide it."

"What about your family?" he continues, trying a different tact. "You think this only affects you? It's fine for you to say that you're just being yourself, but they won't be able to face their friends and neighbors once everyone finds out about you. How can you do this to them?'

"I am doing nothing to them," I shout back, my voice as loud as his. "If they feel any pain out of this, they bring it upon themselves. I'm asking them for nothing more than I'm willing to give them. I don't question how they live their lives, why should they question mine? Besides, they taught me to value truth; how dare they expect me to live a lie now?"

"Bullshit!" His anger is harder, runs deeper than usual this time. "It's not that simple. Your decisions affect them. You know that you could get married and have a family; just have your sex with men quietly on the side."

"And ruin some woman's life by trapping her into a loveless marriage? Leave my true self entombed by your fear? Are you out of your mind?"

"Get serious!" he spits at me, looking me squarely in the eye. What has he been feeding on that has made him so stubborn and hateful this time? "When you were visiting India, you looked with envy at all of the *baraats* (wedding parties). You looked at the grooms on their horses and thought of how neat it would be to marry like that."

I hate the fact that he knows me so well, even if he distorts things. "You're right, I was envious. But I never considered it an option," I respond. "The ritual was seductive, the social validation was enticing, but I never wanted that on any terms but my own. You know that I didn't want to bring a crimson-clothed bride home with me. I wanted another groom beside me, on a matching horse; that's the only ceremony I could take part in."

Rising from the sofa, he walks away from me. Slowly he turns, his face more somber now. "What about kids? You've always wanted to raise one; now you'll never have that experience."

"What makes you think I won't? I don't have to be married to a woman for that; I could raise one with another man, or by myself. It could be my own, or I could adopt."

"What the hell are you going to offer him as a role model?" he shouts, pointing a thin finger at me. "You want him to grow up gay and go through the hell you remember yourself?"

I close my eyes, open them slowly. "You know that's ludicrous. Having a gay parent won't make the kid gay. My parents and yours are straight, remember? Besides, all kids face challenges in life, and being a gay kid in a straight society, or having a gay parent, would just be one more challenge. Whether my kid turns out gay or straight doesn't matter; he would be loved, and that's all that matters."

"So don't get married, if you feel so strongly about it," he says begrudgingly. "Find some guy to have sex with and live quietly. No one has to know."

"But they do, don't you see? As long as I feel a need to hide myself, I'm buying society's crap that there is something wrong with me. There is nothing wrong with me, or with you. I have to let the world know that."

"Look at all of the friends you've lost because they found out that you were gay," he points out.

"If they walked away, then they weren't really friends, were they?" I return. "Look at the friends I've gained by being open."

"But straight people don't go around shouting about their sexuality? Why should you?"

"They don't have to." The frustration in my voice is building. "We're all assumed to be straight until we're open about ourselves. People fear what they don't know. If they can get to know gay people personally, then we can change their attitudes. If someone who hates gay people likes me, then I need to be open with that person so that he or she can see how irrational the hatred is."

"Why? Who's going to listen to a queer here and there? Look at the gay people around you. How many of them scream it out?"

"Not enough." He is young, I tell myself. Have patience. "Don't you see what would happen if we all screamed it out, shattered those damned closet doors? What do you think the world would do to us? Nothing! It could do nothing because there would too many of us. What could the world do to its sons and daughters, sisters and brothers, fathers and mothers, aunts and uncles, grandmothers and grandfathers? No one in this world would be left untouched by our presence."

"Nice dream," he comments sarcastically. "If you were a gambler, you would lose the shirt off your back."

"There are some things that are more important than the shirt on my back," I reply, growing more annoyed.

"That's fucking noble of you," he says acidly, leaning defiantly against the wall. "All because you want to have sex with a guy."

"You know damn well that my being gay involves much more than sex." My patience is nearly exhausted. "What is it that you're afraid of? It's what you remember, isn't?"

He doesn't respond, only turns his back to me.

"Have you forgotten the faces of your own love?" I continue. "The dark-eyed blond boy you ached to hold, whom you still think of today? The pretty boy with the tanned body who filled your senses, made you walk into walls and fall over your own feet? The one you would wrap your arms around if you had the chance even now, when you stand here spouting this fucking poison? Do I have to name them all?"

"Stop it," he whispers softly, his face pressed against the wall.

"You don't have to be afraid," I reply, my voice more gentle. The fight is flowing out of him.

"Yes, I do," he says haltingly. I can see his face, see a moist trail on one cheek. "It hurts when people hate you. I don't want the world to reject me, don't you see? I don't want my family to stop loving me, or my friends to turn away from me."

"But they haven't; if you would just tear down your screen of fear, even if only for a moment, you would see that."

He shakes his head, and I don't press him; I understand. He can't see my point, not through the thick layers of his fear. And his fear is real; as long as it exists in his mind, it is real for him. As always, it leaves me feeling hollow, makes me wish I could do more. He is trembling, wracked with fear and sorrow.

"Come here," I say to him, blinking away the moisture in my eyes and holding my arms out.

He walks slowly into my arms, his body slumps against mine. How fragile he feels, how thin and vulnerable. I wrap my arms around him, as I wish someone had done for me years ago. As I tighten my embrace, his body begins to fade, then disappears altogether. I am left alone, my arms encircling my own body.

293

He is gone, but he has not left me forever. He lives on in some corner of my being. He is my doubts, he is my fears, and he emerges, a bruised memory of the adolescent I once was, each time I face a new challenge as a gay man in a straight world. He is a testament to a lesson of self-hate that the world teaches so well. The lesson that was internalized by a vulnerable youth, rejected when the youth became stronger, but has never been, nor will it ever be, fully banished.

Perhaps it is good that these old fears, these old pains do not wander far from me. Perhaps it is good that the past can be hidden for a time but never fully discarded, for the voice of this frightened adolescent keeps me from growing complacent. His face, full of fear, keeps me from closing my eyes to a world that changes too slowly. This world will not change of its own accord, for it fears any change within its parameters. Thus we who retain the memories of our own wounded and frightened selves from yesterday must bring about this change. We must face these memories, both as individuals and as a people. We must remember the lessons they have taught us, lessons they still teach us. Keeping these pictures and voices of our old selves in mind, we must lift our faces into the wind and shout our outrage, and we must rise to our feet and create a world that would be more kind to the faces of our own past, the faces of others' future.

*Two torsos, one female, one male, arising from the same pelvis, emphasizing the unity rather than the dichotomy of the feminine and the masculine.
(Bronze statue, India)*

Giti Thadani

About the contributors

Biographical information, most of which appears in the author's own words, is presented only for those contributors who have used their full, true names; such information has not been included on other contributors out of respect for their desire for confidentiality.

Raj Ayyar was born in the Indian state of Tamil Nadu and has traveled extensively in the United States. He is currently engaged in graduate studies in counseling in San Francisco, California, where he also continues his pursuit of *yaari*.

Kaushalya Bannerji was born in Calcutta, India, and raised in Canada. She has a master's degree in political science, and is active in the struggle against racism, homophobia, and sexism.

Zariamma Harat is a poet, artist, mother, and political activist. Originally from southern India, Zari and her daughter currently make their home in Berlin, Germany.

At Stanford University, **Ashok Jethanandani** not only learned mechanical engineering, but also how to accept and celebrate his gay identity. He is the publisher of *India Currents,* America's largest circulation Indian magazine, and has been involved with Trikone since its inception. Ashok is also the San Francisco Bay Area's first male to have studied *bharat natyam,* the classical dance of South India.

Arvind Kumar has been one of the pivotal figures in the emergence of the gay and lesbian movement in the United States. He helped to found Trikone and has edited many of its newsletters. Arvind is the editor of *India Currents,* and lives with his life partner, Ashok Jethanandani, in San Jose.

Indian-born **Suniti Namjoshi** has held academic posts in India and Canada, where she has taught at the University of Toronto since 1972. She currently makes her home in Devon, England. Suniti's numerous publications include the books *Conversations with Cow, The Mothers of Maya Diip,* and *The Blue Donkey Fables.* She has also written, with Gillian Hanscombe, a sequence of poems titled *Flesh and Paper.*

Ifti Nasim was born in Pakistan and immigrated to the United States at the age of twenty. He also writes in Urdu and has been widely published in India and Pakistan. Ifti currently resides in Chicago, Illinois, where he is active in gay and human rights causes.

Ian Rashid is a writer, activist, and arts administrator. He was born in Tanzania, raised in Toronto, Canada, and is currently working as a guest editor for *Bazaar* magazine in London, England. Ian has been published many times, the most recent being a collection of his poetry titled *Black Markets, White Boyfriends and Other Acts of Elision.*

Nayan Shah was born in Washington, D.C., and raised in the Maryland suburbs. He studies issues of race and sexuality in U.S. history at the University of Chicago.

Giti Thadani is an independent researcher on traditions of liminal sexualities in the context of Indian history.

Glossary of South Asian terms

All terms are from the Hindi/Urdu/Punjabi language group, unless noted otherwise.

Anamika: Nameless.

Ardhanarishwara: A Hindu god normally depicted as a half-male, half-female figure.

Bindi: A colored dot worn by Indian women on their foreheads.

Dhoti: A piece of cloth, usually plain white, traditionally wrapped by men around the lower body. Also called a *lunghee.*

Deedee: Sister, used in camp talk by South Asian gays.

Dhobi: One who washes clothes for a living.

Ghandoo: Pejorative for gay man.

Hijra: A category variously including hermaphrodites, transsexuals, and sometimes drag queens. Often reviled and feared, *hijras* have sanctioned roles in Indian society as spiritualists and entertainers, and an unsanctioned role as prostitutes.

Kameez: Dresslike blouse worn by South Asian women.

Khush: Gay (a literal translation currently used by some gay and lesbian South Asians to identify their lifestyle).

Lata: A prolific and hugely popular Indian songstress.

Mujra: A type of dance traditionally performed by South Asian courtesans.

Rhada: The consort of the Hindu god Krishna.

Rani: Queen.

Rundi: Whore, slut.

Saheli: A woman's special female friend, normally used in a platonic context.

Salvar: Very baggy pajama pants worn by South Asian women.

Sari: One long piece of cloth, often in brilliant colors, wrapped around the lower body with one end draped across the torso. Worn by Indian women.

Savitri: The consort of the Indian god Vishnu.

Shakti: Principle of active feminine strength.

Shamakami: The love of an equal (from Bengali).

Sita: The consort of the Indian god Rama.

Trikone: Triangle (from Sanskrit).

Yaar: Historically has meant lover or platonic best friend at various times, currently used by some South Asians to describe their lovers.

Yaarana: Currently used by some South Asians to describe their love relationship.

Zenaana: A feminine man, normally used as a pejorative.

Glossary of gay terms

Androgyny: A balance of the feminine and masculine in one person.

Bisexual: An individual who is sexually or romantically attracted to people of either gender.

Butch: A very masculine man or woman.

Chicken: A gay youth, usually under eighteen.

Coming out: Acknowledging that one is gay or lesbian, to oneself or to others.

Cruising: Actively looking for a partner, involves a distinct body and eye language.

Cross-dressing: Wearing the clothes of the other gender.

Closed: When speaking of a relationship, this refers to one that is monogamous.

Dishing: Putting another person down, usually in a spirit of fun.

Dyke: Lesbian. Considered a pejorative when used by nonlesbians.

Drag: Dressing in the clothes of the other gender for the purpose of parody; usually refers to men dressing as women.

Femme: Feminine man or woman.

Faggot: A pejorative term for a gay man.

Gay: A term for homosexual, preferred as a positive self-identification by those who are gay.

Gay-bashing: The physical or verbal assault on someone simply because he or she is gay.

Homophobia: An irrational fear of someone who is homosexual.

Lesbian: A woman who loves other women; preferred by some women to the term *gay*.

Open: When speaking of a relationship, this refers to one that is nonmonogamous.

Queen: A man who is very feminine. A pejorative term when used by nongays.

Queer: Literally meaning "strange," a pejorative term used against both gay men and lesbians.

Role-playing: When two people in a relationship adhere strictly to roles, one traditionally feminine, the other masculine.

Straight: Heterosexual.

Directory of resources for South Asian lesbians and gays

Canada

• **Alliance for South Asian AIDS Prevention,** 320 1/2 Bloor St. W., 2nd Floor, Toronto, Ontario M5S 1W1, Canada.

• **Asian Lesbians of Toronto (ALOT),** Box 23, Station P, Toronto, Ontario M5S 2S7, Canada.

• **Gay Asian AIDS Project,** call (416) 462-1397, Mondays, 7–10 p.m.

• **Gay Asians Toronto,** P.O. Box 752, Station F, Toronto, Ontario M4Y 2N6, Canada.

• **Khush: South Asian Lesbians and Gays of Toronto,** P.O. Box 6172, Station A, Toronto, Ontario M5W 1P6, Canada, or call (416) 461-4105; ask for Nelson. Newsletter: *Khush Khayal.*

• **Lesbiennese Gaies en Couleur de Montreal,** P.O. Box 1546, Place du Park, Montreal, Quebec H2W 2R5, Canada.

• **South Asian AIDS Coalition (SAAC),** P.O. Box 6172, Station A, Toronto, Ontario M5W 1P6, Canada.

India

• **AIDS Bhedbhav Virodhi Andolan (ABVA),** P.O. 5308, Delhi 110 053, India.

- **Bombay Dost,** 105 A Veena Beena Shopping Center, opposite Bandra Station, Bandra West, Bombay 400 050, India.
- **Freedom** (newsletter), P.O. Box 80, Gulbarga 585 102, India.
- **Gays and lesbians in New Delhi** (as-yet-unnamed group), P.O. Box 7032, Sriniwas Puri, New Delhi 110 065, India.
- **Sakhi** (lesbian organization), P.O. Box 7032, Srinawas Puri, New Delhi 110 065, India.

United States
- **Asian Lesbians and Gays Association of Philadelphia (ALGA),** P.O. Box 58815, Philadelphia, PA 19102, USA, or call (215) 735-3793; ask for Jayant.
- **Buddhist Association** (welcomes gay/lesbian members), P.O. Box 1974, Bloomfield, NJ 07003.
- **Sangat** (gay/lesbian organization), Box 268463, Chicago, IL 60626, or call (312) 973-5747; ask for Viru.
- **Shamakami** (South Asian lesbian organization; newsletter), P.O. Box 460456, San Francisco, CA 94146.
- **South Asian Lesbian and Gay Association (SALGA),** 170 E. Third St. #2G, New York, NY 10009, or call (212) 475-6486; ask for Haresh Advani.
- **Trikone: Organization of Gay and Lesbian South Asians**
Los Angeles: Call (818) 895-2238; ask for Nadeem.
San Francisco: P.O. Box 21354, San Jose, CA 95151, USA, or call (408) 270-8776.
Newsletter: *Trikone.*
- **The Arabic Society,** P.O. Box 4971, Washington, DC 20008.

United Kingdom
- **Shakti: South Asian Lesbian and Gay Network of London,** BM Box 4390, London WCIN 3XX, UK, or call 01 993 99001, weekends.
Newsletter: *Shakti Khabar.*
- **Shakti Leicester,** call 0533 550667; ask for Shakti.

Alyson Publications publishes a wide variety
of books with gay and lesbian themes.
For a free catalog, or to be placed on our mailing list,
please write to:
Alyson Publications
40 Plympton St.
Boston, Mass. 02118
Indicate whether you are interested in books for
gay men, for lesbians, or both.